baking & desserts

This is a Starfire book
First published in 2001

02 04 05 03

1 3 5 7 9 10 8 6 4 2

Starfire is part of
The Foundry Creative Media Company Limited
Crabtree Hall, Crabtree Lane, Fulham, London, SW6 6TY

Visit the Foundry website: www.foundry.co.uk/recipes

ISBN: 1-903817-11-0

The CIP record for this book is available from the British Library.

Printed in China

ACKNOWLEDGEMENTS

Authors: Catherine Atkinson, Juliet Barker, Liz Martin, Vicki Smallwood,
Gina Steer, Carol Tennant, Mari Mererid Williams, Elizabeth Wolf-Cohen and Simone Wright
Editorial Consultant: Gina Steer
Project Editor: Karen Fitzpatrick
Photography: Colin Bowling, Paul Forrester and Stephen Brayne
Home Economists and Stylists: Jacqueline Bellefontaine,
Mandy Phipps, Vicki Smallwood and Penny Stephens

All props supplied by Barbara Stewart at Surfaces

NOTE
Recipes using uncooked eggs should be avoided by infants,
the elderly, pregnant women and anyone suffering from an illness.

LET'S COOK

baking & desserts

STAR
FIRE

Contents

BISCUITS, COOKIES, BROWNIES, TRAYBAKES & BUNS

PUDDINGS, PIES & TARTS

EVERYDAY CAKES & DESSERTS

CREAM CAKES & GATEAUX

Hygiene in the Kitchen

It is well worth remembering that many foods can carry some form of bacteria. In most cases, the worst it will lead to is a bout of food poisoning or gastroenteritis, although for certain groups this can be more serious – the risk can be reduced or eliminated by good food hygiene and proper cooking.

Do not buy food that is past its sell-by date and do not consume food that is past its use-by date. When buying food, use the eyes and nose. If the food looks tired, limp or a bad colour or it has a rank, acrid or simply bad smell, do not buy or eat it under any circumstances.

Do take special care when preparing raw meat and fish. A separate chopping board should be used for each; wash the knife, board and the hands thoroughly before handling or preparing any other food.

Regularly clean, defrost and clear out the refrigerator or freezer – it is worth checking the packaging to see exactly how long each product is safe to freeze.

Avoid handling food if suffering from an upset stomach as bacteria can be passed through food preparation.

Dish cloths and tea towels must be washed and changed regularly. Ideally use disposable cloths which should be replaced on a daily basis. More durable cloths should be left to soak in bleach, then washed in the washing machine on a boil wash.

Keep the hands, cooking utensils and food preparation surfaces clean and do not allow pets to climb on to any work surfaces.

BUYING

Avoid bulk buying where possible, especially fresh produce such as meat, poultry, fish, fruit and vegetables. Fresh foods lose their nutritional value rapidly so buying a little at a time minimises loss of nutrients. It also eliminates a packed refrigerator which reduces the effectiveness of the refrigeration process.

When buying prepackaged goods such as cans or pots of cream and yogurts, check that the packaging is intact and not damaged or pierced at all. Cans should not be dented, pierced or rusty. Check the sell-by dates even for cans and packets of dry ingredients such as flour and rice. Store fresh foods in the refrigerator as soon as possible – not in the car or the office.

When buying frozen foods, ensure that they are not heavily iced on the outside and the contents feel completely frozen. Ensure that the frozen foods have been stored in the cabinet at the correct storage level and the temperature is below -18°C/-0.4°F. Pack in cool bags to transport home and place in the freezer as soon as possible after purchase.

PREPARATION

Make sure that all work surfaces and utensils are clean and dry. Hygiene should be given priority at all times. Separate chopping boards should be used for raw and cooked meats, fish and vegetables. Currently, a variety of good-quality plastic boards come in various designs and colours. This makes differentiating easier and the plastic

has the added hygienic advantage of being washable at high temperatures in the dishwasher. (NB: If using the board for fish, first wash in cold water, then in hot to prevent odour!) Also, remember that knives and utensils should always be thoroughly cleaned after use.

When cooking, be particularly careful to keep cooked and raw food separate to avoid any contamination. It is worth washing all fruits and vegetables regardless of whether they are going to be eaten raw or lightly cooked. This rule should apply even to prewashed herbs and salads.

Do not reheat food more than once. If using a microwave, always check that the food is piping hot all the way through. (In theory, the food should reach 70°C/158°F and needs to be cooked at that temperature for at least three minutes to ensure that all bacteria are killed.)

All poultry must be thoroughly thawed before using, including chicken and poussin. Remove the food to be thawed from the freezer and place in a shallow dish to contain the juices. Leave the food in the refrigerator until it is completely thawed. A 1.4 kg/3 lb whole chicken will take about 26–30 hours to thaw. To speed up the process immerse the chicken in cold water. However, make sure that the water is changed regularly. When the joints can move freely and no ice crystals remain in the cavity, the bird is completely thawed.

Once thawed, remove the wrapper and pat the chicken dry. Place the chicken in a shallow dish, cover lightly and store as close to the base of the refrigerator as possible. The chicken should be cooked as soon as possible.

Some foods can be cooked from frozen including many prepacked foods such as soups, sauces, casseroles and breads. Where applicable follow the manufacturers' instructions.

Vegetables and fruits can also be cooked from frozen, but meats and fish should be thawed first. The only time food can be refrozen is when the food has been thoroughly thawed then cooked. Once the food has cooled then it can be frozen again. On such occasions the food can only be stored for one month.

All poultry and game (except for duck) must be cooked thoroughly. When cooked the juices will run clear on the thickest part of the bird – the best area to try is usually the thigh. Other meats, like minced meat and pork should be cooked right the way through. Fish should turn opaque, be firm in texture and break easily into large flakes.

When cooking leftovers, make sure they are reheated until piping hot and that any sauce or soup reaches boiling point first.

STORING, REFRIGERATING AND FREEZING

Meat, poultry, fish, seafood and dairy products should all be refrigerated. The temperature of the refrigerator should be between 1–5°C/ 34–41°F while the freezer temperature should not rise above -18°C/-0.4°F.

To ensure the optimum refrigerator and freezer temperature, avoid leaving the door open for a long time. Try not to overstock the refrigerator as this reduces the airflow inside and affects the effectiveness in cooling the food within.

When refrigerating cooked food, allow it to cool down quickly and completely before refrigerating. Hot food will raise the temperature of the refrigerator and possibly affect or spoil other food stored in it.

Food within the refrigerator and freezer should always be covered. Raw and cooked food should be stored in separate parts of the refrigerator. Cooked food should be kept on the top shelves of the refrigerator, while raw meat, poultry and fish should be placed on bottom shelves to avoid drips and cross-contamination. It is recommended that eggs should be refrigerated in order to maintain their freshness and shelf life.

Take care that frozen foods are not stored in the freezer for too long. Blanched vegetables can be stored for one month; beef, lamb, poultry and pork for six months and unblanched vegetables and fruits in syrup for a year. Oily fish and sausages should be stored for three months. Dairy products can last four to six months while cakes and pastries should be kept in the freezer for three to six months.

HIGH-RISK FOODS

Certain foods may carry risks to people who are considered vulnerable such as the elderly, the ill, pregnant women, babies, young infants and those suffering from a recurring illness.

It is advisable to avoid those foods listed below which belong to a higher-risk category.

There is a slight chance that some eggs carry the bacteria salmonella. Cook the eggs until both the yolk and the white are firm to eliminate this risk. Pay particular attention to dishes and products incorporating lightly cooked or raw eggs which should be eliminated from the diet. Sauces including Hollandaise, mayonnaise, mousses, soufflés and meringues all use raw or lightly cooked eggs, as do custard-based dishes, ice creams and sorbets. These are all considered high-risk foods to the vulnerable groups mentioned above.

Certain meats and poultry also carry the potential risk of salmonella and so should be cooked thoroughly until the juices run clear and there is no pinkness left. Unpasteurised products such as milk, cheese (especially soft cheese), pâté, meat (both raw and cooked) all have the potential risk of listeria and should be avoided.

When buying seafood, buy from a reputable source which has a high turnover to ensure freshness. Fish should have bright clear eyes, shiny skin and bright pink or red gills. The fish should feel stiff to the touch, with a slight smell of sea air and iodine. The flesh of fish steaks and fillets should be translucent with no signs of discolouration. Molluscs such as scallops, clams and mussels are sold fresh and are still alive. Avoid any that are open or do not close when tapped lightly. In the same way, univalves such as cockles or winkles should withdraw back into their shells when lightly prodded. When choosing cephalopods such as squid and octopus they should have a firm flesh and pleasant sea smell.

As with all fish, whether it is shellfish or seafish, care is required when freezing it. It is imperative to check whether the fish has been frozen before. If it has been frozen, then it should not be frozen again under any circumstances.

Essential Ingredients

The quantities may differ, but basic baking ingredients do not vary greatly. Let us take a closer look at the baking ingredients which are essential.

FAT

Butter and firm block margarine are the fats most commonly used in baking. Others can also be used such as white vegetable fat, lard and oil. Low-fat spreads are not recommended as they break down when cooked at a high temperature and are not recommended for baking. Often it is a matter of personal preference which fat you choose when baking but there are a few guidelines that are important to remember.

Unsalted butter is the fat most commonly used in cake making, especially in rich fruit cakes and the heavier sponge cakes such as Madeira or chocolate torte. Unsalted butter gives a distinctive flavour to the cake. Some people favour margarine which imparts little or no flavour to the cake. As a rule, firm margarine and butter should not be used straight from the refrigerator but allowed to come to room temperature before using. Also, it should

be beaten by itself first before creaming or rubbing in. Soft margarine is best suited to one-stage recipes. If oil is used care should be taken – it is a good idea to follow a specific recipe as the proportions of oil to flour and eggs are different.

Fat is an integral ingredient when making pastry, again there are a few specific guidelines to bear in mind.

For shortcrust pastry the best results are achieved by using equal amounts of lard or white vegetable fat with butter or block margarine. The amount of fat used is always half the amount of flour. Other pastries use differing amounts of ingredients. Pâté sucrée (a sweet flan pastry) uses all butter with eggs and a little sugar, while flaky or puff pastry uses a larger proportion of fat to flour and relies on the folding and rolling during making to ensure that the pastry rises and flakes well. When using a recipe, refer to the instructions to obtain the best result.

FLOUR

We can buy a wide range of flour all designed for specific jobs. Strong flour which is rich in gluten, whether it is white or brown (this includes granary and stoneground) is best kept for bread and Yorkshire pudding. It is also recommended for steamed suet puddings as well as puff pastry. 00 flour is designed for pasta making and there is no substitute for this flour. Ordinary flour or weak flour is best for cakes, biscuits and sauces which absorb the fat easily and give a soft light texture. This flour comes in plain white or self-raising, as well as wholemeal. Self-raising flour, which has the raising agent already incorporated is best kept for sponge cakes where it is important that an even rise is achieved. Plain flour can be used for all types of baking and sauces. If using plain flour for scones or cakes and puddings, unless other-wise stated in the recipe, use 1 teaspoon of baking powder to 225 g/8 oz of plain flour. With sponge cakes and light fruit cakes, it is best to use self-raising flour as the raising agent has already been added to the flour. This way there is no danger of using too much which can result in a sunken cake with a sour taste. There are other raising agents that are also used. Some cakes use bicarbonate of soda with or without cream of tartar, blended with warm or sour milk. Whisked eggs also act as a raising agent as the air trapped in the egg ensures that the mixture rises. Generally no other raising agent is required.

Flour also comes ready sifted. There is even a special sponge flour designed especially for whisked sponges. Also, it is possible to buy flours that cater for coeliacs which contain no gluten. Buckwheat, soya and chick pea flours are also available.

EGGS

When a recipe states 1 egg, it is generally accepted this refers to a medium egg. Over the past few years the grading of eggs has changed. For years, eggs were sold as small, standard and large, then this method changed and they were graded in numbers with 1 being the largest. The general feeling by the public was that this system was misleading, so now we buy our eggs as small, medium and large. Due to the slight risk of salmonella, all eggs are now sold date stamped to ensure that the eggs are used in their prime. This applies even to farm eggs which are no longer allowed to be sold straight from the farm. Look for the lion quality stamp (on 75% of all eggs sold) which guarantees that the eggs come from hens vaccinated against salmonella, have been laid in the UK and are produced to the highest food safety and standards. All of these eggs carry a best before date.

There are many types of eggs sold and it really is a question of personal preference which ones are chosen. All offer the same nutritional benefits. The majority of eggs sold in this country are caged eggs. These are the cheapest eggs and the hens have been fed on a manufactured mixed diet.

Barn eggs are from hens kept in barns who are free to roam within the barn. However, their diet is similar to caged hens and the barns may be overcrowded.

It is commonly thought that free-range eggs are from hens that lead a much more natural life and are fed natural foods. This, however, is not always the case and in some instances they may still live in a crowded environment.

Four-grain eggs are from hens that have been fed on grain and no preventative medicines have been included in their diet. Organic eggs are from hens that live in a flock, whose beaks are not clipped and who are completely free to roam. Obviously, these eggs are much more expensive than the others.

Store eggs in the refrigerator with the round end uppermost (as packed in the egg boxes). Allow to come to room temperature before using. Do remember, raw or semi-cooked eggs should not be given to babies, toddlers, pregnant women, the elderly and those suffering from a reccurring illness.

SUGAR

Sugar not only offers taste to baking but also adds texture and volume to the mixture. It is generally accepted that caster sugar is best for sponge cakes, puddings and meringues. Its fine granules disperse evenly when creaming or whisking. Granulated sugar is used for more general cooking, such as stewing fruit, whereas demerara sugar with its toffee taste and crunchy texture is good for sticky puddings and cakes such as flapjacks. For rich fruit cakes, Christmas puddings and cakes, use the muscovado sugars which give a rich intense molasses or treacle flavour. Icing sugar is used primarily for icings and can be used in meringues and in fruit sauces when the sugar needs to dissolve quickly. For a different flavour try flavouring your own sugar. Place a vanilla pod in a screw top jar, fill with caster sugar, screw down the lid and leave for 2–3 weeks before using. Top up after use or use thinly pared lemon or orange rind in the same manner.

If trying to reduce sugar intake then use the unrefined varieties, such as golden granulated, golden caster, unrefined demerara and the muscovado sugars. All of these are a little sweeter than their refined counterparts, so less is required. Alternatively, clear honey or fructose (fruit sugar) can reduce sugar intake as they have similar calories to sugar, but are twice as sweet. Also, they have a slow release so their effect lasts longer. Dried fruits can also be included in the diet to top up sugar intake.

YEAST

There is something very comforting about the aroma of freshly baked bread and the taste is far different and superior to commercially made bread. Bread making is regarded by some as being a time consuming process but with the advent of fast-acting yeast this no longer applies. There are three types of yeast available, fresh yeast, which can now be bought in the instore bakery department of many supermarkets (fresh yeast freezes well), dried yeast which is available in tins and quick-acting yeast which comes in packets.

Fresh yeast should be bought in small quantities; it has a putty-like colour and texture with a slight wine smell. It should be creamed with a little sugar and some warm liquid before being added to the flour.

Dried yeast, can be stored for up to six months and comes in small hard granules. It should be sprinkled on to warm liquid with a little sugar then left to stand, normally between 15–20 minutes, until the mixture froths. When replacing the fresh yeast with dried yeast, use 1 tablespoon of dried yeast for 25 g/1 oz of fresh yeast.

Quick acting yeast cuts down the time of bread making and eliminates the need for proving the bread twice. Also, the yeast can be added straight to the flour without it needing to be activated. When replacing quick-acting yeast for dried yeast, you will need double the amount.

When using yeast the most important thing to remember is that yeast is a living plant and needs food, water and warmth to work.

Equipment

Nowadays, you can get lost in the cookware sections of some of the larger stores – they really are a cook's paradise with gadgets, cooking tools and state-of-the-art electronic blenders, mixers and liquidisers. A few, well-picked, high-quality utensils and pieces of equipment will be frequently used and will therefore be a much wiser buy than cheaper gadgets.

Cooking equipment not only assists in the kitchen, but can make all the difference between success and failure. Take the humble cake tin, although a very basic piece of cooking equipment, it plays an essential role in baking. Using the incorrect size, for example, a tin that is too large will spread the mixture too thinly and the result will be a flat, limp-looking cake. On the other hand, cramming the mixture into a tin which is too small will result in the mixture rising up and out of the tin.

BAKING EQUIPMENT

To ensure successful baking it is worth investing in a selection of high quality tins, which if looked after properly should last for many years. Follow the manufacturers' instructions when first using and ensure that the tins are thoroughly washed and dried after use and before putting away.

Perhaps the most useful of tins for baking are sandwich cake tins, ideal for classics such as Victoria sponge, genoese and coffee and walnut cake. You will need two tins and they are normally 18 cm/7 inches or 20.5 cm/8 inches in diameter and are about 5–7.5cm/2–3 inches deep and are often non stick.

With deep cake tins, it is personal choice whether you buy round or square tins and they vary in size from 12.5–35.5 cm/5–14 inches with a depth of between 12.5–15 cm/5–6 inches. A deep cake tin, for everyday fruit or Madeira cake is a must, a useful size is 20.5 cm/8 inches.

Loaf tins are used for bread, fruit or tea bread and terrines and normally come in two sizes, 450 g/1 lb and 900 g/2 lb.

Good baking sheets are a must for all cooks. Dishes that are too hot to handle such as apple pies should be placed directly on to the baking tray. Meringues, biscuits and cookies are cooked on the tray. Do not confuse with Swiss roll tins which have sides all around, whereas a sheet only has one raised side.

Square or oblong shallow baking tins are also very useful for making tray bakes, fudge brownies, flapjacks and shortbread.

Then there are patty tins; ideal for making small buns, jam tarts or mince pies; individual Yorkshire pudding tins and muffin tins or flan tins. They are available in a variety of sizes.

There are plenty of other tins to choose from, ranging from themed tins, such as a Christmas

trees, numbers from 1–9 as well as tins shaped as petals, ring mould tins, (tins with a hole in the centre) to spring form tins where the sides release after cooking allowing the finished cake to be removed easily.

Three to four different sizes of mixing bowls are also very useful.

Another piece of equipment which is worth having is a wire cooling rack. It is essential when baking to allow biscuits and cakes to cool after being removed from their tins.

A selection of different sized roasting tins are also a worthwhile investment as they can double up as a bain marie, or for cooking larger quantities of cakes such as gingerbread. A few different tins and dishes are required if baking crumbles, soufflés and pies. Ramekin dishes and small pudding basins can be used for a variety of

different recipes as can small tartlet tins and dariole moulds.

When purchasing your implements for baking, perhaps the rolling pin is one of the most important. Ideally it should be long and thin, heavy enough to roll the pastry out easily but not too heavy that it is uncomfortable to use. Pastry needs to be rolled out on a flat surface and although a lightly floured flat surface will do, a marble slab will ensure that the pastry is kept cool and ensures that the fats do not melt while being rolled. This helps to keep the pastry light, crisp and flaky rather than heavy and stodgy which happens if the fat melts before being baked.

Other useful basic pastry implements are tools such as a pastry brush (which can be used to wet pastry or brush on a glaze), a pastry wheel for cutting and a sieve to remove impurities and also

to sift air into the flour, encouraging the pastry or mixture to be lighter in texture.

Basic mixing cutlery is also essential such as a wooden spoon (for mixing and creaming), a spatula (for transferring the mixture from the mixing bowl to the baking tins and spreading the mixture once it is in the tins) and a palette knife (to ease cakes and breads out of their tins before placing them on the wire racks to cool). Measuring spoons are essential for accurate measuring of both dry and wet ingredients.

ELECTRICAL EQUIPMENT

Nowadays help from time-saving gadgets and electrical equipment make baking far easier and quicker. Equipment can be used for creaming, mixing, beating, whisking and kneading, grating and chopping. There is a wide choice of machines available from the most basic to the very sophisticated.

FOOD PROCESSORS

First decide what you need your processor to do when choosing a machine. If you are a novice to baking, it may be a waste to start with a machine which offers a wide range of implements and functions. This can be off putting and result in not using the machine to its ultimate.

In general, while styling and product design play a role in the price, the more you pay, the larger the machine will be with a bigger bowl capacity and many more gadgets attached. Nowadays, you can chop, shred, slice, chip, blend, purée, knead, whisk and cream anything. However, just what basic features should you ensure your machine has before buying it?

When buying a food processor look for measurements on the side of the processor bowl and machines with a removable feed tube which allows food or liquid to be added while the motor is still running. Look out for machines that have the facility to increase the capacity of the bowl (ideal when making soup) and have a pulse button for controlled chopping.

For many, storage is an issue so reversible discs and flex storage, or on more advanced models, a blade storage compartment or box, can be advantageous.

It is also worth thinking about machines which offer optional extras which can be bought as your cooking requirements change. Mini-chopping bowls are available for those wanting to chop small quantities of food. If time is an issue, dishwasher-friendly attachments may be vital. Citrus presses, liquidisers and whisks may all be useful attachments for the individual cook.

BLENDERS

Blenders often come as attachments to food processors and are generally used for liquidising and puréeing foods. There are two main types of blender. The first is known as a goblet blender. The blades of this blender are at the bottom of the goblet with measurements up the sides. The second blender is portable. It is hand-held and should be placed in a bowl to blend.

FOOD MIXERS

These are ideally suited to mixing cakes and kneading dough, either as a table-top mixer or a hand-held mixer. Both are extremely useful and based on the same principle of mixing or whisking in an open bowl to allow more air to get to the mixture and therefore give a lighter texture.

The table-top mixers are freestanding and are capable of dealing with fairly large quantities of mixture. They are robust machines, capable of easily dealing with kneading dough and heavy cake mixing as well as whipping cream, whisking egg whites or making one-stage cakes. These mixers also offer a wide range of attachments ranging from liquidisers, mincers, juicers, can openers and many more and varied attachments.

Hand-held mixers are smaller than freestanding mixers and often come with their own bowl and stand from which they can be lifted off and used as hand-held devices. They have a motorised head with detachable twin whisks. These mixers are particularly versatile as they do not need a specific bowl in which to whisk. Any suitable mixing bowl can be used.

Basic Techniques

There is no mystery to successful baking, it really is easy providing you follow a few simple rules and guidelines. First, read the recipe right through before commencing. There is nothing more annoying than getting to the middle of a recipe and discovering that you are minus one or two of the ingredients. Until you are confident, follow a recipe, do not try a short cut otherwise you may find that you have left out a vital step which means that the recipe really cannot work. Most of all, have patience, baking is easy – if you can read, you can bake.

PASTRY MAKING

Pastry needs to be kept as cool as possible through-out. Cool hands help, but are not essential. Use cold or iced water, but not too much as pastry does not need to be wet. Make sure that your fat is not runny or melted but firm (this is why block fat is the best). Avoid using too much flour when rolling out as this alters the proportions and also avoid handling the dough too much. Roll in one direction as this helps to ensure that the pastry does not shrink Allow to rest, preferably in the refrigerator after rolling. If you follow these guidelines but still your pastry is not as good as you would like it to be, then make in a processor instead.

LINING A FLAN CASE

It is important to choose the right tin to bake with. You will often find that a loose-bottomed metal flan case is the best option as it conducts heat more efficiently and evenly than a ceramic dish. It also has the advantage of a removable base which makes transfering the final flan easy; it simply lifts out keeping the pastry intact.

Roll the pastry out on a lightly floured surface ensuring that it is a few inches larger than the flan case. Wrap the pastry round the rolling pin, lift and place in the tin. Carefully ease the pastry into the base and sides of the tin, ensuring that there are no tears in the pastry. Allow to rest for a few minutes then trim the edge either with a sharp knife or by rolling a rolling pin across the top of the flan tin.

HINTS FOR SUCCESSFUL BAKING

Ensure that the ingredients are accurately measured. A cake that has too much flour or insufficient egg will be dry and crumbly. Take care when measuring the raising agent if used, as too much will mean that the cake will rise too quickly and then sink. Insufficient raising agent means the cake will not rise in the first place.

Ensure that the oven is preheated to the correct temperature, it can take 10 minutes to reach 180°C/350°F/Gas Mark 4. You may find that an oven thermometer is a good investment. Cakes are best if cooked in the centre of the preheated oven. Try to avoid opening the oven door at the start of cooking as a draft can make the cake sink. If using a fan oven refer to the manufacturers' instructions.

Check that the cake is thoroughly cooked by removing from the oven and inserting a clean skewer. Leave for 30 seconds and remove. If clean then the cake is cooked, if there is a little mixture return to the oven for a few minutes.

Other problems while cake making are in-sufficient creaming of the fat and sugar or a curdled creamed mixture (which will result in a fairly solid cake). Flour that has not been folded in carefully enough or has not been mixed with enough raising agent may also result in a fairly heavy consistency. Ensure that the correct size of tin is used as you may end up either with a flat, hard cake or one which has spilled over the edge of the tin. Be aware – especially when cooking with fruit – that if the consistency is too soft, the cake will not be able to support the fruit.

Finally, when you take your cake out of the oven, unless the recipe states that it should be left in the tin until cold, leave for a few minutes, then loosen the edges and turn out on to a wire rack to cool. Cakes which are left in the tin for too long, tend to sink or slightly overcook. When storing, make sure the cake is completely cold before placing it into an airtight tin or plastic container.

BAKING BLIND

The term baking blind means that the pastry case needs to be cooked without the filling, resulting in a crisp pastry shell that is either partially or fully cooked depending on whether the filling needs any cooking. Pastry shells can be prepared ahead of time as they last for several days if stored correctly in an airtight container or longer if frozen.

To bake blind, line a pastry case with the prepared pastry and allow to rest in the refrigerator for 30 minutes. This will help to minimise shrinkage while it is being cooked. Remove from the refrigerator and lightly prick the base all over with a fork (do not do this if the filling is runny). Brush with a little beaten egg if desired or simply line the case with a large square of greaseproof paper, big enough to cover both the base and sides of the pastry case. Fill with either ceramic baking beans or dried beans. Place on a baking sheet and bake in a preheated oven, generally at 200°C/400°F/Gas Mark 6, remembering that ovens can take at least 15 minutes to reach this heat. Cook for 10–12 minutes, then remove from the oven, discard the paper and beans. Return to the oven and continue to cook for a further 5–10 minutes depending on whether the filling needs cooking. Normally unless otherwise stated, individual pastry tartlet cases also benefit from baking blind.

COVERING A PIE DISH

To cover a pie, roll out the pastry until it is about two inches larger than the circumference of the dish. Cut a 2.5 cm/1 inch strip from around the outside of the pastry and then moisten the edge of the pie dish you are using. Place the strip on the edge of the dish and brush with water or beaten egg. Generously fill the pie dish until the surface is slightly rounded. Using the rolling pin, lift the remaining pastry and cover the pie dish. Press together, then seal. Using a sharp knife, trim off any excess pastry from around the edges. Try to avoid brushing the edges of the pastry especially puff pastry as this prevents the pastry rising evenly.

Before placing in the oven make a small hole in the centre of the pie to allow the steam to escape.

The edges of the pie can be forked by pressing the back of a fork around the edge of the pie or instead crimp by pinching the edge crust holding the thumb and index finger of your right hand against the edge while gently pushing with the index finger of your left hand. Other ways of finishing the pie are to knock up (achieved by gently pressing your index finger down on to the rim and, at the same time, tapping a knife horizontally along the edge giving it a flaky appearance), or fluting the edges by pressing your thumb down on the edge of the pastry while gently drawing back an all-purpose knife about 1 cm/⅓ inch and repeating around the rim. Experiment by putting leaves and berries made out of leftover pastry to finish off the pie, then brush the top of the pie with beaten egg.

LINING CAKE TINS

If a recipe states that the tin needs lining do not be tempted to ignore this. Rich fruit cakes and other cakes that take a long time to cook benefit from the tin being lined so that the edges and base do not burn or dry out. Greaseproof or baking parchment paper is ideal for this. It is a good idea to have the paper at least double thickness, or preferably 3–4 thicknesses. Sponge cakes and other cakes that are cooked in 30 minutes or less are also better if the bases are lined as it is far easier to remove them from the tin.

The best way to line a round or square tin is to lightly draw around the base and then cut just inside the markings making it easy to sit in the tin. Next, lightly oil the paper so it easily peels away from the cake. If the sides of the tin also need to be lined, then cut a strip of paper long enough for the tin. This can be measured by wrapping a piece of string around the rim of the tin. Once again, lightly oil the paper, push against the tin and oil once more as this will hold the paper to the sides of the tin. Steamed puddings usually need only a disc of greaseproof paper at the bottom of the dish as the sides come away easily.

Handling Chocolate
Tips & Techniques

There are a few useful techniques for working with chocolate. None of them are very complicated, and all can be mastered easily with a little practice.

These general guidelines apply equally for all types of chocolate.

MELTING CHOCOLATE

All types of chocolate are sensitive to temperature, so care needs to be taken during the melting process. It is also worth noting that different brands of chocolate have different consistencies when melting and when melted. Experiment with different brands to find one that you prefer.

As a general rule, it is important not to allow any water to come into contact with the chocolate. In fact, a drop or two of water is more dangerous than larger amounts, which may blend in. The melted chocolate will seize and it will be impossible to bring it back to a smooth consistency.

Do not overheat chocolate or melt it by itself in a pan over a direct heat. Always use either a double boiler or a heatproof bowl set over a saucepan of water, but do not allow the bottom of the bowl to come into contact with the water as this would overheat the chocolate. Keep an eye on the chocolate, checking it every couple of minutes and reducing or extinguishing the heat under the saucepan, as necessary. Stir the chocolate once or twice during melting until it is smooth and no lumps remain. Do not cover the bowl once the chocolate has melted or condensation will form, water will drop into it and it will be ruined. If the chocolate turns from a glossy, liquid mass into a dull, coarse, textured mess, you will have to start again.

Microwaving is another way of melting chocolate, but again, caution is required. Follow the

oven manufacturer's instructions together with the instructions on the chocolate and proceed with care. Melt the chocolate in bursts of 30–60 seconds, stirring well between bursts until the chocolate is smooth. If possible, stop microwaving before all the chocolate has melted and allow the residual heat in the chocolate to finish the job. The advantage of microwaving is that you do not need to use a saucepan, making the whole job quicker and neater.

MAKING CHOCOLATE DECORATIONS

Curls and caraque Chocolate curls are made using a clean paint scraper. They are usually large, fully formed curls which are useful for decorating gateaux and cakes. Caraque are long thin curls which can be used in the same way, but are less dramatic.

To make either shape, melt the chocolate following your preferred method and then spread it in a thin layer over a cool surface, such as a marble slab, ceramic tile or piece of granite. Leave until just set but not hard.

To make curls, take the clean paint scraper and set it at an angle to the surface of the chocolate, then push, taking a layer off the surface. This will curl until you release the pressure.

To make caraque, use a large sharp knife and hold it at about a 45-degree angle to the chocolate. Hold the handle and the tip and scrape the knife towards you pulling the handle but keeping the tip more or less in the same place. This method makes thinner, tighter, longer curls.

SHAVED CHOCOLATE Using a vegetable peeler, shave a thick block of chocolate to make mini-curls. These are best achieved if the chocolate is a little soft, otherwise it has a tendency to break into little flakes.

CHOCOLATE SHAPES Spread a thin layer of chocolate, as described in the instructions for chocolate curls, and allow to set as before. Use shaped cutters or a sharp knife to cut out shapes. Use to decorate cakes.

CHOCOLATE LEAVES Many types of leaf are suitable, but ensure they are not poisonous before using. Rose leaves are easy to find and make good shapes. Wash and dry the leaves carefully before using. Melt chocolate following the instructions given at the beginning of the section. Using a small paintbrush, paint a thin layer of chocolate on to the back of the leaf. Allow to set before adding another thin layer. When set, carefully peel off the leaf. Chocolate leaves are also very attractive when made using two different types of chocolate, white and dark chocolate, for example. Paint half the leaf first with one type of chocolate and allow to set before painting the other half with the second chocolate. Leave to set then peel off the leaf as above.

CHOCOLATE LACE Make a non stick baking parchment piping bag. Draw an outline of the required shape onto some nonstick baking parchment, a triangle, for example. Pipe chocolate evenly onto the outline, fill in the centre with lacy squiggles and leave until set. Remove the paper to use.

CHOCOLATE SQUIGGLES Use a teaspoon of melted chocolate to drizzle random shapes on to nonstick baking parchment. Leave to set and remove paper to use. Alternatively, pipe a zigzag line about 5 cm/2 inches long on to a piece of nonstick baking parchment. Pipe a straight line slightly longer at either end down the middle of the zigzag.

CHOCOLATE BUTTERFLIES Draw a butterfly shape on a piece of nonstick baking parchment. Fold the paper down the middle of the body of the butterfly to make a crease, then open

the paper out flat. Pipe chocolate on to the outline of the butterfly, then fill in the wings with loose zigzag lines. Carefully fold the paper so the wings are at right-angles, supporting them from underneath in the corner of a large tin or with some other support, and leave until set. Peel away the paper to use.

CHOCOLATE MODELLING paste To make chocolate modelling paste (very useful for cake coverings and for making heavier shapes, like ribbons) put 200 g/7 oz plain chocolate in a bowl and add 3 tablespoons of liquid glucose. Set the bowl over a pan of gently simmering water. Stir until the chocolate is just melted then remove from the heat. Beat until smooth and leave the mixture to cool. When cool enough to handle, knead to a smooth paste on a clean work surface. The mixture can now be rolled and cut to shape. If the paste hardens, wrap it in clingfilm and warm it in the microwave for a few seconds on low.

CARAMEL AND PRALINE DECORATIONS

Caramel Put 75 g/3 oz of granulated sugar into a heavy-based saucepan with about 3 tablespoons of cold water. Over a low heat, stir well until the sugar has dissolved completely. If any sugar clings to the pan, brush it down using a wet brush. Bring the mixture to the boil and cook, without stirring, until the mixture turns golden. You may need to tilt the pan carefully to ensure the sugar colours evenly. As soon as the desired colour is reached, remove the pan from the heat and plunge the base of the pan into cold water to stop it from cooking further.

Praline To make praline, follow the instructions as for caramel but during the final stage do not plunge the pan into cold water. Add nuts to the caramel mixture, do not stir, but pour immediately on to an oiled baking sheet. Leave to set at room temperature. Once cold, the praline can be chopped or broken into pieces as required. Keep leftover praline in a sealed container. It will keep for several months if stored this way.

CARAMEL-DIPPED NUTS Make the caramel, remove the pan from the heat and plunge into cold water as described earlier. Using two skewers or two forks, dip individual nuts into the hot caramel, lift out carefully, allowing excess to run off, then transfer to a foil-covered tray until set. If the caramel becomes too sticky or starts making a lot of sugar strands, reheat gently until liquid again.

CARAMEL SHAPES Make the caramel, remove the pan from the heat and plunge into cold water as described earlier. Using a teaspoon, drizzle or pour spoonfuls of caramel on to an oiled baking sheet. Leave to set before removing from the tray. Do not refrigerate caramel shapes as they will liquefy.

CARAMEL LACE Follow the method for caramel shapes, but use the teaspoon to drizzle threads in a random pattern on to an oiled tray. When set, break into pieces to use as decorations. Do not refrigerate.

Smoked Haddock Tart

1 Preheat the oven to 190°C/ 375°F/Gas Mark 5. Sift the flour and salt into a large bowl. Add the fats and mix lightly. Using the fingertips rub into the flour until the mixture resembles breadcrumbs.

2 Sprinkle 1 tablespoon of cold water into the mixture and with a knife, start bringing the dough together. (It may be necessary to use the hands for the final stage.) If the dough does not form a ball instantly, add a little more water.

3 Put the pastry in a polythene bag and chill for at least 30 minutes.

4 On a lightly floured surface, roll out the pastry and use to line a 18 cm/7 inch lightly oiled quiche or flan tin. Prick the base all over with a fork and bake blind in the preheated oven for 15 minutes.

5 Carefully remove the pastry from the oven, brush with a little of the beaten egg.

6 Return to the oven for a further 5 minutes, then place the fish in the pastry case.

7 For the filling, beat together the eggs and cream. Add the mustard, black pepper and cheese and pour over the fish.

8 Sprinkle with the chives and bake for 35–40 minutes or until the filling is golden brown and set in the centre. Serve hot or cold with the lemon and tomato wedges and salad leaves.

INGREDIENTS
Serves 6

SHORTCRUST PASTRY:
150 g/5 oz plain flour
pinch of salt
25 g/1 oz lard or white vegetable fat, cut into small cubes
40 g/1½ oz butter or hard margarine, cut into small cubes

FOR THE FILLING:
225 g/8 oz smoked haddock, skinned and cubed
2 large eggs, beaten
300 ml/½ pint double cream
1 tsp Dijon mustard
freshly ground black pepper
125 g/4 oz Gruyère cheese, grated
1 tbsp freshly snipped chives

TO SERVE:
lemon wedges
tomato wedges
fresh green salad leaves

Food Fact

Haddock is a good low-fat source of protein as well as containing vitamins B6 and B12 and niacin acid. Where possible it is best to buy the slightly more expensive undyed variety.

Stilton, Tomato & Courgette Quiche

1 Preheat the oven to 190°C/ 375°F/Gas Mark 5. On a lightly floured surface, roll out the pastry and use to line an 18 cm/7 inch lightly oiled quiche or flan tin, trimming any excess pastry with a knife.

2 Prick the base all over with a fork and bake blind in the preheated oven for 15 minutes. Remove the pastry from the oven and brush with a little of the beaten egg. Return to the oven for a further 5 minutes.

3 Heat the butter in a frying pan and gently fry the onion and courgette for about 4 minutes until soft and starting to brown. Transfer into the pastry case.

4 Sprinkle the Stilton over evenly and top with the halved cherry tomatoes. Beat together the eggs and crème fraîche and season to taste with salt and pepper.

5 Pour the filling into the pastry case and bake in the oven for 35–40 minutes, or until the filling is golden brown and set in the centre. Serve the quiche hot or cold.

INGREDIENTS
Serves 4

1 quantity shortcrust pastry (see page 30)
25 g/1 oz butter
1 onion, peeled and finely chopped
1 courgette, trimmed and sliced
125 g/4 oz Stilton cheese, crumbled
6 cherry tomatoes, halved
2 large eggs, beaten
200 ml tub crème fraîche
salt and freshly ground black pepper

Food Fact

Stilton is a very traditional British cheese which often makes an appearance on the cheese board or served with a ploughman's lunch. It gets much of its full pungent flavour, from its veins (created from the steel wires which are inserted into the cheese during the maturing process). It is worth looking for a piece of Stilton with lots of veins that has been matured for longer.

French Onion Tart

1 Preheat the oven to 200°C/ 400°F/Gas Mark 6. Place the butter in the freezer for 30 minutes. Sift the flour and salt into a large bowl. Remove the butter from the freezer and grate using the coarse side of a grater, dipping the butter in the flour every now and again as it makes it easier to grate.

2 Mix the butter into the flour, using a knife, making sure all the butter is coated thoroughly with flour.

3 Add 2 tablespoons of cold water and continue to mix, bringing the mixture together. Use your hands to complete the mixing. Add a little more water if needed to leave a clean bowl. Place the pastry in a polythene bag and chill in the refrigerator for 30 minutes.

4 Heat the oil in a large frying pan, then fry the onions for 10 minutes, stirring occasionally until softened.

5 Stir in the white wine vinegar and sugar. Increase the heat and stir frequently, for another 4–5 minutes until the onions turn a deep caramel colour. Cook for another 5 minutes, then reserve to cool.

6 On a lightly floured surface, roll out the pastry to a 35.5 cm/14 inch circle. Wrap over a rolling pin and move the circle on to a baking sheet.

7 Sprinkle half the cheese over the pastry, leaving a 5 cm/2 inch border around the edge, then spoon the caramelised onions over the cheese.

8 Fold the uncovered pastry edges over the edge of the filling to form a rim and brush the rim with beaten egg or milk.

9 Season to taste with salt and pepper. Sprinkle over the remaining Cheddar and bake for 20–25 minutes. Transfer to a large plate and serve immediately.

INGREDIENTS
Serves 4

QUICK FLAKY PASTRY:
125 g/4 oz butter
175 g/6 oz plain flour
pinch of salt

FOR THE FILLING:
2 tbsp olive oil
4 large onions, peeled and
  thinly sliced
3 tbsp white wine vinegar
2 tbsp muscovado sugar
a little beaten egg or milk
175 g/6 oz Cheddar
  cheese, grated
salt and freshly ground
  black pepper

Tasty Tip

For a milder, nutty taste, substitute the Cheddar cheese for Gruyère and grate a little nutmeg over the layer of cheese in step 7.

Parsnip Tatin

1 Preheat the oven to 200°C/400°F/Gas Mark 6. Heat the butter in a 20.5 cm/8 inch frying pan.

2 Add the parsnips, arranging the cut side down with the narrow ends towards the centre.

3 Sprinkle the parsnips with sugar and cook for 15 minutes, turning halfway through until golden.

4 Add the apple juice and bring to the boil. Remove the pan from the heat.

5 On a lightly floured surface, roll the pastry out to a size slightly larger than the frying pan.

6 Position the pastry over the parsnips and press down slightly to enclose the parsnips.

7 Bake in the preheated oven for 20–25 minutes until the parsnips and pastry are golden.

8 Invert a warm serving plate over the pan and carefully turn the pan over to flip the tart on to the plate. Serve immediately.

INGREDIENTS
Serves 4

1 quantity shortcrust pastry (see page 30)

FOR THE FILLING:

50 g/2 oz butter
8 small parsnips, peeled and halved
1 tbsp brown sugar
75 ml/3 fl oz apple juice

Food Fact

In many parts of Europe parsnips are unpopular. Indeed, in Italy they feed them to the pigs. However, parsnips are great winter warmers especially when mashed with potatoes.

Tasty Tip

This dish is delicious served warm with a Greek salad. Feta cheese is one of the main ingredients in Greek salad and because of its salty taste, it tastes particularly good with the creamy flavour of parsnips in this recipe.

Garlic Wild Mushrooms Galettes

1 Preheat the oven to 220°C/ 425°F/Gas Mark 7. On a lightly floured surface roll out the chilled pastry very thinly.

2 Cut out 6 x 15 cm/6 inch circles and place on a lightly oiled baking sheet.

3 Thinly slice the onion, then divide into rings and reserve.

4 Thinly slice the chilli and slice the garlic into wafer-thin slivers. Add to the onions and reserve.

5 Wipe or lightly rinse the mushrooms. Half or quarter any large mushrooms and keep the small ones whole.

6 Heat the butter in a frying pan and sauté the onion, chilli and garlic gently for about 3 minutes. Add the mushrooms and cook for about 5 minutes, or until beginning to soften.

7 Stir the parsley into the mushroom mixture and drain off any excess liquid.

8 Pile the mushroom mixture on to the pastry circles within 5 mm/¼ inches of the edge. Arrange the sliced mozzarella cheese on top.

9 Bake in the preheated oven for 12–15 minutes, or until golden brown and serve with the tomatoes and salad.

INGREDIENTS
Serves 6

1 quantity quick flaky pastry (see page 34), chilled
1 onion, peeled
1 red chilli, deseeded
2 garlic cloves, peeled
275 g/10 oz mixed mushrooms e.g. oyster, chestnuts, morels, ceps and chanterelles
25 g/1 oz butter
2 tbsp freshly chopped parsley
125 g/4 oz mozzarella cheese, sliced

TO SERVE:
cherry tomatoes
mixed green salad leaves

Helpful Hint

Many supermarkets now stock a variety of wild mushrooms, all of which can be used in this recipe. It is important to maintain as much of the flavour of the mushrooms as possible, so do not peel mushrooms unless they appear old or tough. Either rinse lightly if covered with small pieces of soil or wipe well, trim the stalks and use.

Beef & Red Wine Pie

1 Preheat the oven to 200°C/ 400°F/Gas Mark 6. Toss the beef cubes in the seasoned flour.

2 Heat the oil in a large heavy-based frying pan. Fry the beef in batches for about 5 minutes until golden brown.

3 Return all of the beef to the pan and add the onions, garlic and thyme. Fry for about 10 minutes, stirring occasionally. If the beef begins to stick, add a little water.

4 Add the red wine and stock and bring to the boil. Stir in the Worcestershire sauce, tomato ketchup and bay leaves.

5 Cover and simmer on a very low heat for about 1 hour or until the beef is tender.

6 Heat the butter and gently sauté the mushrooms until golden brown. Add to the stew. Simmer uncovered for a further 15 minutes. Remove the bay leaves. Spoon the beef into a 1.1 litre/2 pint pie dish and reserve.

7 Roll out the pastry on a lightly floured surface. Cut out the lid to 5 mm/¼ inch wider than the dish. Brush the rim with the beaten egg and lay the pastry lid on top. Press to seal, then knock the edges with the back of the knife.

8 Cut a slit in the lid and brush with the beaten egg or milk to glaze. Bake in the preheated oven for 30 minutes, or until golden brown. Garnish with the sprig of parsley and serve immediately.

INGREDIENTS
Serves 4

1 quantity quick flaky pastry (see page 34), chilled
700 g/1½ lb stewing beef, cubed
4 tbsp seasoned plain flour
2 tbsp sunflower oil
2 onions, peeled and chopped
2 garlic cloves, peeled and crushed
1 tbsp freshly chopped thyme
300 ml/½ pint red wine
150 ml/¼ pint beef stock
1–2 tsp Worcestershire sauce
2 tbsp tomato ketchup
2 bay leaves
a knob of butter
225 g/8 oz button mushrooms
beaten egg or milk, to glaze
sprig of parsley, to garnish

Helpful Hint

Shortcrust or puff pastry could also be used to top the pie in this recipe. It is important though, whichever pastry is used, to brush the pie with beaten egg or milk before baking, as this will result in an appetising golden crust.

Moroccan Lamb with Apricots

1 Preheat the oven to 190°C/ 375°F/Gas Mark 5. Pound the ginger, garlic, cardamom and cumin to a paste with a pestle and mortar. Heat 1 tablespoon of the oil in a large frying pan and fry the spice paste for 3 minutes. Remove and reserve.

2 Add the remaining oil and fry the lamb in batches for about 5 minutes, until golden brown. Return all the lamb to the pan and add the onions and spice paste. Fry for 10 minutes, stirring occasionally.

3 Add the chopped tomatoes, cover and simmer for 15 minutes. Add the apricots and chickpeas and simmer for a further 15 minutes.

4 Lightly oil a round 18 cm/7 inch spring form cake tin.

Lay one sheet of filo pastry in the base of the tin, allowing the excess to fall over the sides. Brush with melted butter, then layer five more sheets in the tin and brush each one with butter.

5 Spoon in the filling and level the surface. Layer half the remaining filo sheets on top, again brushing each with butter. Fold the overhanging pastry over the top of the filling. Brush the remaining sheet with butter and scrunch up and place on top of the pie so that the whole pie is completely covered. Brush with melted butter once more.

6 Bake in the preheated oven for 45 minutes, then reserve for 10 minutes. Unclip the tin and remove the pie. Sprinkle with the nutmeg, garnish with the dill sprigs and serve.

INGREDIENTS
Serves 6

5 cm/2 inch piece root ginger,
  peeled and grated
3 garlic cloves, peeled and crushed
1 tsp ground cardamom
1 tsp ground cumin
2 tbsp olive oil
450 g/1 lb lamb neck fillet, cubed
1 large red onion, peeled
400 g can chopped tomatoes
125 g/4 oz ready-to-eat
  dried apricots
400 g can chickpeas, drained
7 large sheets filo pastry
50 g/2 oz butter, melted
pinch of nutmeg
dill sprigs, to garnish

Food Fact

Ready-prepared filo pastry is sold rolled in wafer-thin sheets and is available from most supermarkets and good grocers.

Bacon, Mushroom & Cheese Puffs

1 Preheat the oven to 200°C/400°F/Gas Mark 6. Heat the olive oil in a large frying pan.

2 Add the mushrooms and bacon and fry for 6–8 minutes until golden in colour. Stir in the parsley, season to taste with salt and pepper and allow to cool.

3 Roll the sheet of pastry a little thinner on a lightly floured surface to a 30.5 cm/12 inch square. Cut the pastry into 4 equal squares.

4 Stir the grated Emmenthal cheese into the mushroom mixture. Spoon a quarter of the mixture on to one half of each square.

5 Brush the edges of the square with a little of the beaten egg.

6 Fold over the pastry to form a triangular parcel. Seal the edges well and place on a lightly oiled baking sheet. Repeat until the squares are done

7 Make shallow slashes in the top of the pastry with a knife.

8 Brush the parcels with the remaining beaten egg and cook in the preheated oven for 20 minutes, or until puffy and golden brown.

9 Serve warm or cold, garnished with the salad leaves and served with tomatoes.

INGREDIENTS
Serves 4

1 tbsp olive oil
225 g/8 oz field mushrooms, wiped and roughly chopped
225 g/8 oz rindless streaky bacon, roughly chopped
2 tbsp freshly chopped parsley
salt and freshly ground black pepper
350 g/12 oz ready-rolled puff pastry sheets, thawed if frozen
25 g/1 oz Emmenthal cheese, grated
1 medium egg, beaten
salad leaves such as rocket or watercress, to garnish
tomatoes, to serve

Tasty Tip

The Emmenthal cheese in this recipe can be substituted for any other cheese, but for best results use a cheese such as Cheddar, which like Emmenthal melts easily! The bacon can also be substituted for slices of sweeter cured hams such as pancetta, speck, Parma or prosciutto.

Fennel & Caramelised Shallot Tartlets

1 Preheat the oven to 200°C/ 400°F/Gas Mark 6. Sift the flour into a bowl, then rub in the butter, using the fingertips. Stir in the cheese, then add the egg yolk with about 2 tablespoons of cold water. Mix to a firm dough, then knead lightly. Wrap in clingfilm and chill in the refrigerator for 30 minutes.

2 Roll out the pastry on a lightly floured surface and use to line 6 x 10 cm/ 4 inch individual flan tins or patty tins which are about 2 cm/¾ inch deep.

3 Line the pastry cases with greaseproof paper and fill with baking beans or rice. Bake blind in the preheated oven for about 10 minutes, then remove the paper and beans.

4 Heat the oil in a frying pan, add the shallots and fennel and fry gently for 5 minutes. Sprinkle with the sugar and cook for a further 10 minutes, stirring occasionally until lightly caramelised. Reserve until cooled.

5 Beat together the egg and cream and season to taste with salt and pepper. Divide the shallot mixture between the pastry cases. Pour over the egg mixture and sprinkle with the cheese and cinnamon. Bake for 20 minutes, until golden and set. Serve with the salad leaves.

INGREDIENTS
Serves 6

CHEESE PASTRY:
176 g/6 oz plain white flour
75 g/3 oz slightly salted butter
50 g/2 oz Gruyère cheese, grated
1 small egg yolk

FOR THE FILLING:
2 tbsp olive oil
225 g/8 oz shallots, peeled
  and halved
1 fennel bulb, trimmed and sliced
1 tsp soft brown sugar
1 medium egg
150 ml/¼ pint double cream
salt and freshly ground
  black pepper
25 g/1 oz Gruyère cheese, grated
½ tsp ground cinnamon
mixed salad leaves, to serve

Tasty Tip

Fennel has a very aromatic, almost aniseed flavour, which works particularly well with the sweet shallots and the cheese in this dish. A nice addition, is to add a generous grating of nutmeg to the pie filling in step 5 as this compliments the creamy cheese filling.

Roasted Vegetable Pie

1 Preheat the oven to 220°C/ 425°F/Gas Mark 7. Sift the flour and salt into a large bowl, add the fats and mix lightly. Using the fingertips rub into the flour until the mixture resembles breadcrumbs. Stir in the herbes de Provence. Sprinkle over a tablespoon of cold water and with a knife start bringing the dough together. (It may be necessary to use the hands for the final stage.) If the dough does not form a ball instantly, add a little more water. Place the pastry in a polythene bag and chill for 30 minutes.

2 Place the peppers on a baking tray and sprinkle with 1 tablespoon of oil. Roast in the preheated oven for 20 minutes or until the skins start to blacken. Brush the aubergines, courgettes and leeks with oil and place on another baking tray. Roast in the oven with the peppers for 20 minutes.

3 Place the blackened peppers in a polythene bag and leave the skin to loosen for 5 minutes. When cool enough to handle, peel the skins off the peppers.

4 Roll out half the pastry on a lightly floured surface and use to line a 20.5 cm/8 inch round pie dish. Line the pastry with greaseproof paper and fill with baking beans or rice and bake blind for about 10 minutes. Remove the beans and the paper, then brush the base with a little of the beaten egg. Return to the oven for 5 minutes.

5 Layer the cooked vegetables and the cheese in the pastry case, seasoning each layer. Roll out the remaining pastry on a lightly floured surface, and cut out the lid 5 mm/¼ inch wider than the dish. Brush the rim with the beaten egg and lay the pastry lid on top, press to seal. Knock the edges with the back of a knife. Cut a slit in the lid and brush with the beaten egg. Bake for 30 minutes. Transfer to a large serving dish, garnish with sprigs of mixed herbs and serve immediately.

INGREDIENTS
Serves 4

225 g/8 oz plain flour
pinch of salt
50 g/2 oz white vegetable fat or lard, cut into squares
50 g/2 oz butter, cut into squares
2 tsp herbes de Provence
1 red pepper, deseeded and halved
1 green pepper, deseeded and halved
1 yellow pepper, deseeded and halved
3 tbsp extra-virgin olive oil
1 aubergine, trimmed and sliced
1 courgette, trimmed and halved lengthways
1 leek, trimmed and cut into chunks
1 medium egg, beaten
125 g/4 oz fresh mozzarella cheese, sliced
salt and freshly ground black pepper
sprigs of mixed herbs, to garnish

Helpful Hint

Look out for *buffalo mozzarella* because it is the best around.

Chicken & Ham Pie

1 Preheat the oven to 200°C/ 400°F/Gas Mark 6. Heat the oil in a frying pan and fry the leek and bacon for 4 minutes until soft but not coloured. Transfer to a bowl and reserve.

2 Cut the chicken into bite-sized pieces and add to the leek and bacon. Toss the avocado in the lemon juice, add to the chicken and season to taste with salt and pepper.

3 Roll out half the pastry on a lightly floured surface and use to line a 18 cm/7 inch loose-bottomed deep flan tin. Scoop the chicken mixture into the pastry case.

4 Mix together 1 egg, the yogurt and the chicken

stock. Pour the yogurt mixture over the chicken. Roll out the remaining pastry on a lightly floured surface, and cut out the lid to 5 mm/¼ inch wider than the dish.

5 Brush the rim with the remaining beaten egg and lay the pastry lid on top, pressing to seal.

6 Knock the edges with the back of a knife to seal further. Cut a slit in the lid and brush with the egg.

7 Sprinkle with the poppy seeds and bake in the preheated oven for about 30 minutes, or until the pastry is golden brown. Serve with the onion and mixed salad leaves.

INGREDIENTS
Serves 6

2 quantities shortcrust pastry, (see page 16)
1 tbsp olive oil
1 leek, trimmed and sliced
175 g/6 oz piece of bacon, cut into small dice
225 g/8 oz cooked boneless chicken meat
2 avocados, peeled, pitted and chopped
1 tbsp lemon juice
salt and freshly ground black pepper
2 large eggs, beaten
150 ml/¼ pint natural yogurt
4 tbsp chicken stock
1 tbsp poppy seeds

TO SERVE:
sliced red onion
mixed salad leaves

Helpful Hint

Generally, corn-fed or free-range maize-fed chickens, tend to be more flavoursome and tender than standard supermarket birds. Although these types of chicken are a bit more expensive they really are worth the extra money.

Fish Puff Tart

1 Preheat the oven to 220°C/ 425°F/Gas Mark 7. On a lightly floured surface roll out the pastry into a 20.5 x 25.5 cm/ 8 x 10 inch rectangle.

2 Draw a 18 x 23 cm/7 x 9 inch rectangle in the centre of the pastry, to form a 2.5 cm/ 1 inch border. (Be careful not to cut through the pastry.)

3 Lightly cut criss-cross patterns in the border of the pastry with a knife.

4 Place the fish on a chopping board and with a sharp knife skin the cod and smoked haddock. Cut into thin slices.

5 Spread the pesto evenly over the bottom of the pastry case with the back of a spoon.

6 Arrange the fish, tomatoes and cheese in the pastry case and brush the pastry with the beaten egg.

7 Bake the tart in the preheated oven for 20–25 minutes, until the pastry is well risen, puffed and golden brown. Garnish with the chopped parsley and serve immediately.

INGREDIENTS
Serves 4

350 g/12 oz prepared puff pastry, thawed if frozen
150 g/5 oz smoked haddock
150 g/5 oz cod
1 tbsp pesto sauce
2 tomatoes, sliced
125 g/4 oz goats' cheese, sliced
1 medium egg, beaten
freshly chopped parsley, to garnish

Food Fact

The Scottish name for smoked haddock is *finnan haddie*, named after the Scottish fishing village of Findon near Aberdeen. Smoked haddock has been a favourite breakfast dish in Findon and the rest of Scotland for many years. Although this type of fish was traditionally caught and smoked (sometimes over peat fires) in Scotland, nowadays the fish is produced in New England and other eastern coastal states of the United States.

Spinach, Pine Nut & Mascarpone Pizza

1 Preheat the oven to 220°C/ 425°F/ Gas Mark 7. Sift the flour and salt into a bowl and stir in the yeast. Make a well in the centre and gradually add the water and oil to form soft dough.

2 Knead the dough on a floured surface for about 5 minutes until smooth and elastic. Place in a lightly oiled bowl and cover with clingfilm. Leave to rise in a warm place for 1 hour.

3 Knock the pizza dough with your fist a few times, shape and roll out thinly on a lightly floured board. Place on a lightly floured baking sheet and lift the edge to make a little rim. Place another baking sheet into the preheated oven to heat up.

4 Heat half the oil in a frying pan and gently fry the onion and garlic until soft and starting to change colour.

5 Squeeze out any excess water from the spinach and finely chop. Add to the onion and garlic with the remaining olive oil. Season to taste with salt and pepper.

6 Spread the passata on the pizza dough and top with the spinach mixture. Mix the mascarpone with the pine nuts and dot over the pizza.

7 Slide the pizza on to the hot baking sheet and bake for 15–20 minutes. Transfer to a large plate and serve immediately.

INGREDIENTS
Serves 2–4

BASIC PIZZA DOUGH:
225 g/8 oz strong plain flour
½ tsp salt
¼ tsp quick-acting dried yeast
150 ml/¼ pint warm water
1 tbsp extra-virgin olive oil

FOR THE TOPPING:
3 tbsp olive oil
1 large red onion, peeled and chopped
2 garlic cloves, peeled and finely sliced
450 g/1 lb frozen spinach, thawed and drained
salt and freshly ground black pepper
3 tbsp passata
125 g/4 oz mascarpone cheese
1 tbsp toasted pine nuts

Food Fact
Traditionally, mozzarella cheese is used for pizza topping, but this recipe incorporates another Italian cheese – mascarpone – which gives a creamy textured result to compliment the delicate spinach and pine nut topping.

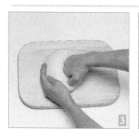

Chilli Beef Calzone

1 Preheat the oven to 220°C/ 425°F/ Gas Mark 7, 15 minutes before baking. Heat the oil in a large saucepan and gently cook the onion and pepper for 5 minutes.

2 Add the minced beef to the saucepan and cook for 10 minutes, until browned.

3 Add the chilli beans and tomatoes and simmer gently for 30 minutes, or until the mince is tender. Place a baking sheet into the preheated oven to heat up.

4 Divide the pizza dough into 4 equal pieces. Cover

3 pieces of the dough with clingfilm and roll out the other piece on a lightly floured board to a 20.5 cm/8 inch round.

5 Spoon a quarter of the chilli mixture on to half of the dough round and dampen the edges with a little water.

6 Fold over the empty half of the dough and press the edges together well to seal.

7 Repeat this process with the remaining dough. Place on the hot baking sheet and bake for 15 minutes. Serve with the salad leaves.

INGREDIENTS
Serves 4

1 quantity pizza dough (see page 54)
1 tbsp sunflower oil
1 onion, peeled and finely chopped
1 green pepper, deseeded and chopped
225 g/8 oz minced beef steak
420 g can chilli beans
220 g can chopped tomatoes
mixed salad leaves, to serve

Tasty Tip

Calzone is a stuffed pizza which originates from Naples. Instead of stuffing with chilli con carne, replace the meat with sliced roasted vegetables such as peppers, onions, courgettes, mushrooms and aubergines. Sprinkle some grated mozzarella cheese over the vegetables and fold the dough over into a half-moon shape as in step 6. Serve with tomato sauce on the side.

Roquefort, Parma & Rocket Pizza

1 Preheat the oven to 220°C/ 425°F/Gas Mark 7. Roll the pizza dough out on a lightly floured board to form a 25.5 cm/ 10 inch round.

2 Lightly cover the dough and reserve while making the sauce. Place a baking sheet in the preheated oven to heat up.

3 Place all of the tomato sauce ingredients in a large heavy-based saucepan and slowly bring to the boil.

4 Cover and simmer for 15 minutes, uncover and cook for a further 10 minutes until the sauce has thickened and reduced by half.

5 Spoon the tomato sauce over the shaped pizza dough. Place on the hot baking sheet and bake for 10 minutes.

6 Remove the pizza from the oven and top with the Roquefort and Parma ham, then bake for a further 10 minutes.

7 Toss the rocket in the olive oil and pile on to the pizza. Sprinkle with the Parmesan cheese and serve immediately.

INGREDIENTS
Serves 2–4

1 quantity pizza dough
(see page 40)

BASIC TOMATO SAUCE:

400 g can chopped tomatoes
2 garlic cloves, peeled and crushed
grated rind of ½ lime
2 tbsp extra-virgin olive oil
2 tbsp freshly chopped basil
½ tsp sugar
salt and freshly ground
black pepper

FOR THE TOPPING:

125 g/4 oz Roquefort cheese, cut
into chunks
6 slices Parma ham
50 g/2 oz rocket leaves, rinsed
1 tbsp extra-virgin olive oil
50 g/2 oz Parmesan cheese,
freshly shaved

Food Fact

To make a thin and crispy-based pizza, roll the dough out to a 12-inch round in step 1, then continue as demonstrated. For a really crispy pizza, remove from the oven 5 minutes before the end of cooking time. Place directly on the grill rack in the oven and cook until the cheese has melted and the pizza base is crispy and golden brown.

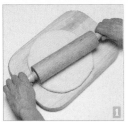

Three Tomato Pizza

1 Preheat the oven to 220°C/ 425°F/Gas Mark 7. Place a baking sheet into the oven to heat up.

2 Divide the prepared pizza dough into 4 equal pieces.

3 Roll out one-quarter of the pizza dough on a lightly floured board to form a 20.5 cm/ 8 inch round.

4 Lightly cover the 3 remaining pieces of dough with clingfilm.

5 Roll out the other 3 pieces into rounds, one at a time. While rolling out any piece of dough, keep the others covered with the clingfilm.

6 Slice the plum tomatoes, halve the cherry tomatoes and chop the sun-dried tomatoes into small pieces.

7 Place a few pieces of each type of tomato on each pizza base then season to taste with the sea salt.

8 Sprinkle with the chopped basil and drizzle with the olive oil. Place a few slices of mozzarella on each pizza and season with black pepper.

9 Transfer the pizza on to the heated baking sheet and cook for 15–20 minutes, or until the cheese is golden brown and bubbling. Garnish with the basil leaves and serve immediately.

INGREDIENTS
Serves 2–4

1 quantity pizza dough (see page 54)
3 plum tomatoes
8 cherry tomatoes
6 sun-dried tomatoes
pinch of sea salt
1 tbsp freshly chopped basil
2 tbsp extra-virgin olive oil
125 g/4 oz buffalo mozzarella cheese, sliced
freshly ground black pepper
fresh basil leaves, to garnish

Food Fact

Buffalo mozzarella is considered the king of mozzarellas. It uses buffalo milk, which results in the cheese tasting extremely mild and creamy. A good mozzarella should come in liquid to keep it moist and should tear easily into chunks.

Smoked Mackerel Vol-au-Vents

1 Preheat the oven to 230°C/450°F/Gas Mark 8. Roll the pastry out on a lightly floured surface and using a 9 cm/3½ inch fluted cutter cut out 12 rounds.

2 Using a 1 cm/½ inch cutter mark a lid in the centre of each round.

3 Place on a damp baking sheet and brush the rounds with a little beaten egg.

4 Sprinkle the pastry with the sesame seeds and bake in the preheated oven for 10–12 minutes, or until golden brown and well risen.

5 Transfer the vol-au-vents to a chopping board and when cool enough to touch carefully remove the lids with a small sharp knife.

6 Scoop out any uncooked pastry from the inside of each vol-au-vent, then return to the oven for 5–8 minutes to dry out. Remove and allow to cool.

7 Flake the mackerel into small pieces and reserve. Peel the cucumber if desired, cut into very small dice and add to the mackerel.

8 Beat the soft cream cheese with the cranberry sauce, dill and lemon rind. Stir in the mackerel and cucumber and use to fill the vol-au-vents. Place the lids on top and garnish dill sprigs.

INGREDIENTS
Serves 1–2

350 g/12 oz prepared puff pastry
1 small egg, beaten
2 tsp sesame seeds
225 g/8 oz peppered smoked mackerel, skinned and chopped
5 cm/2 inch piece cucumber
4 tbsp soft cream cheese
2 tbsp cranberry sauce
1 tbsp freshly chopped dill
1 tbsp finely grated lemon rind
dill sprigs, to garnish
mixed salad leaves, to serve

Food Fact

Mackerel is a relatively cheap fish and one of the richest sources of minerals, oils and vitamins available. This dish is an affordable way to incorporate all these essential nutrients into your diet.

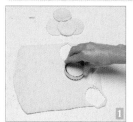

Luxury Fish Pasties

1 Preheat the oven to 200°C/ 400°F/Gas Mark 6. Place the butter in a saucepan and slowly heat until melted.

2 Add the flour and cook, stirring for 1 minute. Remove from the heat and gradually add the milk a little at a time, stirring between each addition.

3 Return to the heat and simmer, stirring continuously until thickened. Remove from the heat and add the salmon, parsley, dill, lime rind, lime juice, prawns and seasoning.

4 Roll out the pastry on a lightly floured surface and cut out 6 x 12.5 cm/5 inch circles and 6 x 15 cm/6 inch circles.

5 Brush the edges of the smallest circle with the beaten egg and place two tablespoons of filling in the centre of each one.

6 Place the larger circle over the filling and press the edges together to seal.

7 Pinch the edge of the pastry between the forefinger and thumb to ensure a firm seal and decorative edge.

8 Cut a slit in each parcel, brush with the beaten egg and sprinkle with sea salt.

9 Transfer to a baking sheet and cook in the preheated oven for 20 minutes, or until golden brown. Serve immediately with some fresh green salad leaves.

INGREDIENTS
Serves 6

2 quantities of quick flaky pastry
  (see page 34), chilled
125 g/4 oz butter
125 g/4oz plain flour
300 ml/½ pint milk
225 g/8 oz salmon fillet, skinned
  and cut into chunks
1 tbsp freshly chopped parsley
1 tbsp freshly chopped dill
grated rind and juice of 1 lime
225 g/8 oz peeled prawns
salt and freshly ground
  black pepper
1 small egg, beaten
1 tsp sea salt
fresh green salad leaves, to serve

Helpful Hint

Salmon is not only full of minerals but is a vital source of calcium as well as being extremely low in fat. Ensure when using raw prawns that the vein that runs along the back of the prawn is removed.

Tomato & Courgette Herb Tart

1 Preheat the oven to 230°C/ 450°F/Gas Mark 8. Heat 2 tablespoons of the oil in a large frying pan.

2 Fry the onion and garlic for about 4 minutes until softened and reserve.

3 Roll out the pastry on a lightly floured surface, and cut out a 30.5 cm/12 inch circle.

4 Brush the pastry with a little beaten egg, then prick all over with a fork.

5 Transfer on to a dampened baking sheet and bake in the preheated oven for 10 minutes.

6 Turn the pastry over and brush with a little more egg. Bake for 5 more minutes, then remove from the oven.

7 Mix together the onion, garlic and herbs with the goats' cheese and spread over the pastry.

8 Arrange the tomatoes and courgettes over the goats' cheese and drizzle with the remaining oil.

9 Bake for 20–25 minutes, or until the pastry is golden brown and the topping bubbling. Garnish with the thyme sprigs and serve immediately.

INGREDIENTS
Serves 4

4 tbsp olive oil
1 onion, peeled and
  finely chopped
3 garlic cloves, peeled and crushed
400 g / 14 oz prepared puff
  pastry, thawed if frozen
1 small egg, beaten
2 tbsp freshly chopped rosemary
2 tbsp freshly chopped parsley
175 g / 6 oz rindless fresh soft
  goats' cheese
4 ripe plum tomatoes, sliced
1 medium courgette, trimmed
  and sliced
thyme sprigs, to garnish

Food Fact

Goats' cheese works particularly well in this recipe, complimenting both the tomato and courgette. Be aware though, that it can tend to be a little acidic, so it is best to try to choose a creamy variety, which will mellow even more once baked.

Olive & Feta Parcels

1 Preheat the oven to 180°C/ 350°F/Gas Mark 4. Preheat the grill, then line the grill rack with tinfoil.

2 Cut the peppers into quarters and remove the seeds. Place skin side up on the foil-lined grill rack and cook under the preheated grill for 10 minutes, turning occasionally until the skins begin to blacken.

3 Place the peppers in a polythene bag and leave until cool enough to handle, then skin and thinly slice.

4 Chop the olives and cut the feta cheese into small cubes. Mix together the olives, feta, sliced peppers and pine nuts.

5 Cut 1 sheet of filo pastry in half then brush with a little of the oil. Place a spoonful of the olive and feta mix about one -third of the way up the pastry.

6 Fold over the pastry and wrap to form a square parcel encasing the filling completely.

7 Place this parcel in the centre of the second half of the pastry sheet. Brush the edges lightly with a little oil, bring up the corners to meet in the centre and twist them loosely to form a purse.

8 Brush with a little more oil and repeat with the remaining filo pastry and filling.

9 Place the parcels on a lightly oiled baking sheet and bake in the preheated oven for 10–15 minutes, or until crisp and golden brown. Serve with the dip.

INGREDIENTS
Makes 30

1 small red pepper
1 small yellow pepper
125 g/4 oz assorted marinated
   green and black olives
125 g/4 oz feta cheese
2 tbsp pine nuts, lightly toasted
6 sheets filo pastry
3 tbsp olive oil
sour cream and chive dip, to serve

Helpful Hint

Feta is generally made from goats' milk and has quite a salty taste. To make the cheese less salty simply soak it in milk, then drain before eating.

Classic White Loaf

1 Preheat the oven to 220°C/ 425°F/Gas Mark 7 15 minutes before baking. Oil and line the base of a 900 g/ 2 lb loaf tin with greaseproof paper. Sift the flour and salt into a large bowl. Rub in the butter, then stir in the sugar and yeast. Make a well in the centre.

2 Add the milk and the warm water to the dry ingredients. Mix to a soft dough, adding a little more water if needed. Turn out the dough and knead on a lightly floured surface for 10 minutes, or until smooth and elastic.

3 Place the dough in an oiled bowl, cover with clingfilm or a clean tea towel and leave in a warm place to rise for 1 hour, or until doubled in size. Knead again for a minute or two to knock out the air.

4 Shape the dough into an oblong and place in the prepared tin. Cover with oiled clingfilm and leave to rise for a further 30 minutes or until the dough reaches the top of the tin. Dredge the top of the loaf with flour or brush with the egg glaze and scatter with kibbled wheat if making the wholemeal version. Bake the loaf on the middle shelf of the preheated oven for 15 minutes.

5 Turn down the oven to 200°C/400°F/Gas Mark 6. Bake the loaf for a further 20–25 minutes, or until well risen and hollow sounding when tapped underneath. Turn out, cool on a wire rack and serve.

INGREDIENTS
Makes 1 x 900 g/2 lb loaf

700 g/1½ lb strong white flour
1 tbsp salt
25 g/1 oz butter, cubed
1 tsp caster sugar
2 tsp easy-blend dried yeast
150 ml/¼ pint milk
300 ml/½ pint warm water
1 tbsp plain flour, to dredge

LIGHT WHOLEMEAL VARIATION:
450 g/1 lb strong wholemeal flour
225 g/8 oz strong white flour
beaten egg, to glaze
1 tbsp kibbled wheat, to finish

Tasty Tip

Every now and then nothing can beat white bread, especially when it is freshly cooked. While the bread is still warm spread generously with fresh butter and eat. It is simply delicious!

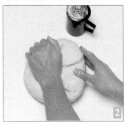

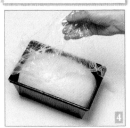

Mixed Grain Bread

1 Preheat the oven to 220°C/ 425°F/Gas Mark 7 15 minutes before baking. Sift the white flour and salt into a large bowl. Stir in the Granary and rye flours, then rub in the butter until the mixture resembles breadcrumbs. Stir in the yeast, oats and seeds and make a well in the centre.

2 Stir the malt extract into the warm water until dissolved. Add the malt water to the dry ingredients. Mix to a soft dough.

3 Turn the dough out on to a lightly floured surface and knead for 10 minutes, until smooth and elastic.

4 Put in an oiled bowl, cover with clingfilm and leave to rise in a warm place for 1½ hours or until doubled in size.

5 Turn out and knead again for a minute or two to knock out the air.

6 Shape into an oval loaf about 30.5 cm/12 inches long and place on a well-oiled baking sheet.

7 Cover with oiled clingfilm and leave to rise for 40 minutes, or until doubled in size

8 Brush the loaf with beaten egg and bake in the preheated oven for 35–45 minutes, or until the bread is well risen, browned and sounds hollow when the base is tapped. Leave to cool on a wire rack, then serve.

INGREDIENTS
Makes 1 large loaf

350 g/12 oz strong white flour
2 tsp salt
225 g/8 oz strong Granary flour
125 g/4 oz rye flour
25 g/1 oz butter, diced
2 tsp easy-blend dried yeast
25 g/1 oz rolled oats
2 tbsp sunflower seeds
1 tbsp malt extract
450 ml/¾ pint warm water (see Helpful Hint)
1 medium egg, beaten

Helpful Hint

The amount of water you need to add to the dry ingredients in this recipe will depend on the type and brand of flour you use. Add just enough water to make a soft elastic dough.

Quick Brown Bread

1 Preheat the oven to 200°C/ 400°F/Gas Mark 6 15 minutes before baking. Oil 2 x 450 g/1 lb loaf tins. Sift the flour, salt and sugar into a large bowl, adding the remaining bran in the sieve. Stir in the yeast, then make a well in the centre.

2 Pour the warm water into the dry ingredients and mix to form a soft dough, adding a little more water if needed.

3 Knead on a lightly floured surface for 10 minutes, until smooth and elastic.

4 Divide in half, shape into 2 oblongs and place in the tins. Cover with oiled clingfilm and leave in a warm place for 40 minutes, or until risen to the top of the tins.

5 Glaze 1 loaf with the beaten egg and dust the other loaf generously with the plain flour.

6 Bake the loaves in the preheated oven for 35 minutes or until well risen and lightly browned. Turn out of the tins and return to the oven for 5 minutes to crisp the sides. Cool on a wire rack.

7 For the onion and caraway seed rolls, gently fry the onion in the oil until soft. Reserve until the onions are cool, then stir into the dry ingredients with 1 tablespoon of the caraway seeds. Make the dough as before.

8 Divide the dough into 16 pieces and shape into rolls. Put on 2 oiled baking trays, cover with oiled clingfilm and prove for 30 minutes.

9 Glaze the rolls with milk and sprinkle with the rest of the seeds. Bake for 25–30 minutes, cool on a wire rack and serve.

INGREDIENTS
Makes 2 x 450 g/1 lb loaves

700 g/1½ lb strong wholemeal flour
2 tsp salt
½ tsp caster sugar
7 g/¼ oz sachet easy-blend dried yeast
450 ml/¾ pint warm water

TO FINISH:
beaten egg, to glaze
1 tbsp plain white flour, to dust

ONION & CARAWAY SEED ROLLS:
1 small onion, peeled and finely chopped
1 tbsp olive oil
2 tbsp caraway seeds
milk, to glaze

Helpful Hint

For most breads the dough is kneaded, left to rise, kneaded, shaped and then left to rise again. This bread does not need the first rising – simply knead, shape, rise and bake.

Rustic Country Bread

1 Preheat the oven to 220°C/ 425°F/Gas Mark 7 15 minutes before baking. For the starter, sift the flour into a bowl. Stir in the yeast and make a well in the centre. Pour in the warm water and mix with a fork.

2 Transfer to a saucepan, cover with a clean tea towel and leave for 2–3 days at room temperature. Stir the mixture and spray with a little water twice a day.

3 For the dough, mix the flours, salt, sugar and yeast in a bowl. Add 225 ml/8 fl oz of the starter, the oil and the warm water. Mix to a soft dough.

4 Knead on a lightly floured surface for 10 minutes until smooth and elastic. Put in an oiled bowl, cover and leave to rise in a warm place for about 1½ hours, or until doubled in size.

5 Turn the dough out and knead for a minute or two. Shape into a round loaf and place on an oiled baking sheet.

6 Cover with oiled clingfilm and leave to rise for 1 hour, or until doubled in size.

7 Dust the loaf with flour, then using a sharp knife make several slashes across the top of the loaf. Slash across the loaf in the opposite direction to make a square pattern.

8 Bake in the preheated oven for 40–45 minutes, or until golden brown and hollow sounding when tapped underneath. Cool on a wire rack and serve.

INGREDIENTS
Makes 1 large loaf

SOURDOUGH STARTER:
225 g/8 oz strong white flour
2 tsp easy-blend dried yeast
300 ml/½ pint warm water

BREAD DOUGH:
350 g/12 oz strong white flour
25 g/1 oz rye flour
1½ tsp salt
½ tsp caster sugar
1 tsp dried yeast
1 tsp sunflower oil
175 ml/6 fl oz warm water

TO FINISH:
2 tsp plain flour
2 tsp rye flour

Helpful Hint

Put the remaining starter in a pan, stir in 125 ml/4 fl oz of warm water and 125 g/4 oz strong white flour. Stir twice a day for 2–3 days and use as a starter for another loaf.

Soft Dinner Rolls

1 Preheat the oven to 220°C/ 425°F/Gas Mark 7 15 minutes before baking. Gently heat the butter, sugar and milk in a saucepan until the butter has melted and the sugar has dissolved. Cool until tepid. Sift the flour and salt into a bowl, stir in the yeast and make a well in the centre. Reserve 1 tablespoon of the beaten eggs. Add the rest to the dry ingredients with the milk mixture. Mix to form a soft dough.

2 Knead the dough on a lightly floured surface for 10 minutes until smooth and elastic. Put in an oiled bowl, cover with clingfilm and leave in a warm place to rise for 1 hour, or until doubled in size. Knead again for a minute or two, then divide into 16 pieces. Shape into plaits, snails, clover leaf and cottage buns (see Helpful Hints). Place on 2 oiled baking sheets, cover with oiled clingfilm and leave to rise for 30 minutes, until doubled in size.

3 Mix the reserved beaten egg with the milk and brush over the rolls. Sprinkle some with sea salt, others with poppy seeds and leave some plain. Bake in the preheated oven for about 20 minutes, or until golden and hollow sounding when tapped underneath. Transfer to a wire rack. Cover with a clean tea towel while cooling to keep the rolls soft and serve.

INGREDIENTS
Makes 16

50 g/2 oz butter
1 tbsp caster sugar
225 ml/8 fl oz milk
550 g/1¼ lb strong white flour
1½ tsp salt
2 tsp easy-blend dried yeast
2 medium eggs, beaten

TO GLAZE & FINISH:
2 tbsp milk
1 tsp sea salt
2 tsp poppy seeds

Helpful Hint

For clover leaf rolls, divide into 3 equal pieces and roll each into a ball. Place the balls together in a triangular shape. For cottage buns, divide the dough into two-thirds and one-third pieces. Shape each piece into a round, then put the smaller one on top of the larger one. Push a floured wooden spoon handle or finger through the middle of the top one and into the bottom one to join together.

Helpful Hint

For plaits, divide into 3 equal pieces and roll each piece of dough into a rope about 9 cm/3½ inches long. Plait, then pinch the ends together to seal. For snails, roll into a 25.5 cm/10 inch rope, then form into a coil, tucking the end under the roll to secure.

Bagels

1 Preheat the oven to 200°C/400°F/Gas Mark 6 15 minutes before baking. Sift the flour and salt into a large bowl. Stir in the yeast, then make a well in the centre. Whisk the eggs together with the honey and oil. Add to the dry ingredients with the tepid water and mix to form a soft dough.

2 Knead the dough on a lightly floured surface for 10 minutes until smooth and elastic. Put in a bowl, cover with clingfilm and leave in a warm place to rise for 45 minutes, or until doubled in size.

3 Briefly knead the dough again to knock out the air. Divide into 12 pieces, form each into a 20.5 cm/8 inch roll, curve into a ring and pinch the edges to seal.

4 Put the rings on an oiled baking sheet, cover with oiled clingfilm and leave to rise in a warm place for 20 minutes, or until risen and puffy.

5 Add the caster sugar to a large saucepan of water. Bring to the boil, then drop in the bagels, one at a time and poach for 15 seconds. Lift out with a slotted spoon and return to the baking tray.

6 Brush the bagels with beaten egg and sprinkle one-third with poppy seeds. Mix together the onion and oil and sprinkle over another third of the bagels. Leave the remaining third plain.

7 Bake in the preheated oven for 12–15 minutes, or until golden brown. Transfer to a wire rack and serve when cool.

INGREDIENTS
Serves 4

450 g/1 lb strong plain flour
1½ tsp salt
2 tsp easy-blend dried yeast
2 medium eggs
1 tsp clear honey
2 tbsp sunflower oil
250 ml/9 fl oz tepid water

TO FINISH:

1 tbsp caster sugar
beaten egg, to glaze
2 tsp poppy seeds
½ small onion, peeled and finely chopped
2 tsp sunflower oil

Tasty Tip

Why not try bagels for breakfast? They are delicious filled with cheese and ham or served toasted with scrambled egg. They are also good with smoked salmon and cream cheese.

Sweet Potato Baps

1 Preheat the oven to 200°C/ 400°F/Gas Mark 6 15 minutes before baking. Peel the sweet potato and cut into large chunks. Cook in a saucepan of boiling water for 12–15 minutes, or until tender.

2 Drain well and mash with the butter and nutmeg. Stir in the milk, then leave until barely warm.

3 Sift the flour and salt into a large bowl. Stir in the yeast. Make a well in the centre.

4 Add the mashed sweet potato and beaten egg and mix to a soft dough. Add a little more milk if needed, depending on the moisture in the sweet potato.

5 Turn out the dough on to a lightly floured surface and knead for about 10 minutes, or until smooth and elastic. Place in

a lightly oiled bowl, cover with clingfilm and leave in a warm place to rise for about 1 hour, or until the dough doubles in size.

6 Turn out the dough and knead for a minute or two until smooth.

7 Divide into 16 pieces, shape into rolls and place on a large oiled baking sheet. Cover with oiled clingfilm and leave to rise for 15 minutes.

8 Brush the rolls with beaten egg, then sprinkle half with rolled oats and leave the rest plain.

9 Bake in the preheated oven for 12–15 minutes, or until well risen, lightly browned and sound hollow when the bases are tapped. Transfer to a wire rack and immediately cover with a clean tea towel to keep the crusts soft.

INGREDIENTS
Makes 16

225 g/8 oz sweet potato
15 g/½ oz butter
freshly grated nutmeg
about 200 ml/7 fl oz milk
450 g/1 lb strong white flour
2 tsp salt
7 g/¼ oz sachet easy-blend yeast
1 medium egg, beaten

TO FINISH:
beaten egg, to glaze
1 tbsp rolled oats

Helpful Hint

There are many varieties of sweet potato, so be sure to choose the correct potato for this recipe as their flavours and textures vary. The sweet potato used in this recipe is dark skinned and has a vibrant orange flesh which cooks to a moist texture.

Rosemary & Olive Focaccia

1 Preheat the oven to 200°C/400°F/Gas Mark 6 15 minutes before baking. Sift the flour, salt and sugar into a large bowl. Stir in the yeast and rosemary. Make a well in the centre.

2 Pour in the warm water and the oil and mix to a soft dough. Turn out on to a lightly floured surface and knead for about 10 minutes, until smooth and elastic.

3 Pat the olives dry on kitchen paper, then gently knead into the dough. Put in an oiled bowl, cover with clingfilm and leave to rise in a warm place for 1½ hours, or until it has doubled in size.

4 Turn out the dough and knead again for a minute or two. Divide in half and roll out each piece to a 25.5 cm/10 inch circle.

5 Transfer to oiled baking sheets, cover with oiled clingfilm and leave to rise for 30 minutes.

6 Using the fingertips, make deep dimples all over the the dough. Drizzle with the oil and sprinkle with sea salt.

7 Bake in the preheated oven for 20–25 minutes, or until risen and golden. Cool on a wire rack and garnish with sprigs of rosemary. Grind over a little black pepper before serving.

INGREDIENTS
Makes 2 loaves

700 g/1½ lb strong white flour
pinch of salt
pinch of caster sugar
7 g/¼ oz sachet easy-blend dried yeast
2 tsp freshly chopped rosemary
450 ml/¾ pint warm water
3 tbsp olive oil
75 g/3 oz pitted black olives, roughly chopped
sprigs of rosemary, to garnish

TO FINISH:
3 tbsp olive oil
coarse sea salt
freshly ground black pepper

Tasty Tip

As a variation to the rosemary used in this bread, replace with a little chopped sun-dried tomatoes. Knead the tomatoes into the dough along with the olives in step 3, then before baking drizzle with the oil and replace the salt with some grated mozzarella cheese.

Daktyla-style Bread

1 Preheat the oven to 220°C/ 425°F/Gas Mark 7 15 minutes before baking. Sift the white and wholemeal flours and salt into a large bowl, adding the bran left in the sieve. Stir in the cornmeal and yeast. Make a well in the centre.

2 Put the honey, oil, milk and water in a saucepan and heat gently until tepid. Add to the dry ingredients and mix to a soft dough, adding a little more water if needed.

3 Knead the dough on a lightly floured surface for 10 minutes, until smooth and elastic. Put in an oiled bowl, cover with clingfilm and leave to rise in a warm place for 1½ hours or until it has doubled in size.

4 Turn the dough out and knead for a minute or two. Shape into a long oval about 25.5 cm/10 inches long. Cut the oval into 6 equal pieces. Shape each piece into an oblong, then on an oiled baking sheet arrange in a row so that all the pieces of dough are touching.

5 Cover with oiled clingfilm and leave for 45 minutes, or until doubled in size.

6 Brush the bread with milk, then scatter with sesame seeds.

7 Bake the bread in the preheated oven for 40–45 minutes, or until golden brown and hollow sounding when tapped underneath. Cool on a wire rack and serve.

INGREDIENTS
Makes 1 loaf

350 g/12 oz strong white flour
125 g/4 oz wholemeal flour
1 tsp salt
50 g/2 oz fine cornmeal
2 tsp easy-blend dried yeast
2 tsp clear honey
1 tbsp olive oil
4 tbsp milk
250 ml/9 fl oz water

TO GLAZE & FINISH:
4 tbsp milk
4 tbsp sesame seeds

Food Fact

Daktyla was traditionally made in Cyprus during Lent. The Cypriots made crisp syrup-soaked fingers of pastry filled with an almond and cinnamon filling. In this recipe the bread is shaped into oblongs and baked so that the bread can be broken into fingers to eat.

Spicy Filled Naan Bread

1 Preheat the oven to 220°C/
450°F/Gas Mark 8 15
minutes before baking and place
a large baking sheet in to heat
up. Sift the flour and salt into
a large bowl. Stir in the yeast
and make a well in the centre.
Add the ghee or melted butter,
honey and the warm water. Mix
to a soft dough.

2 Knead the dough on a
lightly floured surface, until
smooth and elastic. Put in a
lightly oiled bowl, cover with
clingfilm and leave to rise for 1
hour, or until doubled in size.

3 For the filling, melt the
ghee or butter in a frying
pan and gently cook the onion
for about 5 minutes. Stir in the
garlic and spices and season to
taste with salt and pepper. Cook
for a further 6–7 minutes, until

soft. Remove from the heat, stir
in 1 tablespoon of water and
leave to cool.

4 Briefly knead the dough,
then divide into 6 pieces.
Roll out each piece of dough to
12.5 cm/ 5 inch rounds. Spoon
the filling on to one half of
each round.

5 Fold over and press the
edges together to seal.
Re-roll to shape into flat ovals,
about 16 cm/6½ inches long.

6 Cover with oiled clingfilm
and leave to rise for about
15 minutes.

7 Transfer the breads to the
hot baking sheet and cook
in the preheated oven for 10–12
minutes, until puffed up and
lightly browned. Serve hot.

INGREDIENTS
Makes 6

400 g/14 oz strong white flour
1 tsp salt
1 tsp easy-blend dried yeast
15 g/½ oz ghee or unsalted
  butter, melted
1 tsp clear honey
200 ml/7 fl oz warm water

FOR THE FILLING:
25 g/1 oz ghee or unsalted butter
1 small onion, peeled and
  finely chopped
1 garlic clove, peeled and crushed
1 tsp ground coriander
1 tsp ground cumin
2 tsp grated fresh root ginger
pinch of chilli powder
pinch of ground cinnamon
salt and freshly ground
  black pepper

Helpful Hint
Ghee is more expensive than other butters but it has
a longer life and a much higher smoke point (190°C/375°F).
Ghee, therefore, is practical for sautéing and frying.

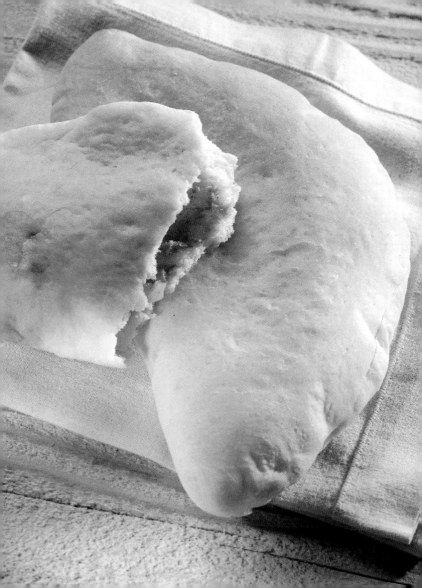

Fruited Brioche Buns

1 Preheat the oven to 220°C/
425°F/Gas Mark 7 15
minutes before baking. Sift the
flour and salt into a bowl. Stir
in the sugar and yeast. Make a
well in the centre. Add the eggs,
butter and 2 tablespoons of warm
water and mix to a soft dough.

2 Knead the dough on a
lightly floured surface for 5
minutes, until smooth and elastic.
Put in an oiled bowl, cover with
clingfilm and leave to rise in a
warm place for 1 hour, or until
it has doubled in size.

3 Mix the ingredients for the
filling together, cover the
bowl and leave to soak while the
dough is rising.

4 Re-knead the dough for a
minute or two, then divide
into 12 pieces. Take 1 piece at a
time and flatten three-quarters
into a 6.5 cm/2½ inch round.

Spoon a little filling in the centre,
then pinch the edges together
to enclose. Put seam-side down
into a well-greased fluted 12-
hole bun tin.

5 Shape the smaller piece of
dough into a round and
place on top of the larger one.

6 Push a finger or floured
wooden spoon handle
through the middle of the top
one and into the bottom one to
join them together. Repeat with
the remaining balls of dough.

7 Cover the brioche with
oiled clingfilm and leave
for about 20 minutes, or until
well risen.

8 Brush the brioches with
beaten egg and bake in
the preheated oven for 10–12
minutes, or until golden. Cool
on a wire rack and serve.

INGREDIENTS
Makes 12

225 g/8 oz strong white flour
pinch of salt
1 tbsp caster sugar
7 g/¼ oz sachet easy-blend
*   dried yeast*
2 large eggs, beaten
50 g/2 oz butter, melted
beaten egg, to glaze

FOR THE FILLING:
40 g/1½ oz blanched
*   almonds, chopped*
50 g/2 oz luxury mixed
*   dried fruit*
1 tsp light soft brown sugar
2 tsp orange liqueur or brandy

Spiced Apple Doughnuts

1 Sift the flour, salt and 1 teaspoon of the cinnamon into a large bowl. Stir in the yeast and make a well in the centre.

2 Add the milk, butter and egg and mix to a soft dough. Knead on a lightly floured surface for 10 minutes, until smooth and elastic.

3 Divide the dough into 8 pieces and shape each into a ball. Put on a floured baking sheet, cover with oiled clingfilm and leave in a warm place for 1 hour, or until doubled in size.

4 To make the filling, put the apples in a saucepan with the sugar, lemon juice and 3 tablespoons of water. Cover and simmer for about 10 minutes, then uncover and cook until fairly dry, stirring occasionally. Mash or blend in a food processor to a purée.

5 Pour enough oil into a deep-fat frying pan to come one-third of the way up the pan. Heat the oil to 180°C/350°F, then deep-fry the doughnuts for 1½–2 minutes on each side, until well browned.

6 Drain the doughnuts on kitchen paper, then roll in the caster sugar mixed with the remaining ½ teaspoon of ground cinnamon. Push a thick skewer into the centre to make a hole, then pipe in the apple filling. Serve warm or cold.

INGREDIENTS
Makes 8

225 g/8 oz strong white flour
½ tsp salt
1½ tsp ground cinnamon
1 tsp easy-blend dried yeast
75 ml/3 fl oz warm milk
25 g/1 oz butter, melted
1 medium egg, beaten
oil, to deep-fry
4 tbsp caster sugar, to coat

FOR THE FILLING:
2 small eating apples, peeled, cored
    and chopped
2 tsp soft light brown sugar
2 tsp lemon juice

Tasty Tip

These doughnuts are also excellent when filled with pears. Simply replace the 2 apples with 2 pears and continue with the recipe. Look out for Comice pears as they are considered to be amongst the best on the market or perhaps stick closer to home and use our own favourite English Conference pears which have lovely tender melting flesh and a delicious flavour.

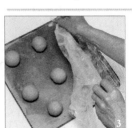

Bacon & Tomato Breakfast Twist

1 Preheat the oven to 200°C/ 400°F/Gas Mark 6 15 minutes before baking. Sift the flour and salt into a large bowl. Stir in the yeast and make a well in the centre. Pour in the milk and butter and mix to a soft dough.

2 Knead on a lightly floured surface for 10 minutes, until smooth and elastic. Put in an oiled bowl, cover with clingfilm and leave to rise in a warm place for 1 hour, until doubled in size.

3 Cook the bacon under a hot grill for 5–6 minutes, turning once until crisp. Leave to cool, then roughly chop.

4 Knead the dough again for a minute or two. Roll it out to a 25.5 x 33 cm/10 x 13 inch rectangle. Cut in half lengthways. Lightly brush with butter, then scatter with the bacon, tomatoes and black pepper, leaving a 1 cm/ ½ inch margin around the edges.

5 Brush the edges of the dough with beaten egg, then roll up each rectangle lengthways.

6 Place the 2 rolls side by side and twist together, pinching the ends to seal.

7 Transfer to an oiled baking sheet and loosely cover with oiled clingfilm. Leave to rise in a warm place for 30 minutes.

8 Brush with the beaten egg and sprinkle with the oatmeal. Bake in the preheated oven for about 30 minutes, or until golden brown and hollow sounding when tapped on the base. Serve the bread warm in thick slices.

INGREDIENTS
Serves 8

450 g/1 lb strong plain flour
½ tsp salt
7 g/¼ oz sachet easy-blend dried yeast
300 ml/½ pint warm milk
15 g/½ oz butter, melted

FOR THE FILLING:
225 g/8 oz back bacon, derinded
15 g/½ oz butter, melted
175 g/6 oz ripe tomatoes, peeled, deseeded and chopped
freshly ground black pepper

TO FINISH:
beaten egg, to glaze
2 tsp medium oatmeal

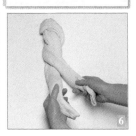

Irish Soda Bread

1 Preheat the oven to 200°C/ 400°F/Gas Mark 6 15 minutes before baking. Sift the flour, salt and bicarbonate of soda into a large bowl. Rub in the butter until the mixture resembles fine breadcrumbs. Stir in the oatmeal and make a well in the centre.

2 Mix the honey, buttermilk and milk together and add to the dry ingredients. Mix to a soft dough.

3 Knead the dough on a lightly floured surface for 2–3 minutes, until the dough is smooth. Shape into a 20.5 cm/ 8 inch round and place on an oiled baking sheet.

4 Thickly dust the top of the bread with flour. Using a sharp knife, cut a deep cross on top, going about halfway through the loaf.

5 Bake in the preheated oven on the middle shelf of the oven for 30–35 minutes or until the bread is slightly risen, golden and sounds hollow when tapped underneath. Cool on a wire rack. Eat on the day of making.

6 For a wholemeal soda bread, use all the wholemeal flour instead of the white flour and add an extra tablespoon of milk when mixing together. Dust the top with wholemeal flour and bake.

INGREDIENTS
Makes 1 loaf

400 g/14 oz plain white flour, plus 1 tbsp for dusting
1 tsp salt
2 tsp bicarbonate of soda
15 g/½ oz butter
50 g/2 oz coarse oatmeal
1 tsp clear honey
300 ml/½ pint buttermilk
2 tbsp milk

WHOLEMEAL VARIATION:
400 g/14 oz plain wholemeal flour, plus 1 tbsp for dusting
1 tbsp milk

Tasty Tip

Soda bread relies on the raising agent bicarbonate of soda, which when combined with the acidic buttermilk enables the bread to rise. For an unusual Irish soda bread, knead a handful of currants and 2 tablespoons of caraway seeds in step 3. According to Irish legend the cross on the top of the bread is intended to scare away the devil.

Traditional Oven Scones

1 Preheat the oven to 220°C/425°F/Gas Mark 7 15 minutes before baking. Sift the flour, baking powder and salt into a large bowl. Rub in the butter until the mixture resembles fine breadcrumbs. Stir in the sugar and mix in enough milk to give a fairly soft dough.

2 Knead the dough on a lightly floured surface for a few seconds until smooth. Roll out until 2 cm/¾ inches thick and stamp out 6.5 cm/ 2½ inch rounds with a floured plain cutter.

3 Place on an oiled baking sheet and brush the tops with milk (do not brush it over the sides or the scones will not rise properly). Dust with a little plain flour.

4 Bake in the preheated oven for 12–15 minutes, or until well risen and golden brown. Transfer to a wire rack and serve warm or leave to cool completely. (The scones are best eaten on the day of baking but may be kept in an airtight tin for up to 2 days.)

5 For lemon and sultana scones, stir in the sultanas and lemon rind with the sugar. Roll out until 2 cm/ ¾ inches thick and cut into 8 fingers, 10 x 2.5 cm/4 x 1 inch in size. Bake the scones as before.

INGREDIENTS
Makes 8

225 g/8 oz self-raising flour
1 tsp baking powder
pinch of salt
40 g/1½ oz butter, cubed
15 g/½ oz caster sugar
150 ml/¼ pint milk, plus
  1 tbsp for brushing
1 tbsp plain flour, to dust

LEMON & SULTANA SCONE VARIATION:
50 g/2 oz sultanas
finely grated rind of ½ lemon
beaten egg, to glaze

Tasty Tip
Nothing beats scones still warm from the oven.
Split the scones open and fill with a layer of juicy
strawberry jam and clotted cream. Serve the scones with
a pot of Earl Grey tea for a delicious afternoon treat.

Cheese-crusted Potato Scones

1 Preheat the oven to 220°C/425°F/Gas Mark 7 15 minutes before baking. Sift the flours, salt and baking powder into a large bowl. Rub in the butter until the mixture resembles fine breadcrumbs.

2 Stir 4 tablespoons of the milk into the mashed potato and season with black pepper.

3 Add the dry ingredients to the potato mixture, mixing together with a fork and adding the remaining 1 tablespoon of milk if needed.

4 Knead the dough on a lightly floured surface for a few seconds until smooth. Roll out to a 15 cm/6 inch round and transfer to an oiled baking sheet.

5 Mark the scone round into 6 wedges, cutting about halfway through with a small sharp knife.

6 Brush with milk, then sprinkle with the cheese and a faint dusting of paprika.

7 Bake on the middle shelf of the preheated oven for 15 minutes, or until well risen and golden brown.

8 Transfer to a wire rack and leave to cool for 5 minutes before breaking into wedges.

9 Serve warm or leave to cool completely. Once cool store the scones in an airtight tin. Garnish with a sprig of basil and serve split and buttered.

INGREDIENTS
Makes 6

200 g/7 oz self-raising flour
25 g/1 oz wholemeal flour
½ tsp salt
1½ tsp baking powder
25 g/1 oz butter, cubed
5 tbsp milk
175 g/6 oz cold mashed potato
freshly ground black pepper

TO FINISH:
2 tbsp milk
40 g/1½ oz mature Cheddar cheese, finely grated
paprika pepper, to dust
sprig of basil, to garnish

Food Fact

The scone supposedly acquired its name from the Stone of Destiny (or Scone) in Scotland where Scottish Kings were once crowned.

Maple, Pecan & Lemon Loaf

1 Preheat the oven to 170°C/ 325°F/Gas Mark 3 10 minutes before baking. Lightly oil and line the base of a 900 g/ 2 lb loaf tin with non-stick baking parchment.

2 Sift the flour and baking powder into a large bowl.

3 Rub in the butter until the mixture resembles fine breadcrumbs. Stir in the caster sugar and pecan nuts.

4 Beat the eggs together with the milk and lemon rind. Stir in the maple syrup. Add to the dry ingredients and gently stir in until mixed thoroughly to make a soft dropping consistency.

5 Spoon the mixture into the prepared tin and level the

top with the back of a spoon. Bake on the middle shelf of the preheated oven for 50–60 minutes, or until the cake is well risen and lightly browned. If a skewer inserted into the centre comes out clean, then the cake is ready.

6 Leave the cake in the tin for about 10 minutes, then turn out and leave to cool on a wire rack. Carefully remove the lining paper.

7 Sift the icing sugar into a small bowl and stir in the lemon juice to make a smooth icing.

8 Drizzle the icing over the top of the loaf, then scatter with the chopped pecans. Leave to set, thickly slice and serve.

INGREDIENTS
Cuts into 12 slices

350 g/12 oz plain flour
1 tsp baking powder
175 g/6 oz butter, cubed
75 g/3 oz caster sugar
125 g/4 oz pecan nuts, roughly
   chopped
3 medium eggs
1 tbsp milk
finely grated rind of 1 lemon
5 tbsp maple syrup

FOR THE ICING:

75 g/3 oz icing sugar
1 tbsp lemon juice
25 g/1 oz pecans,
   roughly chopped

Food Fact

Maple syrup is made using the sap of the maple tree and has an intensely sweet, almost vanilla flavour. It is important to differentiate between the real thing and cheaper imitations which are maple-flavoured syrups, and contain artificial flavours.

Helpful Hint

If the top of the cake starts to brown too much during cooking, loosely cover with a piece of tinfoil.

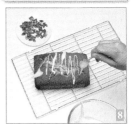

Moist Mincemeat Tea Loaf

1 Preheat the oven to 180°C/350°F/Gas Mark 4 10 minutes before cooking. Oil and line the base of a 900 g/2 lb loaf tin with non-stick baking paper.

2 Sift the flour and mixed spice into a large bowl. Add the butter and rub in until the mixture resembles breadcrumbs.

3 Reserve 2 tablespoons of the flaked almonds and stir in the rest with the glacé cherries and sugar.

4 Make a well in the centre of the dry ingredients. Lightly whisk the eggs, then stir in the mincemeat, lemon zest and brandy or milk.

5 Add the egg mixture and fold together until blended. Spoon into the prepared loaf tin, smooth the top with the back of a spoon, then sprinkle over the reserved flaked almonds.

6 Bake on the middle shelf of the preheated oven for 30 minutes. Cover with tinfoil to prevent the almonds browning too much. Bake for a further 30 minutes, or until well risen and a skewer inserted into the centre comes out clean.

7 Leave the tea loaf in the tin for 10 minutes before removing and cooling on a wire rack. Remove the lining paper, slice thickly and serve.

INGREDIENTS
Cuts into 12 slices

225 g/8 oz self-raising flour
½ tsp ground mixed spice
125 g/4 oz cold butter, cubed
75 g/3 oz flaked almonds
25 g/1 oz glacé cherries, rinsed, dried and quartered
75 g/3 oz light muscovado sugar
2 medium eggs
250 g/9 oz prepared mincemeat
1 tsp lemon zest
2 tsp brandy or milk

Food Fact

Traditionally mincemeat contained cooked lean beef, but this is now omitted. Mince pies are now part of the Christmas fare in Britain. There are many different recipes mostly containing suet. Again traditionally beef suet was used. With the upsurge in vegetarianism, however, vegetarian suet is now often used.

Marbled Chocolate & Orange Loaf

1 Preheat the oven to 180°C/ 350°F/Gas Mark 4. Lightly oil a 450 g/1 lb loaf tin and line the base with a layer of non-stick baking paper.

2 Put the chocolate in a bowl over a saucepan of very hot water. Stir occasionally until melted. Remove and leave until just cool, but not starting to reset.

3 Meanwhile, cream together the butter, sugar and orange zest until pale and fluffy. Gradually add the beaten eggs, beating well after each addition.

4 Sift in the flour, add the orange juice and fold with a metal spoon or rubber spatula. Divide the mixture by half into 2 separate bowls. Gently fold the cocoa powder and chocolate into one half of the mixture.

5 Drop tablespoonfuls of each cake mixture into the prepared tin, alternating between the orange and chocolate mixtures. Briefly swirl the colours together with a knife to give a marbled effect.

6 Bake in the preheated oven for 40 minutes, or until firm and a fine skewer inserted into the centre comes out clean. Leave in the tin for 5 minutes, then turn out and cool on a wire rack. Carefully remove the lining paper.

7 Dust the cake with the icing sugar and then with the cocoa powder. Cut into thick slices and serve.

INGREDIENTS
Cuts into 6 slices

50 g/2 oz plain dark chocolate, broken into squares
125 g/4 oz butter, softened
125 g/4 oz caster sugar
zest of 1 orange
2 medium eggs, beaten
125 g/4 oz self-raising flour
2 tsp orange juice
1 tbsp cocoa powder, sifted

TO FINISH:
1 tbsp icing sugar
1 tsp cocoa powder

Tasty Tip

To make a cream cheese icing for this cake, beat together 75 g/ 3 oz of cream cheese with 1–2 tablespoons of milk until smooth. Add a pinch of salt, 1 teaspoon of vanilla essence and 225 g/8 oz of icing sugar and mix well. Spread on top of the cake when cool.

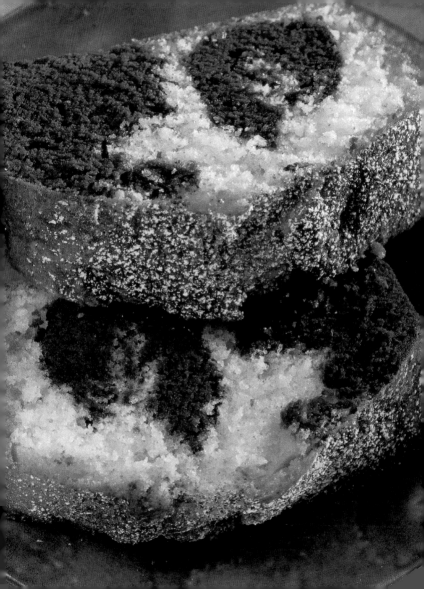

Fruity Apple Tea Bread

1 Preheat the oven to 180°C/ 350°F/Gas Mark 4. Oil and line the base of a 900 g/2 lb loaf tin with non-stick baking paper.

2 Put the butter, sugar, sultanas and apple juice in a small saucepan. Heat gently, stirring occasionally until the butter has melted. Tip into a bowl and leave to cool.

3 Stir in the chopped apple and beaten eggs. Sift the flour, spices and bicarbonate of soda over the apple mixture.

4 Stir into the sultana mixture, spoon into the prepared loaf tin and smooth the top level with the back of a spoon.

5 Toss the apple slices in lemon juice and arrange on top.

6 Bake in the preheated oven for 50 minutes. Cover with tinfoil to prevent the top from browning too much.

7 Bake for 30–35 minutes, or until a skewer inserted into the centre comes out clean.

8 Leave in the tin for 10 minutes before turning out to cool on to a wire rack.

9 Brush the top with golden syrup and leave to cool. Remove the lining paper, cut into thick slices and serve with curls of butter.

INGREDIENTS
Cuts into 12 slices

125 g/4 oz butter
125 g/4 oz soft light brown sugar
275 g/10 oz sultanas
150 ml/¼ pint apple juice
1 eating apple, peeled cored
  and chopped
2 medium eggs, beaten
275 g/10 oz plain flour
½ tsp ground cinnamon
½ tsp ground ginger
2 tsp bicarbonate of soda
curls of butter, to serve

TO DECORATE:

1 eating apple, cored and sliced
1 tsp lemon juice
1 tbsp golden syrup, warmed

Tasty Tip

For an alcoholic version of this cake, soak the sultanas in brandy overnight before adding in step 2. To make the tea bread moister in texture, add 1 grated carrot at the same time as the chopped apple in step 3.

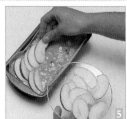

Chocolate Chip Cookies

1 Preheat the oven to 180°C/350°F/Gas Mark 4, 10 minutes before baking. Lightly butter 3–4 large baking sheets with 15 g/½ oz of the butter. Place the remaining butter and both sugars in a food processor and blend until smooth. Add the egg and vanilla essence and blend briefly. Alternatively, cream the butter and sugars together in a bowl, then beat in the egg with the vanilla essence.

2 If using a food processor, scrape out the mixture with a spatula and place the mixture into a large bowl. Sift the flour and bicarbonate of soda together,

then fold into the creamed mixture. When the mixture is blended thoroughly, stir in the chocolate chips.

3 Drop heaped teaspoons of the mixture onto the prepared baking sheets, spaced well apart and bake the cookies in the preheated oven for 10–12 minutes or until lightly golden.

4 Leave to cool for a few seconds, then using a spatula, transfer to a wire rack and cool completely. The cookies are best eaten when just cooked, but can be stored in an airtight tin for a few days.

INGREDIENTS
Makes about 30

140 g/4½ oz butter
50 g/2 oz caster sugar
60 g/2½ oz soft dark brown sugar
1 medium egg, beaten
½ tsp vanilla essence
125 g/4 oz plain flour
½ tsp bicarbonate of soda
150 g/5 oz plain or milk chocolate chips

Helpful Hint

For light-textured, crumbly biscuits, do not over work the biscuit dough. Handle as little as possible and fold the ingredients together gently in a figure of 8 using a metal spoon or rubber spatula. To ring the changes with these basic biscuits, use an equal mixture of chocolate chips and nuts. Alternatively, replace the chocolate chips entirely with an equal quantity of your favourite chopped nuts.

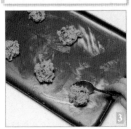

Chewy Choc & Nut Cookies

1 Preheat the oven to 180°C/ 350°F/Gas Mark 4, 10 minutes before baking. Lightly butter several baking sheets with the butter and line with a sheet of nonstick baking parchment. Place the egg whites in a large grease-free bowl and whisk with an electric mixer until the egg whites are very frothy.

2 Add the sugar, with the cocoa powder, the flour and coffee powder and whisk again until the ingredients are blended thoroughly. Add 1 tablespoon of water and continue to whisk on the highest speed until the mixture is very thick. Fold in the chopped walnuts.

3 Place tablespoons of the mixture onto the prepared baking sheets, leaving plenty of space between them as they expand greatly during cooking.

4 Bake in the preheated oven for 12–15 minutes, or until the tops are firm, golden and quite cracked. Leave to cool for 30 seconds, then using a spatula, transfer to a wire rack and leave to cool. Store in an airtight tin.

INGREDIENTS
Makes 18

15 g/½ oz butter
4 medium egg whites
350 g/12 oz icing sugar
75 g/3 oz cocoa powder
2 tbsp plain flour
1 tsp instant coffee powder
125 g/4 oz walnuts, finely
  chopped

Food Fact

When the Spanish brought the cocoa bean home they also brought the word 'cacao' as well. In every other European country it is still known as cacao – it is only in English that it is known as cocoa.

Tasty Tip

Although the walnuts in these biscuits are excellent, hazelnuts or mixed nuts would also go very well with both the chocolate and the coffee flavours.

White Chocolate Cookies

1 Preheat the oven to 180°C/ 350°F/Gas Mark 4, 10 minutes before baking. Lightly butter several baking sheets with 15 g/½ oz of the butter. Place the remaining butter with both sugars into a large bowl and beat with a wooden spoon or an electric mixer until soft and fluffy.

2 Beat the egg, then gradually beat into the creamed mixture. Sift the flour and the bicarbonate of soda together, then carefully fold into the creamed mixture with a few drops of vanilla essence.

3 Roughly chop the chocolate and hazelnuts into small pieces, add to the bowl and gently stir into the mixture. Mix together lightly to blend.

4 Spoon heaped teaspoons of the mixture onto the prepared baking sheets, making sure that there is plenty of space in between each one as they will spread a lot during cooking.

5 Bake the cookies in the preheated oven for 10 minutes or until golden, then remove from the oven and leave to cool for 1 minute. Using a spatula, carefully transfer to a wire rack and leave to cool completely. The cookies are best eaten on the day they are made. Store in an airtight tin.

INGREDIENTS
Makes about 24

140 g/4½ oz butter
40 g/1½ oz caster sugar
60 g/2½ oz soft dark brown
  sugar
1 medium egg
125 g/4 oz plain flour
½ tsp bicarbonate of soda
few drops of vanilla essence
150 g/5 oz white chocolate
50 g/2 oz whole hazelnuts,
  shelled

Helpful Hint

White chocolate is available in bars as well as in chips. As there are no cocoa solids in white chocolate, look for one with a good percentage of cocoa butter, as it is the cocoa butter that gives the chocolate its luscious, creamy texture.

Fudgy Chocolate Bars

1 Preheat the oven to 180°C/ 350°F/Gas Mark 4, 10 minutes before baking. Lightly oil a 18 cm/7 inch square tin and line the base with nonstick baking parchment. Rinse the glacé cherries thoroughly, dry well on absorbent kitchen paper and reserve.

2 Place the nuts on a baking tray and roast in the preheated oven for 10 minutes, or until light golden brown. Leave to cool slightly, then chop roughly and reserve.

3 Break the chocolate into small pieces, place with the butter and salt into the top of a double boiler or in a bowl set over a saucepan of gently simmering water. Heat gently

stirring until melted and smooth. Alternatively, melt the chocolate in the microwave, according to the manufacturer's instructions.

4 Chop the biscuits into 5 mm/¼ inch pieces and cut the cherries in half. Add to the chocolate mixture with the nuts and stir well. Spoon the mixture into the prepared tin and level the top.

5 Chill in the refrigerator for 30 minutes, remove from the tin, discard the baking parchment and cut into 14 bars. Cover lightly, return to the refrigerator and keep chilled until ready to serve. To serve, lightly sprinkle the bars with sifted icing sugar if using. Store covered in the refrigerator.

INGREDIENTS
Makes 14

25 g/1 oz glacé cherries
60 g/2½ oz shelled hazelnuts
150 g/5 oz plain dark chocolate
150 g/5 oz unsalted butter
¼ tsp salt
150 g/5 oz digestive biscuits
1 tbsp icing sugar, sifted, optional

Tasty Tip

For these bars, it is best to use a plain chocolate with around 50 per cent cocoa solids. Dark chocolate would not give a good flavour as it is too bitter.

Chocolate Shortcake

1 Preheat the oven to 170°C/ 325°F/Gas Mark 3, 10 minutes before baking. Lightly oil several baking sheets and line with nonstick baking parchment. Place the butter, icing sugar and vanilla essence together in a food processor and blend briefly until smooth. Alternatively, using a wooden spoon, cream the butter, icing sugar and vanilla essence in a large bowl.

2 Sift the flour, cocoa powder and salt together then either add to the food processor bowl and blend quickly to form a dough, or add to the bowl and, using your hands, mix together until a smooth dough is formed.

3 Turn the dough out onto a clean board lined with clingfilm. Place another sheet

of clingfilm over the top and roll the dough out until it is 1 cm/½ inch thick. Transfer the whole board to the refrigerator and chill for 1½–2 hours.

4 Remove the top piece of clingfilm and use a 5 cm/ 2 inch cutter to cut the dough into 30–32 rounds. Place the rounds on the prepared baking sheets and bake in the preheated oven for about 15 minutes or until firm.

5 Cool for 1 minute, then using a spatula, carefully remove the shortcakes from the baking parchment and transfer to a wire rack. Leave to cool completely. Sprinkle the short-cakes with sifted icing sugar before serving. Store in an airtight tin for a few days.

INGREDIENTS
Makes 30–32

225 g/8 oz unsalted butter, softened
150 g/5 oz icing sugar
1 tsp vanilla essence
250 g/9 oz plain flour
25 g/1 oz cocoa powder
¼ tsp salt
extra icing sugar, to decorate

Food Fact

Using icing sugar instead of caster sugar helps to give these biscuits a really crumbly texture. Do make sure that you use butter rather than margarine to ensure that you get the classic shortbread texture.

Chocolate Macaroons

1 Preheat the oven to 180°C/ 350°F/Gas Mark 4, 10 minutes before baking. Lightly oil several baking sheets and line with sheets of nonstick baking parchment. Melt the chocolate in a heatproof bowl set over a saucepan of simmering water. Alternatively, melt in the microwave according to the manufacturer's instructions. Stir until smooth, then cool slightly.

2 Place the ground almonds in a food processor and add the sugar, almond essence, cocoa powder and 1 of the egg whites. Add the melted chocolate and a little of the other egg white and blend to make a soft smooth paste. Alternatively, place the ground almonds with the sugar, almond essence and cocoa powder in a bowl and make a well in the centre. Add the melted chocolate with sufficient egg white and gradually blend together to form a smooth but not sticky paste.

3 Shape the dough into small balls the size of large walnuts and place them on the prepared baking sheets. Flatten them slightly, then brush with a little water. Sprinkle over a little icing sugar and bake in the preheated oven for 10–12 minutes or until just firm.

4 Using a spatula, carefully lift the macaroons off the baking parchment and transfer to a wire rack to cool. These are best served immediately, but can be stored in an airtight container.

INGREDIENTS
Makes 20

650 g/2½ oz plain dark chocolate
125 g/4 oz ground almonds
125 g/4 oz caster sugar
¼ tsp almond essence
1 tbsp cocoa powder
2 medium egg whites
1 tbsp icing sugar

Helpful Hint

If you prefer, you could bake these biscuits on edible rice paper, available from the baking section of supermarkets. Cover the baking sheet with rice paper and drop the mixture onto the paper as directed above. Bake in the preheated oven, then tear the paper to release the macaroons.

Chocolate & Ginger Florentines

1 Preheat the oven to 180°C/ 350°F/Gas Mark 4, 10 minutes before baking. Lightly oil several baking sheets. Melt the butter, cream and sugar together in a saucepan and bring slowly to the boil. Remove from the heat and stir in the almonds and the glacé ginger.

2 Leave to cool slightly, then mix in the flour and the salt. Blend together, then place heaped teaspoons of the mixture on the baking sheets. Make sure they are spaced well apart as they expand during cooking. Flatten them slightly with the back of a wet spoon.

3 Bake in the preheated oven for 10–12 minutes or until just brown at the edges. Leave to cool slightly. Using a spatula, carefully transfer the Florentines to a wire rack and leave to cool.

4 Melt the chocolate in a heatproof bowl set over a saucepan of gently simmering water. Alternatively, melt the chocolate in the microwave according to the manufacturer's instructions, until just liquid and smooth. Spread thickly over one side of the Florentines, then mark wavy lines through the chocolate using a fork and leave until firm.

INGREDIENTS
Makes 14–16

40 g/1½ oz butter
5 tbsp double cream
50 g/2 oz caster sugar
60 g/2½ oz chopped almonds
25 g/1 oz flaked almonds
40 g/1½ oz glacé ginger, chopped
25 g/1 oz plain flour
pinch of salt
150 g/5 oz plain dark chocolate

Helpful Hint

These biscuits spread quite a lot in the oven. To make evenly sized, nicely shaped biscuits, try forming the biscuits in a plain 7.5 cm/3 inch pastry cutter as soon as they come out of the oven and are still very hot and pliable. When making these Florentines, only place 3–4 on each baking sheet, to ensure that they can be removed easily from the sheet after cooking. Leave to cool for about 1 minute, then with a round-bladed knife, gently ease round the outside edge of each Florentine. Once they lift easily, transfer to a wire cooling rack.

Italian Biscotti

1 Preheat the oven to 190°C/ 375°F/Gas Mark 5, 10 minutes before baking. Lightly oil 3–4 baking sheets and reserve. Cream the butter and sugar together in a bowl and mix in the vanilla essence. When it is light and fluffy beat in the egg with the cinnamon, lemon rind and the ground almonds. Stir in the flour to make a firm dough.

2 Knead lightly until smooth and free from cracks. Shape the dough into rectangular blocks about 4 cm/1½ inches in diameter, wrap in greaseproof paper and chill in the refrigerator for at least 2 hours.

3 Cut the chilled dough into 5 mm/¼ inch slices, place on the baking sheets and cook in the preheated oven for 12–15 minutes or until firm. Remove from the oven, cool slightly, then transfer to wire racks to cool.

4 When completely cold, melt the chocolate in a heatproof bowl set over a saucepan of simmering water. Alternatively, melt the chocolate in the microwave according to the manufacturer's instructions. Spoon into a piping bag and pipe over the biscuits. Leave to dry on a sheet of nonstick baking parchment before serving.

INGREDIENTS
Makes 26–28

150 g/5 oz butter
200 g/7 oz caster sugar
¼ tsp vanilla essence
1 small egg, beaten
¼ tsp ground cinnamon
grated rind of 1 lemon
15 g/½ oz ground almonds
150 g/5 oz plain flour
150 g/5 oz plain dark chocolate

Helpful Hint

When using vanilla essence, do use essence, and not vanilla flavouring which is a cheap substitute. Alternatively, use vanilla caster sugar which is very easy to make. Simply place a vanilla pod in a clean screw top jar and fill with caster sugar. Secure and leave in a cool, dark place and leave for 2–3 weeks before using.

Food Fact

In Italy, these deliciously crunchy little biscuits are traditionally served with a sweet dessert wine called Vin Santo.

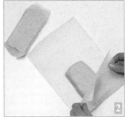

Chocolate & Nut Refrigerator Biscuits

1 Preheat the oven to 190°C/ 375°F/Gas Mark 5, 10 minutes before baking. Lightly grease several baking sheets with 15 g/½ oz of the butter. Cream the remaining butter and both sugars in a large bowl until light and fluffy, then gradually beat in the egg.

2 Sift the flour, bicarbonate of soda and cocoa powder together then gradually fold into the creamed mixture together with the chopped pecans. Mix thoroughly until a smooth but stiff dough is formed.

3 Place the dough on a lightly floured surface or pastry board and roll into sausage shapes about 5 cm/2 inches in diameter. Wrap in clingfilm and chill in the refrigerator for at least 12 hours, or preferably overnight.

4 Cut the dough into thin slices and place on the prepared baking sheets. Bake in the preheated oven for 8–10 minutes or until firm. Remove from the oven and leave to cool slightly. Using a spatula, transfer to a wire rack to cool. Store in an airtight tin.

Helpful Hint

This dough will keep in the refrigerator for 4–5 days if well wrapped. Cut off and bake a few biscuits as required. When oiling or greasing baking sheets for biscuits, be careful about how much oil or butter you use, especially if using nonstick baking sheets. Very rich mixtures, that use a high proportion of fat, will not need to be baked on oiled baking sheets. If they are, there is the probability that the biscuits will spread too much.

Chocolate & Hazelnut Cookies

1 Preheat the oven to 180°C/ 350°F/Gas Mark 4,10 minutes before baking. Lightly oil and flour 2–3 baking sheets. Chop 25 g/1 oz of the hazelnuts and reserve. Blend the remaining hazelnuts with the caster sugar in a food processor until finely ground. Add the butter to the processor bowl and blend until pale and creamy.

2 Add the salt, cocoa powder and the double cream and mix well. Scrape the mixture into a bowl, using a spatula, and stir in the egg whites. Sift the flour, then stir into the mixture together with the rum.

3 Spoon heaped tablespoons of the batter onto the baking sheets and sprinkle over a few of the reserved hazelnuts. Bake in the preheated oven for 5–7 minutes or until firm. Remove the cookies from the oven and leave to cool for 1–2 minutes. Using a spatula, transfer to wire racks and leave to cool.

4 When the biscuits are cold, melt the chocolate in a heatproof bowl set over a saucepan of simmering water. Stir until smooth, then drizzle a little of the chocolate over the top of each biscuit. Leave to dry on a wire rack before serving.

INGREDIENTS
Makes 12

75 g/3 oz blanched hazelnuts
100 g/3½ oz caster sugar
50 g/2 oz unsalted butter
pinch of salt
5 tsp cocoa powder
3 tbsp double cream
2 large egg whites
40 g/1½ oz plain flour
2 tbsp rum
75 g/3 oz white chocolate

Helpful Hint

Be careful not to chop the hazelnuts for too long in the food processor as this tends to make them very oily. To blanch hazelnuts or any nut, simply place on a baking sheet and heat in a hot oven for 10 minutes. Remove, then place in a clean tea towel and rub off the brown skins. Do not rub too many at a time, otherwise they may escape from the tea towel.

Chocolate & Almond Biscuits

1 Preheat the oven to 200°C/
400°F/Gas Mark 6, 15
minutes before baking. Lightly
oil several baking sheets. Cream
the butter and icing sugar
together until light and fluffy,
then gradually beat in the egg,
beating well after each addition.
When all the egg has been
added, stir in the milk and
lemon rind.

2 Sift the flour then stir into
the mixture together with
the chopped almonds to form a
smooth and pliable dough. Wrap
in clingfilm and chill in the
refrigerator for 2 hours.

3 Roll the dough out on a
lightly floured surface, in a
large oblong about 5 mm/¼ inch

thick. Cut into strips, about
6.5 cm/2½ inches long and
4 cm/1½ inches wide and place
on the prepared baking sheets

4 Bake in the preheated oven
for 15 minutes, or until
golden, then remove from the
oven and leave to cool for a few
minutes. Transfer to a wire rack
and leave to cool completely.

5 Melt the chocolate in a
heatproof bowl set over a
saucepan of simmering water.
Alternatively, melt the chocolate
in the microwave according to the
manufacturer's instructions, until
smooth. Spread the chocolate
thickly over the biscuits, sprinkle
over the toasted flaked almonds
and leave to set before serving.

INGREDIENTS
Makes 18–20

140 g/4½ oz butter
60 g/2½ oz icing sugar
1 medium egg, beaten
1 tbsp milk
grated rind of 1 lemon
250 g/9 oz plain flour
100 g/3½ oz blanched almonds,
  chopped
125 g/4 oz plain dark chocolate
75 g/3 oz flaked almonds, toasted

Tasty Tip
As an alternative to flaked almonds for decorating
these biscuits, use slivered almonds. They are easy to make;
simply cut whole blanched almonds into thin slivers.

Fig & Chocolate Bars

1 Preheat the oven to 180°C/ 350°F/Gas Mark 4, 10 minutes before baking. Lightly oil a 18 cm/7 inch square cake tin. Place the butter and the flour in a large bowl and, using your fingertips, rub the butter into the flour until it resembles fine breadcrumbs.

2 Stir in the sugar, then using your hand, bring the mixture together to form a smooth dough. Knead until smooth then press the dough into the prepared tin. Lightly prick the base with a fork and bake in the preheated oven for 20–30 minutes or until golden. Remove from the oven and leave the shortbread to cool in the tin until completely cold.

3 Meanwhile, place the dried figs, lemon juice, 125 ml/ 4 fl oz water and the ground cinnamon in a saucepan and bring to the boil. Cover and simmer for 20 minutes or until soft, stirring occasionally during cooking. Cool slightly, then purée in a food processor until smooth. Cool, then spread over the cooked shortbread.

4 Melt the chocolate in a heatproof bowl set over a saucepan of simmering water. Alternatively, melt the chocolate in the microwave, according to the manufacturer's instructions. Stir until smooth, then spread over the top of the fig filling. Leave to become firm, then cut into 12 bars and serve.

INGREDIENTS
Makes 12

125 g/4 oz butter
150 g/5 oz plain flour
50 g/2 oz soft light brown sugar
225 g/8 oz ready-to-eat dried
  figs, halved
juice of ½ a large lemon
1 tsp ground cinnamon
125 g/4 oz plain dark chocolate

Helpful Hint

If you are unable to find ready-to-eat figs, soak dried figs in boiling water for 20 minutes until plump. Drain well and use as above.

Chocolate-covered Flapjack

1 Preheat the oven to 180°C/ 350°F/Gas Mark 4, 10 minutes before baking. Lightly oil a 33 x 23 cm/13 x 9 inch Swiss roll tin and line with nonstick baking parchment. Place the flour, rolled oats, the light muscovado sugar, bicarbonate of soda and salt into a bowl and stir well together.

2 Melt the butter and golden syrup together in a heavy-based saucepan and stir until smooth, then add to the oat mixture and mix together thoroughly. Spoon the mixture into the prepared tin and press down firmly and level the top.

3 Bake in the preheated oven for 15–20 minutes or until golden. Remove from the oven

and leave the flapjack to cool in the tin. Once cool, remove from the tin. Discard the parchment.

4 Melt the chocolate in a heatproof bowl set over a saucepan of gently simmering water. Alternatively, melt chocolate in the microwave according to the manufacturer's instructions. Once the chocolate has melted quickly beat in the cream, then pour over the flapjack. Mark patterns over the chocolate with a fork when almost set.

5 Chill the flapjack in the refrigerator for at least 30 minutes before cutting into bars. When the chocolate has set, serve. Store in an airtight container for a few days.

INGREDIENTS
Makes 24

215 g/7½ oz plain flour
150 g/5 oz rolled oats
225 g/8 oz light muscovado sugar
1 tsp bicarbonate of soda
pinch of salt
150 g/5 oz butter
2 tbsp golden syrup
250 g/9 oz plain dark chocolate
5 tbsp double cream

Helpful Hint

Try lightly oiling your measuring spoon before dipping it into the golden syrup. The syrup will slide off the spoon easily. Alternatively, warm the syrup slightly before measuring.

Shortbread Thumbs

1 Preheat the oven to 150°C/ 300°F/Gas Mark 2, 10 minutes before baking. Lightly oil 2 baking sheets. Sift the flour into a large bowl, cut 75 g/3 oz of the butter and the white vegetable fat into small cubes, add to the flour, then, using your fingertips, rub in until the mixture resembles fine breadcrumbs.

2 Stir in the granulated sugar, sifted cornflour and 4 table-spoons of cocoa powder and bring the mixture together with your hand to form a soft and pliable dough.

3 Place on a lightly floured surface and shape into 12 small balls. Place onto the baking sheets at least 5 cm/2 inches apart, then press each one with a clean thumb to make a dent.

4 Bake in the preheated oven for 20–25 minutes or until light golden brown. Remove from the oven and leave for 1–2 minutes to cool. Transfer to a wire rack and leave until cold.

5 Sift the icing sugar and the remaining cocoa powder into a bowl and add the remaining softened butter. Blend to form a smooth and spreadable icing with 1–2 tablespoons of hot water. Spread a little icing over the top of each biscuit and place half a cherry on each. Leave until set before serving.

INGREDIENTS
Makes 12

125 g/4 oz self-raising flour
125 g/4 oz butter, softened
25 g/1 oz white vegetable fat
50 g/2 oz granulated sugar
25 g/1 oz cornflour, sifted
5 tbsp cocoa powder, sifted
125 g/4 oz icing sugar
6 assorted coloured glacé cherries,
*   rinsed, dried and halved*

Helpful Hint

After baking, remove the cooked biscuits as soon as possible from the baking sheets as they will continue to cook and could overcook. Cool completely on wire cooling racks before storing in airtight tins.

Food Fact

Using a combination of butter and vegetable fat gives these biscuits a softer texture than using all butter.

Chequered Biscuits

1 Preheat the oven to 190°C/ 375°F/Gas Mark 5, 10 minutes before baking. Lightly oil 3–4 baking sheets. Place the butter and icing sugar in a bowl and cream together until light and fluffy.

2 Add the salt, then gradually add the flour, beating well after each addition. Mix well to form a firm dough. Cut the dough in half and knead the cocoa powder into one half. Wrap both portions of dough separately in clingfilm and then leave to chill in the refrigerator for 2 hours.

3 Divide each piece of dough into 3 portions. Roll each portion of dough into a long roll and arrange these rolls on top of each other to form a chequer-board design, sealing them with egg white. Wrap in clingfilm and refrigerate for 1 hour.

4 Cut the dough into 5 mm/ ¼ inch thick slices, place on the baking sheets and bake in the preheated oven for 10–15 minutes. Remove from the oven, and leave to cool for a few minutes. Transfer to a wire rack and leave until cold before serving. Store in an airtight tin.

INGREDIENTS
Makes 20

150 g/5 oz butter
75 g/3 oz icing sugar
pinch of salt
200 g/7 oz plain flour
25 g/1 oz cocoa powder
1 small egg white

Helpful Hint

When baking biscuits, use a fish slice or spatula to transfer the cut-out biscuits from the work surface to the baking sheets. Use heavy-duty baking sheets that will not bend or warp in the oven. The nonstick silicone baking sheets that are now readily available are ideal for baking biscuits. Follow the manufacturers' instructions for oiling.

Food Fact

Recipes for sweet biscuits and pastries often contain a pinch of salt. This helps to enhance the sweet flavour without making it savoury.

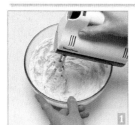

Coconut & Almond Munchies

1 Preheat the oven to 150°C/ 300°F/Gas Mark 2, 10 minutes before baking. Line several baking sheets with rice paper. Place the egg whites in a clean, grease-free bowl and whisk until stiff and standing in peaks. Sift the icing sugar, then carefully fold half of the sugar into the whisked egg whites together with the ground almonds. Add the coconut, the remaining icing sugar and the lemon rind and mix together to form a very sticky dough.

2 Place the mixture in a piping bag and pipe the mixture into walnut-sized mounds onto the rice paper, then sprinkle with a little extra icing sugar. Bake in the preheated oven for 20–25 minutes, or until set and golden on the outside. Remove from the oven and leave to cool slightly. Using a spatula, carefully transfer to a wire rack and leave until cold.

3 Break the milk and white chocolate into pieces and place in 2 separate bowls. Melt both chocolates set over saucepans of gently simmering water. Alternatively, melt in the microwave, according to the manufacturer's instructions. Stir until smooth and free from lumps. Dip one edge of each munchie in the milk chocolate and leave to dry on nonstick baking parchment. When dry, dip the other side into the white chocolate. Leave to set, then serve as soon as possible.

INGREDIENTS
Makes 26–30

5 medium egg whites
250 g/9 oz icing sugar, plus extra
  to sprinkle
225 g/8 oz ground almonds
200 g/7 oz desiccated coconut
grated rind of 1 lemon
125 g/4 oz milk chocolate
125 g/4 oz white chocolate

Helpful Hint

You could, if preferred, drop spoonfuls of this mixture onto the rice paper. However, piping the dough ensures that the munchies will be more evenly sized.

Honey & Chocolate Hearts

1 Preheat the oven to 220°C/ 425°F/Gas Mark 7, 15 minutes before baking. Lightly oil 2 baking sheets. Heat the sugar, butter and honey together in a small saucepan until everything has melted and the mixture is smooth.

2 Remove from the heat and stir until slightly cooled, then add the beaten egg with the salt and beat well. Stir in the mixed peel or glacé ginger, ground cinnamon, ground cloves, the flour and the baking powder and mix well until a dough is formed. Wrap in clingfilm and chill in the refrigerator for 45 minutes.

3 Place the chilled dough on a lightly floured surface, roll out to about 5 mm/¼ inch thickness and cut out small heart shapes. Place onto the prepared baking sheets and bake in the preheated oven for 8–10 minutes. Remove from the oven and leave to cool slightly. Using a spatula, transfer to a wire rack until cold.

4 Melt the chocolate in a heatproof bowl set over a saucepan of simmering water. Alternatively, melt the chocolate in the microwave according to the manufacturer's instructions, until smooth. Dip one half of each biscuit in the melted chocolate. Leave to set before serving.

INGREDIENTS
Makes about 20

60 g/2½ oz caster sugar
15 g/½ oz butter
125 g/4 oz thick honey
1 small egg, beaten
pinch of salt
1 tbsp mixed peel or chopped
  glacé ginger
¼ tsp ground cinnamon
pinch of ground cloves
225 g/8 oz plain flour, sifted
½ tsp baking powder, sifted
75 g/3 oz milk chocolate

Helpful Hint

When cutting out the hearts start at the outside edge working into the centre, cutting out the biscuits as close as possible to minimise the wastage. Press the trimmings lightly together and and roll out once more. Discard any remaining dough as it will be tougher and give a heavier biscuit, which will break up easily.

Tasty Tip

Try different types of honey to vary the flavour of the biscuits. Acacia honey, for example, is very mild while heather honey has a more pronounced flavour.

Chocolate Orange Biscuits

1 Preheat the oven to 200°C/ 400°F/Gas Mark 6, 15 minutes before baking. Lightly oil several baking sheets. Coarsely grate the chocolate and reserve. Beat the butter and sugar together until creamy. Add the salt, beaten egg and half the orange zest and beat again.

2 Sift the flour and baking powder, add to the bowl with the grated chocolate and beat to form a dough. Shape into a ball, wrap in clingfilm and chill in the refrigerator for 2 hours.

3 Roll the dough out on a lightly floured surface to 5 mm/¼ inch thickness and cut into 5 cm/2 inch rounds. Place the rounds on the prepared baking sheets, allowing room for expansion. Bake in the preheated oven for 10–12 minutes or until firm. Remove the biscuits from the oven and leave to cool slightly. Using a spatula, transfer to a wire rack and leave to cool.

4 Sift the icing sugar into a small bowl and stir in sufficient orange juice to make a smooth, spreadable icing. Spread the icing over the biscuits, leave until almost set, then sprinkle on the remaining grated orange zest before serving.

INGREDIENTS
Makes 30

100 g/3½oz plain dark chocolate
125 g/4 oz butter
125 g/4 oz caster sugar
pinch of salt
1 medium egg, beaten
grated zest of 2 oranges
200 g/7 oz plain flour
1 tsp baking powder
125 g/4 oz icing sugar
1–2 tbsp orange juice

Helpful Hint

To get the maximum amount of juice from citrus fruits, heat the whole fruit in the microwave for about 40 seconds, then cool slightly before squeezing. Alternatively, roll the fruit on the table, pressing lightly before squeezing out the juice. It is important to add the orange juice gradually to the icing mixture because you may not need all of it to obtain a spreadable consistency.

Rum & Chocolate Squares

1 Preheat the oven to 190°C/ 350°F/Gas Mark 5, 10 minutes before baking. Lightly oil several baking sheets. Cream the butter, sugar and salt together in a large bowl until light and fluffy. Add the egg yolks and beat well until smooth.

2 Sift together 175 g/6 oz of the flour, the cornflour and the baking powder and add to the mixture and mix well with a wooden spoon until a smooth and soft dough is formed.

3 Halve the dough and knead the cocoa powder into one-half and the rum and the remaining plain flour into the other half. Place the

2 mixtures in 2 separate bowls, cover with clingfilm and chill in the refrigerator for 1 hour.

4 Roll out both pieces of dough separately on a well floured surface into 2 thin rectangles. Place one on top of the other, cut out squares approximately 5 cm/2 inch x 5 mm/¼ inch and place on the prepared baking sheets.

5 Bake in the preheated oven, half with the chocolate uppermost and the other half, rum side up, for 10–12 minutes or until firm. Remove from the oven and leave to cool slightly. Using a spatula, transfer to a wire rack and leave to cool, then serve.

INGREDIENTS
Makes 14–16

125 g/4 oz butter
100 g/3½ oz caster sugar
pinch of salt
2 medium egg yolks
225 g/8 oz plain flour
50 g/2 oz cornflour
¼ tsp baking powder
2 tbsp cocoa powder
1 tbsp rum

Tasty Tip

If you prefer, you could substitute rum flavouring for the rum in this recipe. However, you would need to reduce the amount to about 1 teaspoon.

Chocolate Whirls

1 Preheat the oven to 180°C/350°F/Gas Mark 4, 10 minutes before baking. Lightly oil 2 baking sheets. Cream the margarine, butter and icing sugar together until the mixture is light and fluffy.

2 Stir the chocolate until smooth, then beat into the creamed mixture. Stir in the cornflour. Sift the flours together, then gradually add to the creamed mixture, a little at a time, beating well between each addition. Beat until the consistency is smooth and stiff enough for piping.

3 Put the mixture in a piping bag fitted with a large star nozzle and pipe 40 small whirls onto the prepared baking sheets.

4 Bake the whirls in the preheated oven for 12–15 minutes or until firm to the touch. Remove from the oven and leave to cool for about 2 minutes. Using a spatula, transfer the whirls to wire racks and leave to cool.

5 Meanwhile, make the butter cream. Cream the butter with the vanilla essence until soft. Gradually beat in the icing sugar and add a little cooled boiled water, if necessary, to give a smooth consistency.

6 When the whirls are cold, pipe or spread on the prepared butter cream, sandwich together and serve.

INGREDIENTS
Makes 20

125 g/4 oz soft margarine
75 g/3 oz unsalted butter, softened
75 g/3 oz icing sugar, sifted
75 g/3 oz plain dark chocolate, melted and cooled
15 g/½ oz cornflour, sifted
125 g/4 oz plain flour
125 g/4 oz self-raising flour

FOR THE BUTTER CREAM:
125 g/4 oz unsalted butter, softened
½ tsp vanilla essence
225 g/8 oz icing sugar, sifted

Helpful Hint

It is important that the fats are at room temperature and the flours are sifted. Do not put too much mixture into the piping bag. If liked, the butter cream can be replaced with whipped cream, but the whirls should be eaten on the day they are filled.

Chunky Chocolate Muffins

1 Preheat the oven to 200°C/
400°F/Gas Mark 6, 15
minutes before baking. Line a
muffin or deep bun tin tray with
7 paper muffin cases or oil the
individual compartments well.
Place the plain chocolate in a
large heatproof bowl set over a
saucepan of very hot water and
stir occasionally until melted.
Remove the bowl and leave to
cool for a few minutes.

2 Stir the sugar and butter into
the melted chocolate, then
the milk, vanilla essence and egg.
Sift in the flour, baking powder
and salt together. Add the chopped

white chocolate, then using a
metal spoon, fold together quickly,
taking care not to overmix.

3 Divide the mixture between
the paper cases, piling it up
in the centre. Bake on the centre
shelf of the preheated oven for
20–25 minutes, or until well
risen and firm to the touch.

4 Lightly dust the tops of the
muffins with icing sugar as
soon as they come out of the
oven, if using. Leave the muffins
in the tins for a few minutes,
then transfer to a wire rack.
Serve warm or cold.

INGREDIENTS
Makes 7

*50 g/2 oz plain dark chocolate,
 roughly chopped*
50 g/2 oz light muscovado sugar
25 g/1 oz butter, melted
*125 ml/4 fl oz milk, heated to
 room temperature*
½ tsp vanilla essence
1 medium egg, lightly beaten
150 g/5 oz self-raising flour
½ tsp baking powder
pinch of salt
*75 g/3 oz white chocolate,
 chopped*
2 tsp icing sugar (optional)

Helpful Hint

Measuring dry ingredients when baking is very important, too
much or too little of any ingredient can change the end result
quite substantially. This applies especially to raising agents like
baking powder, bicarbonate of soda and cream of tartar. It is a
good idea to invest in a set of cooks measuring spoons and
remember to use either metric or Imperial measurements. Do
not mix the two when weighing out the ingredients.

Helpful Hint

If you do not have a large
muffin or deep bun tin,
you can use an ordinary
bun tin with cake cases, in
which case the quantities
given will make 10–12
smaller muffins.

Fudgy & Top Hat Chocolate Buns

1 Preheat the oven to 190°C/ 375°F/Gas Mark 5, 10 minutes before baking. Sift the flour, cocoa powder and baking powder into a bowl. Add the butter, sugar, egg and milk. Beat for 2–3 minutes or until light and fluffy.

2 Divide the mixture equally between 12 paper cases arranged in a bun tin tray. Bake on the shelf above the centre in the preheated oven for 15–20 minutes, or until well risen and firm to the touch. Leave in the bun tin for a few minutes, then transfer to a wire rack and leave to cool completely.

3 For the fudgy icing, mix together the melted butter, milk, cocoa powder and icing sugar. Place a spoonful of icing on the top of 6 of the buns, spreading out to a circle with the back of the spoon. Sprinkle with grated chocolate.

4 To make the top hats, use a sharp knife to cut and remove a circle of sponge, about 3 cm/1¼ inch across from each of the 6 remaining cakes. Whip the cream, orange liqueur and 1 teaspoon of icing sugar together until soft peaks form.

5 Spoon the filling into a piping bag fitted with a large star nozzle and pipe a swirl in the centre of each cake. Replace the tops, then dust with the remaining icing sugar and serve with the other buns.

INGREDIENTS
Makes 12

50 g/2 oz self-raising flour
25 g/1 oz cocoa powder
½ tsp baking powder
75 g/3 oz butter, softened
75 g/3 oz soft light brown sugar
1 medium egg, lightly beaten
1 tbsp milk

FOR THE FUDGY ICING:

15 g/½ oz unsalted butter, melted
1 tbsp milk
15 g/½ oz cocoa powder, sifted
40 g/1½ oz icing sugar, sifted
25 g/1 oz plain dark chocolate, coarsely grated

FOR THE TOP HAT FILLING:

150 ml/¼ pint whipping cream
2 tsp orange liqueur
1 tbsp icing sugar, sifted

Helpful Hint

When grating chocolate, grate onto a piece of nonstick baking parchment using the coarse side of a box grater. It is then easier to sprinkle onto the buns from the paper.

Chocolate & Orange Rock Buns

1 Preheat the oven to 200°C/ 400°F/Gas Mark 6, 15 minutes before baking. Lightly oil 2 baking sheets, or line them with nonstick baking parchment. Sift the flour, cocoa powder and baking powder into a bowl. Cut the butter into small squares. Add to the dry ingredients, then, using your hands, rub in until the mixture resembles fine breadcrumbs.

2 Add the granulated sugar, pineapple, apricots and cherries to the bowl and stir to mix. Lightly beat the egg together with the grated orange rind and juice. Drizzle the egg mixture over the dry ingredients and stir to combine. The mixture should be fairly stiff but not too dry, add a little more orange juice, if needed.

3 Using 2 teaspoons, shape the mixture into 12 rough heaps on the prepared baking sheets. Sprinkle generously with the demerara sugar. Bake in the preheated oven for 15 minutes, switching the baking sheets around after 10 minutes. Leave on the baking sheets for 5 minutes to cool slightly, then transfer to a wire rack to cool. Serve warm or cold.

INGREDIENTS
Makes 12

200 g/7 oz self-raising flour
25 g/1 oz cocoa powder
½ tsp baking powder
125 g/4 oz butter
40 g/1½ oz granulated sugar
50 g/2 oz candied pineapple, chopped
50 g/2 oz ready-to-eat dried apricots, chopped
50 g/2 oz glacé cherries, quartered
1 medium egg
finely grated rind of ½ orange
1 tbsp orange juice
2 tbsp demerara sugar

Helpful Hint

When making rock buns it is important that you do not over mix the ingredients and do not add too much liquid, otherwise the 'rocky' texture of the buns will be lost. Vary the ingredients according to personal preference. If liked add some nuts for extra crunch and texture. These buns are best eaten within a day of being made, as they do not keep very well.

Rich Chocolate Cup Cakes

1 Preheat the oven to 180°C/ 350°F/Gas Mark 4, 10 minutes before baking. Line a 12 hole muffin or deep bun tin tray with paper muffin cases. Sift the flour and cocoa powder into a bowl. Stir in the sugar, then add the melted butter, eggs and vanilla essence. Beat together with a wooden spoon for 3 minutes or until well blended.

2 Divide half the mixture between 6 of the paper cases. Dry the cherries thoroughly on absorbent kitchen paper, then fold into the remaining mixture and spoon into the rest of the paper cases.

3 Bake on the shelf above the centre of the preheated oven for 20 minutes, or until a skewer

inserted into the centre of a cake comes out clean. Transfer to a wire rack and leave to cool.

4 For the chocolate icing, melt the chocolate and butter in a heatproof bowl set over a saucepan of hot water. Remove from the heat and leave to cool for 3 minutes, stirring occasionally. Stir in the icing sugar. Spoon over the 6 plain chocolate cakes and leave to set.

5 For the cherry icing, sift the icing sugar into a bowl and stir in 1 tablespoon of boiling water, the butter and cherry syrup. Spoon the icing over the remaining 6 cakes, decorate each with a halved cherry and leave to set.

INGREDIENTS
Makes 12

175 g/6 oz self-raising flour
25 g/1 oz cocoa powder
175 g/6 oz soft light brown sugar
75 g/3 oz butter, melted
2 medium eggs, lightly beaten
1 tsp vanilla essence
40 g/1½ oz maraschino cherries, drained and chopped

FOR THE CHOCOLATE ICING:

50 g/2 oz plain dark chocolate
25 g/1 oz unsalted butter
25 g/1 oz icing sugar, sifted

FOR THE CHERRY ICING:

125 g/4 oz icing sugar
7 g/¼ oz unsalted butter, melted
1 tsp syrup from the maraschino cherries
3 maraschino cherries, halved, to decorate

Tasty Tip

Do not expect the cakes to rise to the top of the cake cases; they should only come about three-quarters of the way up and have fairly flat tops to allow for the thick icing to spoon over.

Chocolate Madeleines

1 Preheat the oven to 180°C/ 350°F/Gas Mark 4, 10 minutes before baking. Lightly oil 10 dariole moulds and line the bases of each with a small circle of nonstick baking parchment. Stand the moulds on a baking tray. Cream the butter and sugar together until light and fluffy. Gradually add the eggs, beating well between each addition. Beat in the almond essence and ground almonds.

2 Sift the flour, cocoa powder and baking powder over the creamed mixture. Gently fold in using a metal spoon. Divide the mixture equally between the prepared moulds; each should be about half full.

3 Bake on the centre shelf of the preheated oven for 20 minutes, or until well risen and firm to the touch. Leave in the tins for a few minutes, then run a small palette knife round the edge and turn out onto a wire rack to cool. Remove the paper circles from the sponges.

4 Heat the conserve with the liqueur, brandy or juice in a small saucepan. Sieve to remove any lumps. If necessary, trim the sponge bases, so they are flat. Brush the tops and sides with warm conserve, then roll in the coconut. Top each with a chocolate button, fixed by brushing its base with conserve.

INGREDIENTS
Makes 10

125 g/4 oz butter
125 g/4 oz soft light brown sugar
2 medium eggs, lightly beaten
1 drop almond essence
1 tbsp ground almonds
75 g/3 oz self-raising flour
20 g/¾ oz cocoa powder
1 tsp baking powder

TO FINISH:
5 tbsp apricot conserve
1 tbsp amaretto liqueur, brandy or
* orange juice*
50 g/2 oz desiccated coconut
10 large chocolate buttons
* (optional)*

Helpful Hint

Oil the tins well and if liked, dust with a little flour, shaking off any excess flour. Place a small circle of nonstick baking parchment in the bases before filling to make removing the cooked cakes easier. Remove the buns as soon as possible after baking, as they have a tendency to stick.

Chocolate Chelsea Buns

1 Preheat the oven to 190°C/ 375°F/Gas Mark 5, 10 minutes before baking. Lightly oil an 18 cm/7 inch square tin. Place the pears in a bowl with the fruit juice, stir then cover and leave to soak while making the dough.

2 Sift the flour, cinnamon and salt into a bowl, rub in 25 g/1 oz of the butter then stir in the yeast and make a well in the middle. Add the milk and egg and mix to a soft dough. Knead on a floured surface for 10 minutes, until smooth and elastic, then place in a bowl. Cover with clingfilm and leave in a warm place to rise for 1 hour or until doubled in size.

3 Turn out on a lightly floured surface and knead the dough lightly before rolling out

to a rectangle, about 30.5 x 23 cm/12 x 9 inches. Melt the remaining butter and brush over. Spoon the pears and chocolate evenly over the dough leaving a 2.5 cm/1 inch border, then roll up tightly, starting at a long edge. Cut into 12 equal slices, then place, cut-side up in the tin. Cover and leave to rise for 25 minutes, or until doubled in size.

4 Bake on the centre shelf of the preheated oven for 30 minutes, or until well risen and golden brown. Cover with tinfoil after 20 minutes, if the filling is starting to brown too much.

5 Brush with the maple syrup while hot, then leave in the tin for 10 minutes to cool slightly. Turn out onto a wire rack and leave to cool. Separate the buns and serve warm.

INGREDIENTS
Makes 12

75 g/3 oz dried pears, finely chopped
1 tbsp apple or orange juice
225 g/8 oz strong plain flour
1 tsp ground cinnamon
½ tsp salt
40 g/1½ oz butter
1½ tsp easy-blend dried yeast
125 ml/4 fl oz warm milk
1 medium egg, lightly beaten
75 g/3 oz plain dark chocolate, chopped
3 tbsp maple syrup

Tasty Tip

As an alternative replace the pears and juice with an equal weight of chopped hazelnuts or almonds.

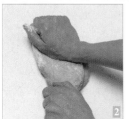

Fruit & Spice Chocolate Slice

1 Preheat the oven to 180°C/ 350°F/Gas Mark 4, 10 minutes before baking. Oil and line a deep 18 cm/7 inch square tin with nonstick baking parchment. Sift the flour and mixed spice into a large bowl. Cut the butter into small squares and, using your hands, rub in until the mixture resembles fine breadcrumbs.

2 Add the chocolate, dried mixed fruit, apricots and nuts to the dry ingredients. Reserve 1 tablespoon of the sugar, then add the rest to the bowl and stir together. Add the eggs and half of the milk and mix together, then add enough of the remaining milk to give a soft dropping consistency.

3 Spoon the mixture into the prepared tin, level the surface with the back of a spoon and sprinkle with the reserved demerara sugar. Bake on the centre shelf of the preheated oven for 50 minutes. Cover the top with tinfoil to prevent the cake from browning too much and bake for a further 30–40 minutes, or until it is firm to the touch and a skewer inserted into the centre of the cake comes out clean.

4 Leave the cake in the tin for 10 minutes to cool slightly, then turn out onto a wire rack and leave to cool completely. Cut into 10 slices and serve. Store in an airtight container.

INGREDIENTS
Makes 10 slices

350 g/12 oz self-raising flour
1 tsp ground mixed spice
175 g/6 oz butter, chilled
125 g/4 oz plain dark chocolate,
  roughly chopped
125 g/4 oz dried mixed fruit
75 g/3 oz dried apricots, chopped
75 g/3 oz chopped mixed nuts
175 g/6 oz demerara sugar
2 medium eggs, lightly beaten
150 ml/¼ pint milk

Helpful Hint

When chopping dried apricots into small pieces it is far easier if you use scissors as dried apricots are sticky. Keep dipping the scissors into flour to stop the apricots from sticking together. This applies to all sticky ingredients such as glacé cherries, candied peel and other ready-to-eat dried fruits.

Helpful Hint

This cake is made by the rubbing-in method and will keep for several days wrapped in greaseproof paper, then in tinfoil.

Chocolate Pecan Traybake

1 Preheat the oven to 180°C/ 350°F/Gas Mark 4, 10 minutes before baking. Lightly oil and line a 28 x 18 x 2.5 cm/11 x 7 x 1 inch cake tin with nonstick baking parchment. Beat the butter and sugar together until light and fluffy. Sift in the flours and cocoa powder and mix together to form a soft dough.

2 Press the mixture evenly over the base of the prepared tin. Prick all over with a fork, then bake on the shelf above the centre of the preheated oven for 15 minutes.

3 Put the butter, sugar, golden syrup, milk and vanilla essence in a small saucepan and heat gently until melted. Remove from the heat and leave to cool for a few minutes, then stir in the eggs and pour over the base. Sprinkle with the nuts.

4 Bake in the preheated oven for 25 minutes or until dark golden brown, but still slightly soft. Leave to cool in the tin. When cool, carefully remove from the tin, then cut into 12 squares and serve. Store in an airtight container.

INGREDIENTS
Makes 12

175 g/6 oz butter
75 g/3 oz icing sugar, sifted
175 g/6 oz plain flour
25 g/1 oz self-raising flour
25 g/1 oz cocoa powder

FOR THE PECAN TOPPING:

75 g/3 oz butter
50 g/2 oz light muscovado sugar
2 tbsp golden syrup
2 tbsp milk
1 tsp vanilla essence
2 medium eggs, lightly beaten
125 g/4 oz pecan halves

Helpful Hint

When a recipe calls for butter or margarine, the solid block variety (not the soft tub alternative, which has had air beaten in) must be used. Low-fat spreads break down on heating and, as they contain a large proportion of water, the end result will not be correct and the cake or tart will be disappointing.

Tasty Tip

Pecans are perfect in this recipe, but if they are unavailable, substitute walnut halves instead.

Chocolate Brazil & Polenta Squares

1 Preheat the oven to 180°C/ 350°F/Gas Mark 4, 10 minutes before baking. Oil and line a deep 18 cm/7 inch square tin with nonstick baking parchment. Finely chop 50 g/ 2 oz of the Brazil nuts and reserve. Roughly chop the remainder. Cream the butter and sugar together until light and fluffy. Gradually add the eggs, beating well between each addition.

2 Sift the flour, cocoa powder, cinnamon, baking powder and salt into the creamed mixture and gently fold in using a large metal spoon or spatula. Add the milk, polenta and the 75 g/3 oz of roughly chopped Brazil nuts. Fold into the mixture.

3 Turn the mixture into the prepared tin, levelling the surface with the back of the spoon. Sprinkle the reserved 50 g/2 oz of finely chopped Brazil nuts over the top. Bake the cake on the centre shelf of the preheated oven for 45–50 minutes, or until well risen and lightly browned and when a clean skewer inserted into the centre of the cake for a few seconds comes out clean.

4 Leave the cake in the tin for 10 minutes to cool slightly, then turn out onto a wire rack and leave to cool completely. Cut the cake into 9 equal squares and serve. Store in an airtight container.

INGREDIENTS
Makes 9 squares

150 g/5 oz shelled Brazil nuts
150 g/5 oz butter, softened
150 g/5 oz soft light brown sugar
2 medium eggs, lightly beaten
75 g/3 oz plain flour
25 g/1 oz cocoa powder
¼ tsp ground cinnamon
1 tsp baking powder
pinch of salt
5 tbsp milk
60 g/2½ oz instant polenta

Tasty Tip

Check the cake after 35 minutes of cooking; if the nuts are starting to brown too much, loosely cover with tinfoil and continue cooking.

Moist Mocha & Coconut Cake

1 Preheat the oven to 170°C/ 325°F/Gas Mark 3, 10 minutes before baking. Lightly oil and line a deep 20.5 cm/8 inch square tin with nonstick baking parchment. Place the ground coffee in a small bowl and pour over the hot milk. Leave to infuse for 5 minutes, then strain through a tea-strainer or a sieve lined with muslin. You will end up with about 4 table-spoons of liquid. Reserve.

2 Put the butter, golden syrup, sugar and coconut in a small heavy-based saucepan and heat gently until the butter has melted and the sugar dissolved. Sift the flour, cocoa powder and bicarbonate of soda together and stir into the melted mixture with the eggs and 3 tablespoons of the coffee-infused milk.

3 Pour the mixture into the prepared tin. Bake on the centre shelf of the preheated oven for 45 minutes, or until the cake is well risen and firm to the touch. Leave in the tin for 10 minutes to cool slightly, then turn out onto a wire rack to cool completely.

4 For the icing, gradually add the icing sugar to the softened butter and beat together until mixed. Add the remaining 1 tablespoon of coffee-infused milk and beat until light and fluffy.

5 Carefully spread the coffee icing over the top of the cake, then cut into 9 squares. Decorate each square with a small piece of chocolate flake and serve.

INGREDIENTS
Makes 9 squares

3 tbsp ground coffee
5 tbsp hot milk
75 g/3 oz butter
175 g/6 oz golden syrup
25 g/1 oz soft light brown sugar
40 g/1½ oz desiccated coconut
150 g/5 oz plain flour
25 g/1 oz cocoa powder
½ tsp bicarbonate of soda
2 medium eggs, lightly beaten
2 chocolate flakes, to decorate

FOR THE COFFEE ICING:

225 g/8 oz icing sugar, sifted
125 g/4 oz butter, softened

Helpful Hint

It is important to use a very fine strainer to remove as much of the coffee as possible or the cake will have an unpleasant gritty texture.

Chocolate Walnut Squares

1 Preheat the oven to 170°C/ 325°F/Gas Mark 3, 10 minutes before baking. Oil and line a 28 x 18 x 2.5 cm/11 x 7 x 1 inch cake tin with nonstick baking parchment. Place the butter, chocolate, sugar, vanilla essence and 225 ml/8 fl oz of cold water in a heavy-based saucepan. Heat gently, stirring occasionally, until the chocolate and butter have melted, but do not allow to boil.

2 Sift the flours and cocoa powder into a large bowl and make a well in the centre. Add the mayonnaise and about one-third of the chocolate mixture and beat until smooth. Gradually beat in the remaining chocolate mixture.

3 Pour into the prepared tin and bake on the centre shelf of the preheated oven for 1 hour, or until slightly risen and firm to the touch. Place the tin on a wire rack and leave to cool. Remove the cake from the tin and peel off the parchment paper.

4 To make the chocolate glaze, place the chocolate and butter in a small saucepan with 1 tablespoon of water and heat very gently, stirring occasionally until melted and smooth. Leave to cool until the chocolate has thickened, then spread evenly over the cake. Chill the cake in the refrigerator for about 5 minutes, then mark into 24 squares.

5 Lightly dust the walnut halves with a little icing sugar and place one on the top of each square. Cut into pieces and store in an airtight container until ready to serve.

INGREDIENTS
Makes 24

125 g/4 oz butter
150 g/5 oz plain dark chocolate, broken into squares
450 g/1 lb caster sugar
½ tsp vanilla essence
200 g/7 oz plain flour
75 g/3 oz self-raising flour
50 g/2 oz cocoa powder
225 g/8 oz mayonnaise, at room temperature

FOR THE CHOCOLATE GLAZE:
125 g/4 oz plain dark chocolate, broken into squares
40 g/1½ oz unsalted butter
24 walnut halves
1 tbsp icing sugar for dusting

Tasty Tip
Mayonnaise is used in this recipe instead of eggs. Make sure you use a plain and not flavoured mayonnaise.

Nanaimo Bars

1 Oil and line a 28 x 18 x 2.5 cm/11 x 7 x 1 inch cake tin with nonstick baking parchment. Place the butter and chocolate in a heatproof bowl set over a saucepan of almost boiling water until melted, stirring occasionally. Stir in the crushed biscuits, coconut and nuts into the chocolate mixture and mix well. Spoon into the prepared tin and press down firmly. Chill in the refrigerator for 20 minutes.

2 For the filling, place the egg yolk and milk in a heatproof bowl set over a saucepan of almost boiling water, making sure the bowl does not touch the water. Whisk for 2–3 minutes. Add the butter and vanilla essence to the bowl and continue whisking until

fluffy, then gradually whisk in the icing sugar. Spread over the chilled base, smoothing with the back of a spoon and chill in the refrigerator for a further 30 minutes.

3 For the topping, place the chocolate and sunflower oil in a heatproof bowl set over a saucepan of almost boiling water. Melt, stirring occasionally, until smooth. Leave to cool slightly, then pour over the filling and tilt the tin, so that the chocolate spreads evenly.

4 Chill in the refrigerator for about 5 minutes, or until the chocolate topping is just set but not too hard, then mark into 15 bars. Chill again in the refrigerator for 2 hours, then cut into slices and serve.

INGREDIENTS
Makes 15

75 g/3 oz unsalted butter
125 g/4 oz plain dark chocolate,
  roughly chopped
75 g/3 oz digestive biscuits,
  crushed
75 g/3 oz desiccated coconut
50 g/2 oz chopped mixed nuts

FOR THE FILLING:

1 medium egg yolk
1 tbsp milk
75 g/3 oz unsalted butter,
  softened
1 tsp vanilla essence
150 g/5 oz icing sugar

FOR THE TOPPING:

125 g/4 oz plain dark chocolate,
  roughly chopped
2 tsp sunflower oil

Food Fact

These rich chocolate-topped squares originated in Nanaimo in British Columbia. Versions of this recipe are now popular all over Canada, including a version with a mint-flavoured filling.

Marbled Toffee Shortbread

1 Preheat the oven to 180°C/ 350°F/Gas Mark 4, 10 minutes before baking. Oil and line a 20.5 cm/8 inch square cake tin with nonstick baking parchment. Cream the butter and sugar until light and fluffy then sift in the flour and cocoa powder. Add the semolina and mix together to form a soft dough. Press into the base of the prepared tin. Prick all over with a fork, then bake in the preheated oven for 25 minutes. Leave to cool.

2 To make the toffee filling, gently heat the butter, sugar and condensed milk together until the sugar has dissolved. Bring to the boil, then simmer for 5 minutes, stirring constantly. Leave for 1 minute, then spread over the shortbread and leave to cool.

3 For the topping, place the different chocolates in separate heatproof bowls and melt one at a time, set over a saucepan of almost boiling water. Drop spoonfuls of each on top of the toffee and tilt the tin to cover evenly. Swirl with a knife for a marbled effect.

4 Leave the chocolate to cool. When just set mark into fingers using a sharp knife. Leave for at least 1 hour to harden before cutting into fingers.

INGREDIENTS
Makes 12

175 g/6 oz butter
75 g/3 oz caster sugar
175 g/6 oz plain flour
25 g/1 oz cocoa powder
75 g/3 oz fine semolina

FOR THE TOFFEE FILLING:

50 g/2 oz butter
50 g/2 oz soft light brown sugar
397 g can condensed milk

FOR THE CHOCOLATE TOPPING:

75 g/3 oz plain dark chocolate
75 g/3 oz milk chocolate
75 g/3 oz white chocolate

Helpful Hint

Make sure the toffee filling turns a rich golden colour or it will not set. Cook for 3–4 minutes if necessary to obtain a good colour. Take care that the mixture does not burn. If preferred, place the ingredients in a glass bowl and heat in the microwave on a medium setting in 30-second bursts until the sugar has melted; stir well after each burst of cooking. Once melted, heat on high for 2–4 minutes; again in 30-second bursts, until golden.

Indulgent Chocolate Squares

1 Preheat the oven to 180°C/ 350°F/Gas Mark 4, 10 minutes before baking. Oil and line a deep 20.5 cm/8 inch square cake tin with nonstick baking parchment. Melt 225 g/ 8 oz of the dark chocolate in a heatproof bowl set over a saucepan of almost boiling water. Stir until smooth, then leave until just cool, but not beginning to set.

2 Beat the butter and sugar until light and fluffy. Stir in the melted chocolate, ground almonds, egg yolks, cocoa powder and breadcrumbs. Whisk the egg whites until stiff peaks form, then stir a large spoonful into the chocolate mixture. Gently fold in the rest, then pour the mixture into the prepared tin.

3 Bake on the centre shelf in the preheated oven for 1¼ hours, or until firm, covering the top with tinfoil after 45 minutes, to prevent it over-browning. Leave in the tin for 20 minutes, then turn out onto a wire rack and leave to cool.

4 Melt the remaining 125 g/ 4 oz plain chocolate with the cream in a heatproof bowl set over a saucepan of almost boiling water, stirring occasionally. Leave to cool for 20 minutes or until thickened slightly.

5 Spread the topping over the cake. Scatter over the white and milk chocolate and leave to set. Cut into 16 squares and serve decorated with a few freshly sliced strawberries, then serve.

INGREDIENTS
Makes 16

350 g/12 oz plain dark chocolate
175 g/6 oz butter, softened
175 g/6 oz soft light brown sugar
175 g/6 oz ground almonds
6 large eggs, separated
3 tbsp cocoa powder, sifted
75 g/3 oz fresh brown breadcrumbs
125 ml/4 fl oz double cream
50 g/2 oz white chocolate, chopped
50 g/2 oz milk chocolate, chopped
few freshly sliced strawberries, to decorate

Helpful Hint

To prevent the tinfoil from coming off the top of the tin, especially in a fan assisted oven, fold the tinfoil around the edge, rather than simply laying it on top.

Fruit & Nut
Refrigerator Fingers

1 Lightly oil and line the base of a 18 cm/7 inch tin with nonstick baking parchment. Using oiled kitchen scissors, snip each marshmallow into 4 or 5 pieces over a bowl. Add the dried mixed fruit, orange peel, cherries and walnuts to the bowl. Sprinkle with the brandy and stir together. Add the crushed biscuits and stir until mixed.

2 Break the chocolate into squares and put in a heatproof bowl with the butter set over a saucepan of almost boiling water. Stir occasionally until melted, then remove from the heat. Pour the melted chocolate mixture over the dry ingredients and mix together well. Spoon into the prepared tin, pressing down firmly.

3 Chill in the refrigerator for 15 minutes, then mark into 12 fingers using a sharp knife. Chill in the refrigerator for a further 1 hour or until set. Turn out of the tin, remove the lining paper and cut into fingers. Dust with icing sugar before serving.

INGREDIENTS
Makes 12

14 pink and white marshmallows
75 g/3 oz luxury dried mixed fruit
25 g/1 oz candied orange peel, chopped
75 g/3 oz glacé cherries, quartered
75 g/3 oz walnuts, chopped
1 tbsp brandy
175 g/6 oz digestive biscuits, crushed
225 g/8 oz plain dark chocolate
125 g/4 oz unsalted butter
1 tbsp icing sugar, for dusting, optional

Helpful Hint

Why not try storing nuts in the freezer? Stored this way, whole nuts will keep for 3 years, shelled nuts for 1 year and ground nuts, such as ground almonds, for 3 months. Whole nuts will crack far easier when frozen, as their shells are far more brittle.

Helpful Hint

If you are using whole candied peel, rather than ready-chopped, use kitchen scissors to snip it into small pieces.

Crunchy-topped Citrus Chocolate Slices

1 Preheat the oven to 170°C/ 325°F/Gas Mark 3, 10 minutes before baking. Oil and line a 28 x 18 x 2.5 cm/11 x 7 x 1 inch cake tin with nonstick baking parchment. Place the butter, sugar and orange rind into a large bowl and cream together until light and fluffy. Gradually add the eggs, beating after each addition, then beat in the ground almonds.

2 Sift the flour and baking powder into the creamed mixture. Add the grated chocolate and milk, then gently fold in using a metal spoon. Spoon the mixture into the prepared tin.

3 Bake on the centre shelf of the preheated oven for 35–40 minutes, or until well risen and firm to the touch. Leave in the tin for a few minutes to cool slightly. Turn out onto a wire rack and remove the baking parchment.

4 Meanwhile, make the crunchy topping, place the sugar with the lime and orange juices into a small jug and stir together. Drizzle the sugar mixture over the hot cake, ensuring the whole surface is covered. Leave until completely cold, then cut into 12 slices and serve.

INGREDIENTS
Makes 12 slices

175 g/6 oz butter
175 g/6 oz soft light brown sugar
finely grated rind of 1 orange
3 medium eggs, lightly beaten
1 tbsp ground almonds
175 g/6 oz self-raising flour
¼ tsp baking powder
125 g/4 oz plain dark chocolate, coarsely grated
2 tsp milk

FOR THE CRUNCHY TOPPING:

125 g/4 oz granulated sugar
juice of 2 limes
juice of 1 orange

Helpful Hint

Store all dry ingredients, such as flour, baking powder and sugar, in airtight containers in a cool, dry place.

Helpful Hint

It is important that the cake is still hot from the oven when the citrus topping is added, otherwise it will simply sit on the cake.

All-in-one Chocolate Fudge Cakes

1 Preheat the oven to 180°C/ 350°F/Gas Mark 4, 10 minutes before baking. Oil and line a 28 x 18 x 2.5 cm/ 11 x 7 x 1 inch cake tin with nonstick baking parchment.

2 Place the soft brown sugar and butter in a bowl and sift in the flour, cocoa powder, baking powder and salt. Add the eggs and golden syrup, then beat with an electric whisk for 2 minutes, before adding 2 tablespoons of warm water and beating for a further 1 minute.

3 Turn the mixture into the prepared tin and level the top with the back of a spoon. Bake on the centre shelf of the preheated oven for 30 minutes, or until firm to the

touch. Turn the cake out onto a wire rack and leave to cool before removing the baking parchment.

4 To make the topping, gently heat the sugar and evaporated milk in a saucepan, stirring frequently, until the sugar has dissolved. Bring the mixture to the boil and simmer for 6 minutes, without stirring.

5 Remove the mixture from the heat. Add the chocolate and butter and stir until melted and blended. Pour into a bowl and chill in the refrigerator for 1–2 hours or until thickened. Spread the topping over the cake, then sprinkle with the chopped fudge. Cut the cake into 15 squares before serving.

INGREDIENTS
Makes 15 squares

175 g/6 oz soft dark brown sugar
175 g/6 oz butter, softened
150 g/5 oz self-raising flour
25 g/1 oz cocoa powder
½ tsp baking powder
pinch of salt
3 medium eggs, lightly beaten
1 tbsp golden syrup

FOR THE FUDGE TOPPING:

75 g/3 oz granulated sugar
150 ml/¼ pint evaporated milk
175 g/6 oz plain dark chocolate, roughly chopped
40 g/1½ oz unsalted butter, softened
125 g/4 oz soft fudge sweets, finely chopped

Tasty Tip
Use a mixture of fudge sweets for the topping on this cake, including chocolate, vanilla and toffee flavours.

Marbled Chocolate Traybake

1 Preheat the oven to 180°C/ 350°F/Gas Mark 4, 10 minutes before baking. Oil and line a 28 x 18 x 2.5 cm/11 x 7 x 1 inch cake tin with nonstick baking parchment. Cream the butter, sugar and vanilla essence until light and fluffy. Gradually add the eggs, beating well after each addition. Sift in the flour and baking powder and fold in with the milk.

2 Spoon half the mixture into the prepared tin, spacing the spoonfuls apart and leaving gaps in between. Blend the cocoa powder to a smooth paste with 2 table-spoons of warm water. Stir this into the remaining cake mixture. Drop small spoonfuls between the

vanilla cake mixture to fill in all the gaps. Use a knife to swirl the mixtures together a little.

3 Bake on the centre shelf of the preheated oven for 35 minutes, or until well risen and firm to the touch. Leave in the tin for 5 minutes to cool, then turn out onto a wire rack and leave to cool. Remove the parchment.

4 For the icing, place the plain and white chocolate in separate heatproof bowls and melt each over a saucepan of almost boiling water. Spoon into separate nonstick baking parchment piping bags, snip off the tips and drizzle over the top. Leave to set before cutting into squares.

INGREDIENTS
Makes 18 squares

175 g/6 oz butter
175 g/6 oz caster sugar
1 tsp vanilla essence
3 medium eggs, lightly beaten
200 g/7 oz self-raising flour
½ tsp baking powder
1 tbsp milk
1½ tbsp cocoa powder

FOR THE CHOCOLATE ICING:
75 g/3 oz plain dark chocolate, broken into pieces
75 g/3 oz white chocolate, broken into pieces

Tasty Tip
To marble the topping, spread the dark chocolate evenly over the top of the cake. Put the white chocolate into a small piping bag or a greaseproof piping bag and drizzle over the dark chocolate in random circles. Use a cocktail stick or skewer to drag the 2 chocolates together.

Triple Chocolate Brownies

1 Preheat the oven to 190°C/ 375°F/Gas Mark 5, 10 minutes before baking. Oil and line a 28 x 18 x 2.5 cm/11 x 7 x 1 inch cake tin with nonstick baking parchment. Place the plain chocolate in a heatproof bowl with the butter set over a saucepan of almost boiling water and stir occasionally until melted. Remove from the heat and leave until just cool, but not beginning to set.

2 Place the caster sugar, eggs, vanilla essence and coffee in a large bowl and beat together until smooth. Gradually beat in the chocolate mixture. Sift the flour into the chocolate mixture. Add the pecans and the white and milk chocolate and gently fold in until mixed thoroughly.

3 Spoon the mixture into the prepared tin and level the top. Bake on the centre shelf of the preheated oven for 45 minutes, or until just firm to the touch in the centre and crusty on top. Leave to cool in the tin, then turn out onto a wire rack. Trim off the crusty edges and cut into 15 squares. Store in an airtight container.

INGREDIENTS
Makes 15

350 g/12 oz plain dark
  chocolate, broken into pieces
225 g/8 oz butter, cubed
225 g/8 oz caster sugar
3 large eggs, lightly beaten
1 tsp vanilla essence
2 tbsp very strong black coffee
100 g/3½ oz self-raising flour
125 g/4 oz pecans, roughly
  chopped
75 g/3 oz white chocolate,
  roughly chopped
75 g/3 oz milk chocolate, roughly
  chopped

Food Fact

Brownies have a high proportion of sugar, giving the brownie its distinctive crusty topping. Underneath, the rich, gooey texture is produced by the small amount of flour used in comparison to the rest of ingredients.

Tasty Tip

Take care not to overcook; the outside crust should be crisp and the centre of the brownies moist and gooey.

Light White Chocolate & Walnut Blondies

1 Preheat the oven to 190°C/ 375°F/Gas Mark 5, 10 minutes before baking. Oil and line a 28 x 18 x 2.5 cm/11 x 7 x 1 inch cake tin with nonstick baking parchment. Place the butter and demerara sugar into a heavy-based saucepan and heat gently until the butter has melted and the sugar has started to dissolve. Remove from the heat and leave to cool.

2 Place the eggs, vanilla essence and milk in a large bowl and beat together. Stir in the butter and sugar mixture, then sift in the 125 g/4oz of flour, the baking powder and salt. Gently stir the mixture twice.

3 Toss the walnuts and chocolate drops in the remaining 1 tablespoon of flour to coat. Add to the bowl and stir the ingredients together gently.

4 Spoon the mixture into the prepared tin and bake on the centre shelf of the preheated oven for 35 minutes, or until the top is firm and slightly crusty. Place the tin on a wire rack and leave to cool.

5 When completely cold, remove the cake from the tin and lightly dust the top with icing sugar. Cut into 15 blondies, using a sharp knife, and serve.

INGREDIENTS
Makes 15

75 g/3 oz unsalted butter
200 g/7 oz demerara sugar
2 large eggs, lightly beaten
1 tsp vanilla essence
2 tbsp milk
125 g/4 oz plain flour,
   plus 1 tbsp
1 tsp baking powder
pinch of salt
75 g/3 oz walnuts, roughly
   chopped
125 g/4 oz white chocolate drops
1 tbsp icing sugar

Tasty Tip

For a chocolate topping, mix together about 50 g/2 oz each of white, milk and plain chocolate chips. Sprinkle over the hot blondies as soon as they are removed from the oven. Leave the cake to cool. Cut into squares and serve from the tin.

Chocolate Chip Cookies

1 Preheat the oven to 190°C/ 375°F/Gas Mark 5 10 minutes before baking. Lightly oil a large baking sheet.

2 In a large bowl, sift together the flour, salt, baking powder and bicarbonate of soda.

3 Cut the butter or margarine into small pieces and add to the flour mixture.

4 Using 2 knives or the fingertips, rub in the butter or margarine until the mixture resembles coarse breadcrumbs.

5 Add the light brown sugar, golden syrup and chocolate chips. Mix together until a smooth dough forms.

6 Shape the mixture into small balls and arrange on the baking sheet, leaving enough space to allow them to expand. (These cookies do not increase in size by a great deal, but allow a little space for expansion.)

7 Flatten the mixture slightly with the fingertips or the heel of the hand.

8 Bake in the preheated oven for 12–15 minutes, or until golden and cooked through.

9 Allow to cool slightly, then transfer the biscuits on to a wire rack to cool. Serve when cold or otherwise store in an airtight tin.

INGREDIENTS
Makes 36 biscuits

175 g/6 oz plain flour
pinch of salt
1 tsp baking powder
¼ tsp bicarbonate of soda
75 g/3 oz butter or margarine
50 g/2 oz soft light brown sugar
3 tbsp golden syrup
125 g/4 oz chocolate chips

Tasty Tip

This is a good basic cookie recipe to which many ingredients, like nuts, glacé cherries, chopped angelica, banana chips, dried cranberries or raisins, can be added instead of chocolate chips.

Chocolate Florentines

1 Preheat the oven to 180°C/ 350°F/Gas Mark 4 10 minutes before baking. Lightly oil a baking sheet.

2 Melt the butter or margarine with the sugar and double cream in a small saucepan over a very low heat. Do not boil.

3 Remove from the heat and stir in the almonds, hazelnuts, sultanas and cherries.

4 Drop teaspoonfuls of the mixture on to the baking sheet. Transfer to the preheated oven and bake for 10 minutes, until golden.

5 Leave the biscuits to cool on the baking sheet for

about 5 minutes, then carefully transfer to a wire rack to cool.

6 Melt the plain, milk and white chocolates in separate bowls, either in the microwave following the manufacturers' instructions or in a small bowl, placed over a saucepan of gently simmering water.

7 Spread one-third of the biscuits with the plain chocolate, one-third with the milk chocolate and one-third with the white chocolate.

8 Mark out wavy lines on the chocolate when almost set with the tines of a fork. Or dip some of the biscuits in chocolate to half coat and serve.

INGREDIENTS
Makes 20

125 g/4 oz butter or margarine
125 g/4 oz soft light brown sugar
1 tbsp double cream
50 g/2 oz blanched almonds,
  roughly chopped
50 g/2 oz hazelnuts,
  roughly chopped
75 g/3 oz sultanas
50 g/2 oz glacé cherries,
  roughly chopped
50 g/2 oz plain, dark chocolate,
  roughly chopped or broken
50 g/2 oz milk chocolate, roughly
  chopped or broken
50 g/2 oz white chocolate,
  roughly chopped or broken

Helpful Hint

When melting chocolate for coating, as in this recipe, it is important not to overheat it or it will develop a white bloom when it resets. If melting the chocolate over simmering water, make sure the bottom of the bowl is not touching the water. If using the microwave, melt in short bursts, stirring in between to ensure that melting is even.

Tasty Tip

Rich and fruity, these Florentines rely on their raw ingredients, so try to use a good-quality chocolate and natural glacé cherries, which have a fruitier taste and are more natural in colour.

Ginger Snaps

1 Preheat the oven to 190°C/ 375°F/Gas Mark 5 10 minutes before baking. Lightly oil a baking sheet.

2 Cream together the butter or margarine and the sugar until light and fluffy.

3 Warm the treacle in the microwave for 30–40 seconds, then add gradually to the butter mixture with the egg. Beat until combined well.

4 In a separate bowl, sift the flour, bicarbonate of soda, salt, ground ginger, ground cloves and ground cinnamon. Add to the butter mixture and mix together to form a firm dough.

5 Chill in the refrigerator for 1 hour. Shape the dough into small balls and roll in the granulated sugar. Place well apart on the oiled baking sheet.

6 Sprinkle the baking sheet with a little water and transfer to the preheated oven.

7 Bake for 12 minutes, until golden and crisp. Transfer to a wire rack to cool and serve.

INGREDIENTS
Makes 40

300 g/11 oz butter or margarine, softened
225 g/8 oz soft light brown sugar
75 g/3 oz black treacle
1 medium egg
400 g/14 oz plain flour
2 tsp bicarbonate of soda
½ tsp salt
1 tsp ground ginger
1 tsp ground cloves
1 tsp ground cinnamon
50 g/2 oz granulated sugar

Tasty Tip

Ginger snaps are great biscuits to use in other recipes. Try crushing them, mixing with melted butter and using as the base for a cheesecake.

Tasty Tip

Ginger snaps are also delicious roughly broken up and added to home-made ice cream – particularly ginger or chocolate ice cream, as they have light, honeycomb textures.

Oatmeal Raisin Cookies

1 Preheat the oven to 200°C/ 400°F/Gas Mark 6 15 minutes before baking. Lightly oil a baking sheet.

2 Mix together the flour, oats, ground ginger, baking powder, bicarbonate of soda, sugar and the raisins in a large bowl.

3 In another bowl, mix the egg, oil and milk together. Make a well in the centre of the dry ingredients and pour in the egg mixture.

4 Mix the mixture together well with either a fork or a wooden spoon to make a soft but not sticky dough.

5 Place spoonfuls of the dough well apart on the oiled baking sheet and flatten the tops down slightly with the tines of a fork.

6 Transfer the biscuits to the preheated oven and bake for 10–12 minutes until golden.

7 Remove from the oven, leave to cool for 2–3 minutes, then transfer the biscuits to a wire rack to cool. Serve when cold or otherwise store in an airtight tin.

INGREDIENTS
Makes 24

175 g/6 oz plain flour
150 g/5 oz rolled oats
1 tsp ground ginger
½ tsp baking powder
½ tsp bicarbonate of soda
125 g/4 oz soft light-brown sugar
50 g/2 oz raisins
1 medium egg, lightly beaten
150 ml/¼ pint vegetable or
   sunflower oil
4 tbsp milk

Food Fact

This dough can be made, wrapped in clingfilm then stored in the refrigerator for up to 1 week before baking. When ready to bake, simply cut off the dough and bake as above.

Food Fact

If desired, add 50 g/2 oz of roughly chopped mixed nuts and replace half of the raisins with dried cranberries or cherries.

Almond Macaroons

1 Preheat the oven to 150°C/ 300°F/Gas Mark 2 10 minutes before baking. Line a baking sheet with the rice paper.

2 Mix the caster sugar, ground almonds, ground rice and almond essence together and reserve.

3 Whisk the egg white until stiff then gently fold in the caster sugar mixture with a metal spoon or rubber spatula.

4 Mix to form a stiff but not sticky paste. (If the mixture is very sticky, add a little extra ground almonds.)

5 Place small spoonfuls of the mixture, about the size of an apricot, well apart on the rice paper.

6 Place a half-blanched almond in the centre of each. Place in the preheated oven and bake for 25 minutes, or until just pale golden.

7 Remove the biscuits from the oven and leave to cool for a few minutes on the baking sheet. Cut or tear the rice paper around the macaroons to release them. Once cold, serve or otherwise store them in an airtight tin.

INGREDIENTS
Makes 12

rice paper
125 g/4 oz caster sugar
50 g/2 oz ground almonds
1 tsp ground rice
2–3 drops almond essence
1 medium egg white
8 blanched almonds, halved

Tasty Tip

Rice paper is an edible paper made from the pith of the Chinese tree. These macaroons are deliciously chewy and are fantastic when broken up and sprinkled in desserts such as trifles. Serve with cream and tart fresh fruits such as raspberries.

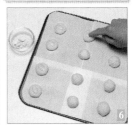

Pumpkin Cookies with Brown Butter Glaze

1 Preheat the oven to 190°C/ 375°F/Gas Mark 5 10 minutes before baking. Lightly oil a baking sheet and reserve.

2 Using an electric mixer, beat the butter until light and fluffy. Add the flour, sugar, pumpkin, beaten egg and beat with the mixer until mixed well.

3 Stir in the ground cinnamon, 1 teaspoon of the vanilla essence and then sift in the baking powder, bicarbonate of soda and grated nutmeg. Beat the mixture until combined well, scraping down the sides of the bowl.

4 Add the wholemeal flour, chopped nuts and raisins to the mixture and fold in with a metal spoon or rubber spatula until mixed thoroughly together.

5 Place teaspoonfuls about 5 cm/2 inches apart on to the baking sheet. Bake in the pre-heated oven for 10–12 minutes, or until the cookie edges are firm.

6 Remove the biscuits from the oven and leave to cool on a wire rack. Meanwhile, melt the butter in a small saucepan over a medium heat, until pale and just turning golden brown.

7 Remove from the heat. Add the sugar, remaining vanilla essence and milk, stirring. Drizzle over the cooled cookies and serve.

INGREDIENTS
Makes 48

125 g/4 oz butter, softened
150 g/5 oz plain flour
175 g/6 oz soft light brown sugar, lightly packed
225 g/8 oz canned pumpkin or cooked pumpkin
1 medium egg, beaten
2 tsp ground cinnamon
2½ tsp vanilla essence
½ tsp baking powder
½ tsp bicarbonate of soda
½ tsp freshly grated nutmeg
125 g/4 oz wholemeal flour
75 g/3 oz pecans, roughly chopped
100 g/3½ oz raisins
50 g/2 oz unsalted butter
225 g/8 oz icing sugar
2 tbsp milk

Helpful Hint

To cook pumpkin, take a slice off the top of the pumpkin. Scrape out the seeds and discard. Cut the pumpkin vertically into quarters and remove the dark orange skin with a potato peeler. Cut the flesh into chunks and steam or microwave until tender. Purée to use in the above recipe.

Spiced Palmier Biscuits with Apple Purée

1 Preheat the oven to 200°C/400°F/Gas Mark 6 15 minutes before baking. Roll out the pastry on a lightly floured surface to form a 25.5 x 30.5 cm/10 x 12 inch rectangle. Trim the edges with a small sharp knife.

2 Sift together the caster sugar, icing sugar, cinnamon, ginger and nutmeg into a bowl. Generously dust both sides of the pastry sheet with about a quarter of the sugar mixture.

3 With a long edge facing the body, fold either side halfway towards the centre. Dust with a third of the remaining sugar mixture.

4 Fold each side again so that they almost meet in the centre and dust again with about half the remaining sugar mixture. Fold the 2 sides together down the centre of the pastry to give 6 layers altogether. Wrap the pastry in clingfilm and refrigerate for

1–2 hours until firm. Reserve the remaining spiced sugar.

5 Remove the pastry from the refrigerator, unwrap and roll in the remaining sugar to give a good coating all round. Using a sharp knife, cut the roll into about 20 thin slices. Place the cut side down on to a baking sheet and place in the pre-heated oven.

6 Cook for 10 minutes, turn the biscuits and cook for a further 5–10 minutes, or until golden and crisp. Remove from the oven and transfer to a wire rack. Allow to cool completely.

7 Meanwhile, combine the remaining ingredients in a saucepan. Cover and cook gently for 15 minutes until the apple is completely soft. Stir well and allow to cool. Serve the palmiers with a spoonful of the apple purée and a little of the whipped double cream.

INGREDIENTS
Makes 20

250 g/9 oz prepared puff pastry, thawed if frozen
40 g/1½ oz caster sugar
25 g/1 oz icing sugar
1 tsp ground cinnamon
¼ tsp ground ginger
¼ tsp freshly grated nutmeg
450 g/1 lb Bramley cooking apples, roughly chopped
50 g/2 oz sugar
25 g/1 oz raisins
25 g/1 oz dried cherries
zest of 1 orange
double cream, lightly whipped, to serve

Food Fact

Palmiers are so called as they are thought to resemble palm leaves – *palmier* being the French word for a palm tree. Palmiers are often served sandwiched together with whipped cream and jam.

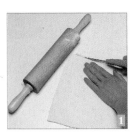

Peanut Butter Truffle Cookies

1 Preheat the oven to 180°C/ 350°F/Gas Mark 4 10 minutes before baking. Make the chocolate filling by breaking the chocolate into small pieces and placing in a heatproof bowl.

2 Put the double cream into a saucepan and heat to boiling point. Immediately pour over the chocolate.

3 Leave to stand for 1–2 minutes, then stir until smooth. Set aside to cool until firm enough to scoop. Do not refrigerate.

4 Lightly oil a baking sheet. Cream together the butter or margarine and the sugar until light and fluffy. Blend in the peanut butter, followed by the golden syrup and milk.

5 Sift together the flour and bicarbonate of soda. Add to the peanut butter mixture, mix well and knead until smooth.

6 Flatten 1–2 tablespoons of the cookie mixture on a chopping board.

7 Put a spoonful of the chocolate mixture into the centre of the cookie dough, then fold the dough around the chocolate to enclose completely.

8 Put the balls on to the baking sheet and flatten slightly. Bake in the preheated oven for 10–12 minutes until golden.

9 Remove from the oven and transfer to a wire rack to cool completely and serve.

INGREDIENTS
Makes 18

125 g/4 oz plain dark chocolate
150 ml/¼ pint double cream
125 g/4 oz butter or
  margarine, softened
125 g/4 oz caster sugar
125 g/4 oz crunchy or smooth
  peanut butter
4 tbsp golden syrup
1 tbsp milk
225 g/8 oz plain flour
½ tsp bicarbonate of soda

Helpful Hint

Measure golden syrup either by warming a metal measuring spoon in boiling water, then dipping it into the syrup, or place the tin in a warm oven or saucepan half-filled with hot water.

Whipped Shortbread

1 Preheat the oven to 180°C/350°F/Gas Mark 4 10 minutes before baking. Lightly oil a baking sheet.

2 Cream the butter and icing sugar until fluffy. Gradually add the flour and continue beating for a further 2–3 minutes until it is smooth and light.

3 Roll into balls and place on a baking sheet. Cover half of the dough mixture with hundreds and thousands, sugar strands, chocolate drops or silver balls. Keep the other half plain.

4 Bake in the preheated oven for 6–8 minutes, until the bottoms are lightly browned. Remove from the oven and transfer to a wire rack to cool.

5 Sift the icing sugar into a small bowl. Add the lemon juice and blend until a smooth icing forms.

6 Using a small spoon swirl the icing over the cooled plain cookies. Decorate with either the extra hundreds and thousands, chocolate drops or silver balls and serve.

INGREDIENTS
Makes 36

225 g/8 oz butter, softened
75 g/3 oz icing sugar
175 g/6 oz flour
hundreds and thousands
sugar strands
chocolate drops
silver balls
50 g/2 oz icing sugar
2–3 tsp lemon juice

Helpful Hint

Although these biscuits have the flavour of classic shortbread, the texture is much lighter. They literally melt in the mouth. These biscuits are great for children. However, for a smarter-looking biscuit which is more appealing to adults, spoon the mixture into a piping bag fitted with a large star nozzle and pipe the biscuits on to the baking sheet. Bake as above.

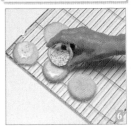

Oatmeal Coconut Cookies

1 Preheat the oven to 180°C/350°F/Gas Mark 4 10 minutes before baking. Lightly oil a baking sheet.

2 Cream together the butter or margarine and sugars until light and fluffy.

3 Gradually stir in the egg and vanilla essence and beat until well blended.

4 Sift together the flour, baking powder and bicarbonate of soda in another bowl.

5 Add to the butter and sugar mixture and beat together until smooth. Fold in the rolled oats and coconut with a metal spoon or rubber spatula.

6 Roll heaped teaspoonfuls of the mixture into balls and place on the baking sheet about 5 cm/2 inches apart and flatten each ball slightly with the heel of the hand.

7 Transfer to the preheated oven and bake for 12–15 minutes, until just golden.

8 Remove from the oven and transfer the biscuits to a wire rack to completely cool and serve.

INGREDIENTS
Makes 40

225 g/8 oz butter or margarine
125 g/4 oz soft light brown sugar
125 g/4 oz caster sugar
1 large egg, lightly beaten
1 tsp vanilla essence
225 g/8 oz plain flour
1 tsp baking powder
½ tsp bicarbonate of soda
125 g/4 oz rolled oats
75 g/3 oz desiccated coconut

Helpful Hint

The raising agent in this recipe, bicarbonate of soda, lightens the texture of these biscuits, resulting in a crisp yet melting result. These biscuits will last for 3–4 days if stored in an airtight tin or jar.

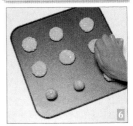

Chocolate Biscuit Bars

1 Lightly oil a 20.5 cm/ 8 inch square tin and line with clingfilm.

2 Place the sultanas into a small bowl and pour over the brandy, if using. Leave to soak for 20–30 minutes.

3 Meanwhile, break the chocolate into small pieces and put into a heatproof bowl.

4 Place the bowl over a saucepan of simmering water, making sure that the bottom of the bowl does not touch the water.

5 Leave the chocolate until melted, stirring occasionally. Remove from the heat.

6 Add the butter, golden syrup and double cream to a small saucepan and heat until the butter has melted.

7 Remove the saucepan from the heat and add the melted chocolate, biscuits, nuts, cherries, orange zest, sultanas and the brandy mixture.

8 Mix thoroughly and pour into the prepared tin. Smooth the top and chill in the refrigerator for at least 4 hours, or until firm.

9 Turn out the cake and remove the clingfilm. Dust liberally with the cocoa powder then cut into bars to serve. Store lightly covered in the refrigerator.

INGREDIENTS
Makes 20 slices

50 g/2 oz sultanas
3–4 tbsp brandy (optional)
100 g/3½ oz plain dark chocolate
125 g/4 oz unsalted butter
2 tbsp golden syrup
90 ml/3 fl oz double cream
6 digestive biscuits,
* roughly crushed*
50 g/2 oz shelled pistachio nuts,
* toasted and roughly chopped*
50 g/2 oz blanched almonds,
* toasted and roughly chopped*
50 g/2 oz glacé cherries,
* roughly chopped*
grated zest of 1 orange
cocoa powder, sifted

Helpful Hint

You may find these bars slice more easily if you heat the knife first. Run the blade of the knife under hot water and wipe dry with a clean tea towel, then slice.

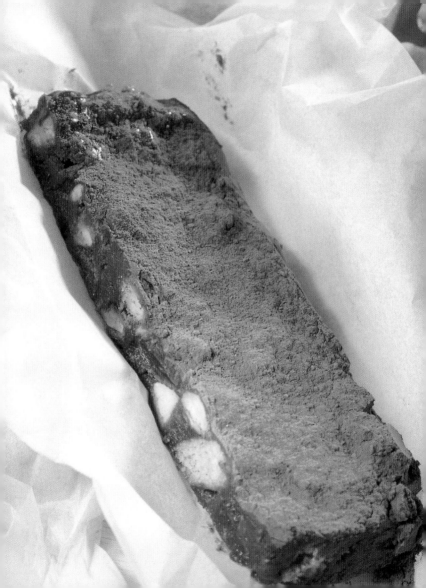

Nanaimo Bars

1 Lightly oil a 23 cm/9 inch square tin and line with clingfilm. Mix together the butter, sugar, cocoa powder, egg, biscuit crumbs, coconut and walnuts until combined thoroughly. Press into the prepared tin very firmly. Chill in the refrigerator for at least 1 hour.

2 For the filling, cream together the butter, custard powder and vanilla essence. Add the milk and icing sugar alternately, about one-third at a time, until smooth. Spread this mixture over the chilled base. Return

to the refrigerator and chill again for a further hour.

3 For the topping, melt the dark chocolate together with the butter. Stir together until combined well. Pour over the filling and spread quickly to cover the base and filling thinly.

4 Leave for 5–10 minutes until starting to set, then mark the chocolate with a sharp knife into 18 squares. Refrigerate until set. Cut through the marks, dividing the cake into squares. Serve the bars chilled.

INGREDIENTS
Makes 18

125 g/4 oz melted butter
40 g/1½ oz granulated sugar
25 g/1 oz cocoa powder
1 large egg, lightly beaten
175 g/6 oz digestive
  biscuit crumbs
75 g/3 oz flaked or
  desiccated coconut
75 g/3 oz chopped walnuts

FOR THE FILLING:

50 g/2 oz butter
2 tbsp custard powder
1 tsp vanilla essence
3 tbsp milk
225 g/8 oz icing sugar, sifted

FOR THE TOPPING:

75 g/3 oz plain
  dark chocolate
1 tbsp butter

Helpful Hint

These bars originate in western Canada in a town called Nanaimo. It is important to use dark chocolate which has not been sweetened too much because the filling layer is very sweet and rich. Do be careful when melting the dark chocolate for this recipe as the plain chocolate used has a fairly high cocoa content and if the melting process is rushed and the heat is too high, the result will be a powdery looking finish to the chocolate topping!

Miracle Bars

1 Preheat the oven to 180°C/ 350°F/Gas Mark 4 10 minutes before baking. Generously butter a 23 cm/9 inch square tin and line with non-stick baking paper.

2 Pour the butter into the prepared tin and sprinkle the biscuit crumbs over in an even layer.

3 Add the chocolate chips, coconut and nuts in even layers and drizzle over the condensed milk.

4 Transfer the tin to the preheated oven and bake for 30 minutes, until golden brown. Allow to cool in the tin, then cut into 12 squares and serve.

INGREDIENTS
Makes 12

100 g/3½ oz butter, melted, plus 1–2 tsp extra for oiling
125 g/4 oz digestive biscuit crumbs
175 g/6 oz chocolate chips
75 g/3 oz shredded or desiccated coconut
125 g/4 oz chopped mixed nuts
400 g can sweetened condensed milk

Food Fact

Condensed milk is pasteurised, homogenised milk that has been reduced to about two-thirds of its original volume by boiling under strictly controlled conditions. It is no longer advised to boil the can of condensed milk when wishing to convert the milk to a golden toffee filling as in banoffee pie. Instead, either place the milk in a heavy-based saucepan and boil gently, or place in a glass bowl, cover with clingfilm, pierce and cook on medium for 1–2 minutes at a time in a microwave. Keep checking to ensure the milk does not burn.

Apple & Cinnamon Crumble Bars

1 Preheat the oven to 190°C/ 375°F/Gas Mark 5 10 minutes before baking. Place the apples, raisins, sugar, cinnamon and lemon zest into a saucepan over a low heat.

2 Cover and cook for about 15 minutes, stirring occasionally, until the apple is cooked through. Remove the cover, stir well to break up the apple completely with a wooden spoon.

3 Cook for a further 15–30 minutes over a very low heat until reduced, thickened and slightly darkened. Allow to cool. Lightly oil and line a 20.5 cm/8 inch square cake tin with greaseproof or baking paper.

4 Mix together the flour, sugar, bicarbonate of soda, rolled oats and butter until combined well and crumbly.

5 Spread half of the flour mixture into the bottom of the prepared tin and press down. Pour over the apple mixture.

6 Sprinkle over the remaining flour mixture and press down lightly. Bake in the preheated oven for 30–35 minutes, until golden brown.

7 Remove from the oven and allow to cool before cutting into slices. Serve the bars warm or cold with crème fraîche or whipped cream.

INGREDIENTS
Makes 16

450 g/1 lb Bramley cooking apples, roughly chopped
50 g/2 oz raisins
50 g/2 oz caster sugar
1 tsp ground cinnamon
zest of 1 lemon
200 g/7 oz plain flour
250 g/9 oz soft light brown sugar
½ tsp bicarbonate of soda
150 g/5 oz rolled oats
150 g/5 oz butter, melted
crème fraîche or whipped cream, to serve

Tasty Tip

The apple filling in this recipe is very similar to American apple butter. To make apple butter, cook the filling in step 2 for a further 30 minutes over a very low heat, stirring often. When reduced to one-third of its original volume (it should be quite dark) then it is ready. It is also delicious spread on toast.

Lemon Bars

1 Preheat the oven to 170°C/
325°F/Gas Mark 3 10
minutes before baking. Lightly
oil and line a 20.5 cm/8 inch
square cake tin with greaseproof
or baking paper.

2 Rub together the flour and
butter until the mixture
resembles breadcrumbs. Stir in
the granulated sugar and mix.

3 Turn the mixture into the
prepared tin and press
down firmly. Bake in the
preheated oven for 20
minutes, until pale golden.

4 Meanwhile, in a food
processor, mix together the
caster sugar, flour, baking
powder, salt, eggs, lemon juice
and rind until smooth. Pour
over the prepared base.

5 Transfer to the preheated
oven and bake for a further
20–25 minutes, until nearly set
but still a bit wobbly in the centre. Remove from the oven and
cool in the tin on a wire rack.

6 Dust with icing sugar and
cut into squares. Serve cold
or store in an airtight tin.

INGREDIENTS
Makes 24

175 g/6 oz flour
125 g/4 oz butter
50 g/2 oz granulated sugar
200 g/7 oz caster sugar
2 tbsp flour
½ tsp baking powder
¼ tsp salt
2 medium eggs, lightly beaten
juice and finely grated rind of
* 1 lemon*
sifted icing sugar, to decorate

Food Fact

Baking Powder is a chemically prepared raising agent
consisting of cream of tartar and bicarbonate of soda,
which is then mixed with a dried starch or flour. It is
very important to measure accurately, otherwise the
mixture could either not rise, or rise too quickly and
then collapse, and give a sour taste to the dish.

Lemon-iced Ginger Squares

1 Preheat the oven to 200°C/ 400°F/Gas Mark 6 15 minutes before baking. Lightly oil a 20.5 cm/8 inch square cake tin and sprinkle with a little flour.

2 Mix together the caster sugar, butter and treacle. Stir in the egg whites.

3 Mix together the flour, bicarbonate of soda, cloves, cinnamon, ginger and salt.

4 Stir the flour mixture and buttermilk alternately into the butter mixture until blended well.

5 Spoon into the prepared tin and bake in the

preheated oven for 35 minutes, or until a skewer inserted into the centre of the cake comes out clean.

6 Remove from the oven and allow to cool for 5 minutes in the tin before turning out on to a wire rack over a large plate. Using a cocktail stick make holes on the top of the cake.

7 Meanwhile, mix together the icing sugar with enough lemon juice to make a smooth pourable icing.

8 Carefully pour the icing over the hot cake, then leave until cold. Cut the ginger cake into squares and serve.

INGREDIENTS
Makes 12

225 g/8 oz caster sugar
50 g/2 oz butter, melted
2 tbsp black treacle
2 medium egg whites,
  lightly whisked
225 g/8 oz plain flour
1 tsp bicarbonate of soda
½ tsp ground cloves
1 tsp ground cinnamon
¼ tsp ground ginger
pinch of salt
225 ml/8 fl oz buttermilk
175 g/6 oz icing sugar
lemon juice

Food Fact

Buttermilk is the liquid that remains after churning cream into butter. It is considered a healthy alternative to sour cream as it does not contain the fat of the cream. It contains lactic acid and when mixed with bicarbonate of soda it acts as a raising agent.

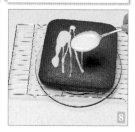

Pecan Caramel
Millionaire's Shortbread

1 Preheat the oven to 180°C/ 350°F/Gas Mark 4 10 minutes before baking. Lightly oil and line an 18 cm x 28 cm/ 7 x 11 inch tin with greaseproof or baking paper.

2 Cream together the butter, peanut butter and sugar until light. Sift in the cornflour and flour together and mix in to make a smooth dough.

3 Press the mixture into the prepared tin and prick all over with a fork. Bake in the preheated oven for 20 minutes, until just golden. Remove from the oven.

4 Meanwhile, for the topping, combine the sugar, butter, golden syrup, glucose, water and milk in a heavy-based saucepan.

5 Stir constantly over a low heat without boiling until the sugar has dissolved. Increase

the heat, boil steadily, stirring constantly, for about 10 minutes until the mixture turns a golden caramel colour.

6 Remove the saucepan from the heat and add the pecans. Pour over the shortbread base immediately. Allow to cool, then refrigerate for at least 1 hour.

7 Break the chocolate into small pieces and put into a heatproof bowl with the butter.

8 Place over a saucepan of barely simmering water, ensuring that the bowl does not come into contact with the water. Leave until melted, then stir together well.

9 Remove the shortbread from the refrigerator and pour the chocolate evenly over the top, spreading thinly to cover. Leave to set, cut into squares and serve.

INGREDIENTS
Makes 20

125 g/4 oz butter, softened
2 tbsp smooth peanut butter
75 g/3 oz caster sugar
75 g/3 oz cornflour
175 g/6 oz plain flour

FOR THE TOPPING:
200 g/7 oz caster sugar
125 g/4 oz butter
2 tbsp golden syrup
75 g/3 oz liquid glucose
75 ml/3 fl oz water
400 g can sweetened
  condensed milk
175 g/6 oz pecans,
  roughly chopped
75 g/3 oz plain dark chocolate
1 tbsp butter

Tasty Tip

Any type of nut can be used in this recipe. Why not try replacing the pecans with a variety of chopped walnuts, almonds and brazil nuts?

Fruit & Nut Flapjacks

1 Preheat the oven to 180°C/350°F/Gas Mark 4 10 minutes before baking. Lightly oil a 23 cm/9 inch square cake tin.

2 Melt the butter or margarine with the sugar and syrup in a small saucepan over a low heat. Remove from the heat.

3 Stir the raisins, walnuts and oats into the syrup mixture and mix together well.

4 Spoon evenly into the prepared tin and press down well. Transfer to the preheated oven and bake for 20–25 minutes.

5 Remove from the oven and leave to cool in the tin. Cut into bars while still warm.

6 Sift the icing sugar into a small bowl then gradually beat in the lemon juice a little at a time to form a thin icing.

7 Place into an icing bag fitted with a writing nozzle then pipe thin lines over the flapjacks. Allow to cool and serve.

INGREDIENTS
Makes 12

75 g/3 oz butter or margarine
125 g/4 oz soft light brown sugar
3 tbsp golden syrup
50 g/2 oz raisins
50 g/2 oz walnuts,
  roughly chopped
175 g/6 oz rolled oats
50 g/2 oz icing sugar
1–1½ tbsp lemon juice

Tasty Tip

These flapjacks are packed with energy, but why not increase the nutritional value by adding a few tablespoons of seeds, such as sesame, sunflower and pumpkin seeds, then add some chopped up ready-to-eat fruit such as apricot, pineapple or mango. You can also add chocolate cooking chips, chopped glacé fruits as well as currants and sultanas.

Food Fact

The rolled oats used in flapjacks can also be used when making porridge, as can oatmeal which is an integral part of haggis, oatcakes and the whisky drink Athol Brose: all great Scottish dishes.

Chocolate Fudge Brownies

1 Preheat the oven to 180°C/350°F/Gas Mark 4 10 minutes before baking. Lightly oil and line a 20.5 cm/8 inch square cake tin with greaseproof or baking paper.

2 Slowly melt the butter and chocolate together in a heatproof bowl set over a saucepan of simmering water. Transfer the mixture to a large bowl.

3 Stir in the sugar and vanilla essence, then stir in the eggs. Sift over the flour and fold together well with a metal spoon or rubber spatula. Pour into the prepared tin.

4 Transfer to the preheated oven and bake for 30 minutes until just set. Remove the cooked mixture from the oven and leave to cool in the tin before turning it out on to a wire rack.

5 Sift the icing sugar and cocoa powder into a small bowl and make a well in the centre.

6 Place the butter in the well then gradually add about 2 tablespoons of hot water. Mix to form a smooth spreadable icing.

7 Pour the icing over the cooked mixture. Allow the icing to set before cutting into squares. Serve the brownies when they are cold.

INGREDIENTS
Makes 16

125 g/4 oz butter
175 g/6 oz plain dark chocolate, roughly chopped or broken
225 g/8 oz caster sugar
2 tsp vanilla essence
2 medium eggs, lightly beaten
150 g/5 oz plain flour
175 g/6 oz icing sugar
2 tbsp cocoa powder
15 g/½ oz butter

Food Fact

Chocolate is obtained from the bean of the cacao tree and was introduced to Europe in the 16th Century. It is available in many different forms from cocoa powder to couverture, which is the best chocolate to use for cooking as it has a high cocoa butter content and melts very smoothly.

Chocolate Nut Brownies

1 Preheat the oven to 180°C/ 350°F/Gas Mark 4 10 minutes before baking. Lightly oil and line a 20.5 cm/8 inch square cake tin with greaseproof or baking paper.

2 Combine the butter, sugar and chocolate in a small saucepan and heat gently until the sugar and chocolate have melted, stirring constantly. Reserve and cool slightly.

3 Mix together the peanut butter, eggs and peanuts in a large bowl.

4 Stir in the cooled chocolate mixture. Sift in the flour and fold together with a metal spoon or rubber spatula until combined.

5 Pour into the prepared tin and bake in the preheated oven for about 30 minutes, or until just firm.

6 Cool for 5 minutes in the tin before turning out on to a wire rack to cool.

7 To make the topping, melt the chocolate in a heatproof bowl over a saucepan of simmering water, making sure that the base of the bowl does not touch the water.

8 Cool slightly, then stir in the soured cream until smooth and glossy. Spread over the brownies, refrigerate until set, then cut into squares. Serve the brownies cold.

INGREDIENTS
Makes 16

125 g/4 oz butter
150 g/5 oz soft light brown sugar, firmly packed
50 g/2 oz plain dark chocolate, roughly chopped or broken
2 tbsp smooth peanut butter
2 medium eggs
50 g/2 oz unsalted roasted peanuts, finely chopped
100 g/3 ½ oz self-raising flour

FOR THE TOPPING:

125 g/4 oz plain dark chocolate, roughly chopped or broken
50 ml/2 fl oz soured cream

Tasty Tip

For those with a really sweet tooth, replace the plain dark chocolate used for the topping with white chocolate. As with plain dark chocolate, buy a good quality white chocolate and take care when melting; it burns very easily in the microwave.

Nutty Date Pudding with Chocolate Sauce

1 Lightly oil a 1.1 litre/2 pint pudding basin and line the base with a small circle of nonstick baking parchment. Cream the butter and sugar together in a large bowl until light and fluffy. Add the beaten eggs a little at a time, adding 1 tablespoon of the flour after each addition. When all the eggs have been added, stir in the remaining flour.

2 Add the grated chocolate and mix in lightly, then stir in the milk together with the hazelnuts and dates. Stir lightly until mixed together well.

3 Spoon the mixture into the prepared pudding basin and level the surface. Cover with a double sheet of baking parchment with a pleat in the centre, allowing for expansion, then cover either with a pudding cloth or a double sheet of tinfoil, again with a central pleat. Secure with string.

4 Place in the top of a steamer, set over a saucepan of gently simmering water and steam for 2 hours, or until cooked and firm to the touch. Remember to top up the water if necessary. Remove the pudding from the saucepan and leave to rest for 5 minutes, before turning out onto a serving plate. Discard the small circle of baking parchment, then sprinkle with the chopped toasted hazelnuts. Keep warm.

5 Meanwhile, make the sauce. Place the butter, sugar and chocolate in a saucepan and heat until the chocolate has melted. Stir in the cream and simmer for 3 minutes until thickened. Pour over the pudding and serve.

INGREDIENTS
Serves 6–8

125 g/4 oz butter, softened
125 g/4 oz golden caster sugar
3 medium eggs, beaten
175 g/6 oz self-raising flour, sifted
50 g/2 oz plain dark chocolate, grated
3 tbsp milk
75 g/3 oz hazelnuts, roughly chopped
75 g/3 oz stoned dates, roughly chopped
chopped toasted hazelnuts, to serve

FOR THE CHOCOLATE SAUCE:
50 g/2 oz unsalted butter
50 g/2 oz soft light brown sugar
50 g/2 oz plain dark chocolate, broken into pieces
125 ml/4 fl oz double cream

Chocolate Brioche Bake

1 Preheat the oven to 180°C/ 350°F/Gas Mark 4, 10 minutes before baking. Lightly oil or butter a 1.7 litre/3 pint ovenproof dish. Melt the chocolate with 25 g/1 oz of the butter in a heatproof bowl set over a saucepan of simmering water. Stir until smooth.

2 Arrange half of the sliced brioche in the ovenproof dish, overlapping the slices slightly, then pour over half of the melted chocolate. Repeat the layers, finishing with a layer of chocolate.

3 Melt the remaining butter in a saucepan. Remove from the heat and stir in the orange oil or rind, the nutmeg and the beaten eggs. Continuing to stir, add the sugar and finally the milk. Beat thoroughly and pour over the brioche. Leave to stand for 30 minutes before baking.

4 Bake on the centre shelf in the preheated oven for 45 minutes, or until the custard is set and the topping is golden brown. Leave to stand for 5 minutes, then dust with cocoa powder and icing sugar. Serve warm.

INGREDIENTS
Serves 6

200 g/7 oz plain dark chocolate, broken into pieces
75 g/3 oz unsalted butter
225 g/8 oz brioche, sliced
1 tsp pure orange oil or 1 tbsp grated orange rind
½ tsp freshly grated nutmeg
3 medium eggs, beaten
25 g/1 oz golden caster sugar
600 ml/1 pint milk
cocoa powder and icing sugar for dusting

Helpful Hint

Croissants, fruit buns or fruit loaves are also suitable for this recipe. It is important that the dish is left to stand for 30 minutes before baking – do not be tempted to omit this step.

Food Fact

Brioche is a type of French bread, enriched with eggs, butter and sugar. It is available as a large round loaf, as a plait or in a long loaf shape and also as individual buns. Any type is suitable for this recipe.

Mocha Pie

1 Place the prepared pastry case on a large serving plate and reserve. Melt the chocolate in a heatproof bowl set over a saucepan of simmering water. Ensure the water is not touching the base of the bowl. Remove from the heat, stir until smooth and leave to cool.

2 Cream the butter, soft brown sugar and vanilla essence until light and fluffy, then beat in the cooled chocolate. Add the strong black coffee, pour into the pastry case and chill in the refrigerator for about 30 minutes.

3 For the topping, whisk the cream until beginning to thicken, then whisk in the sugar and vanilla essence. Continue to whisk until the cream is softly peaking. Spoon just under half of the cream into a separate bowl and fold in the dissolved coffee.

4 Spread the remaining cream over the filling in the pastry case. Spoon the coffee-flavoured whipped cream evenly over the top, then swirl it decoratively with a palate knife. Sprinkle with grated chocolate and chill in the refrigerator until ready to serve.

Helpful Hint

Try storing well-wrapped brown sugar in the freezer. This will keep the sugar soft when thawed and prevent the sugar from sticking together in big lumps. If the sugar has already stuck together in lumps, soften in the microwave for a short time.

Helpful Hint

Using a ready-made pastry case makes this a quickly made store cupboard pie that looks very impressive.

INGREDIENTS
Serves 4–6

1 x 23 cm/9 inch ready-made sweet pastry case

FOR THE FILLING:
125 g/4 oz plain dark chocolate, broken into pieces
175g/6 oz unsalted butter
225 g/8 oz soft brown sugar
1 tsp vanilla essence
3 tbsp strong black coffee

FOR THE TOPPING:
600 ml/1 pint double cream
50 g/2 oz icing sugar
2 tsp vanilla essence
1 tsp instant coffee dissolved in 1 tsp boiling water and cooled
grated plain and white chocolate, to decorate

Individual Steamed Chocolate Puddings

1 Preheat the oven to 180°C/ 350°F/Gas Mark 4, 10 minutes before baking. Lightly oil and line the bases of 8 individual 175 ml/6 fl oz pudding basins with a small circle of nonstick baking parchment. Cream the butter with 50 g/2 oz of the sugar and the nutmeg until light and fluffy.

2 Sift the flour and cocoa powder together, then stir into the creamed mixture. Beat in the egg yolks and mix well, then fold in the ground almonds and the breadcrumbs.

3 Whisk the egg whites in a clean grease-free bowl until stiff and standing in peaks then gradually whisk in the remaining sugar. Using a metal spoon, fold a quarter of the egg whites into the chocolate mixture and mix well, then fold in the remaining egg whites.

4 Spoon the mixture into the prepared basins, filling them two-thirds full to allow for expansion. Cover with a double sheet of tinfoil and secure tightly with string. Stand the pudding basins in a roasting tin and pour in sufficient water to come halfway up the sides of the basins.

5 Bake in the centre of the preheated oven for 30 minutes, or until the puddings are firm to the touch. Remove from the oven, loosen around the edges and invert onto warmed serving plates. Serve immediately with Greek yogurt and chocolate curls.

INGREDIENTS
Serves 8

150 g/5 oz unsalted butter, softened
175 g/6 oz light muscovado sugar
½ tsp freshly grated nutmeg
25 g/1 oz plain white flour, sifted
4 tbsp cocoa powder, sifted
5 medium eggs, separated
125 g/4 oz ground almonds
50 g/2 oz fresh white breadcrumbs

TO SERVE:
Greek yogurt
orange-flavoured chocolate curls

Helpful Hint

Look for individual plastic pudding basins for making this recipe. They are very easy to unmould, as you simply squeeze them to release the pudding.

Chocolate Pear Pudding

1 Preheat the oven to 190°C/375°F/Gas Mark 5, 10 minutes before baking. Butter a 20.5 cm/8 inch sandwich tin with 15 g/½ oz of the butter and sprinkle the base with the soft brown sugar. Arrange the drained pear halves on top of the sugar, cut-side down. Fill the spaces between the pears with the walnut halves, flat-side upwards.

2 Cream the remaining butter with the caster sugar then gradually beat in the beaten eggs, adding 1 tablespoon of the flour after each addition. When all the eggs have been added, stir in the remaining flour.

3 Sift the cocoa powder and baking powder together, then stir into the creamed mixture with 1–2 tablespoons of the reserved pear juice to give a smooth dropping consistency.

4 Spoon the mixture over the pear halves, smoothing the surface. Bake in the preheated oven for 20–25 minutes, or until well risen and the surface springs back when lightly pressed.

5 Remove from the oven and leave to cool for 5 minutes. Using a palate knife, loosen the sides and invert onto a serving plate. Serve with custard.

INGREDIENTS
Serves 6

140 g/4½ oz butter, softened
2 tbsp soft brown sugar
400 g can of pear halves, drained and juice reserved
25 g/1 oz walnut halves
125 g/4 oz golden caster sugar
2 medium eggs, beaten
75 g/3 oz self-raising flour, sifted
50 g/2 oz cocoa powder
1 tsp baking powder
prepared chocolate custard, to serve

Helpful Hint

To soften butter or margarine quickly, pour hot water in a mixing bowl to warm, leave for a few minutes, then drain and dry. Cut the butter or margarine into small pieces and leave at room temperature for a short time. Do not attempt to melt in the microwave as this will make the fat oily and affect the texture of the finished cake.

Tasty Tip

You could substitute fresh pears for the tinned ones in this recipe. However, they would need to be poached first in a light syrup otherwise they would discolour in the oven.

Peach & Chocolate Bake

1 Preheat the oven to 170°C/325°F/Gas Mark 3, 10 minutes before baking. Lightly oil a 1.7 litre/3 pint ovenproof dish.

2 Break the chocolate and butter into small pieces and place in a small heatproof bowl set over a saucepan of gently simmering water. Ensure the water is not touching the base of the bowl and leave to melt. Remove the bowl from the heat and stir until smooth.

3 Whisk the egg yolks with the sugar until very thick and creamy, then stir the melted chocolate and butter into the whisked egg yolk mixture and mix together lightly.

4 Place the egg whites in a clean grease-free bowl and whisk until stiff, then fold 2 tablespoons of the whisked egg whites into the chocolate mixture. Mix well, then add the remaining egg white and fold in very lightly.

5 Fold the peach slices and the cinnamon into the mixture, then spoon the mixture into the prepared dish. Do not level the mixture, leave a little uneven.

6 Bake in the preheated oven for 35–40 minutes, or until well risen and just firm to the touch. Sprinkle the bake with the icing sugar and serve immediately with spoonfuls of crème fraîche.

INGREDIENTS
Serves 6

200 g/7 oz plain dark chocolate
125 g/4 oz unsalted butter
4 medium eggs, separated
125 g/4 oz caster sugar
425 g can peach slices, drained
½ tsp ground cinnamon
1 tbsp icing sugar, sifted, to decorate
crème fraîche, to serve

Helpful Hint

As this cake contains no flour, it has a very light texture. It is very important to fold the ingredients together very lightly otherwise the air will be knocked out of the mixture.

Sticky Chocolate Surprise Pudding

1 Preheat the oven to 180°C/ 350°F/Gas Mark 4, 10 minutes before baking. Lightly oil a 1.4 litre/2½ pint ovenproof soufflé dish. Sift the flour and cocoa powder into a large bowl and stir in the caster sugar and the chopped mint-flavoured chocolate and make a well in the centre.

2 Whisk the milk, vanilla essence and the melted butter together, then beat in the egg. Pour into the well in the dry ingredients and gradually mix together, drawing the dry ingredients in from the sides of the bowl. Beat well until mixed thoroughly. Spoon into the prepared soufflé dish.

3 To make the sauce, blend the dark muscovado sugar and the cocoa powder together and spoon over the top of the pudding. Carefully pour the hot water over the top of the pudding, but do not mix.

4 Bake in the preheated oven for 35–40 minutes, or until firm to the touch and the mixture has formed a sauce underneath. Decorate with mint and serve immediately.

INGREDIENTS
Serves 6–8

150 g/5 oz self-raising flour
25 g/1 oz cocoa powder
200 g/7 oz golden caster sugar
75 g/3 oz mint-flavoured
  chocolate, chopped
175 ml/6 fl oz full cream milk
2 tsp vanilla essence
50 g/2 oz unsalted butter, melted
1 medium egg
sprig of fresh mint, to decorate

FOR THE SAUCE:
175 g/6 oz dark muscovado
  sugar
125 g/4 oz cocoa powder
600 ml/1 pint very hot water

Helpful Hint

All ovens vary, so it is important when baking to be aware of this. Always check the dish about 10 minutes before the end of the cooking time. If cooked, remove and make a note by the recipe. This is especially important if cooking with a fan oven as they cook between 10–20 degrees hotter than conventional ovens. Most baked puddings and cakes are best if cooked in the centre of the oven in the middle of the shelf.

Food Fact

The surprise is that this pudding separates during cooking to give a sticky chocolate cake with a chocolate custard sauce underneath.

Spicy White Chocolate Mousse

1 Tap the cardamom pods lightly so they split. Remove the seeds, then, using a pestle and mortar, crush lightly. Pour the milk into a small saucepan and add the crushed seeds and the bay leaves. Bring to the boil gently over a medium heat. Remove from the heat, cover and leave in a warm place for at least 30 minutes to infuse.

2 Break the chocolate into small pieces and place in a heatproof bowl set over a saucepan of gently simmering water. Ensure the water is not touching the base of the bowl. When the chocolate has melted remove the bowl from the heat and stir until smooth.

3 Whip the cream until it has slightly thickened and holds its shape, but does not form peaks. Reserve. Whisk the egg whites in a clean, grease-free bowl until stiff and standing in soft peaks.

4 Strain the milk through a sieve into the cooled, melted chocolate and beat until smooth. Spoon the chocolate mixture into the egg whites, then using a large metal spoon, fold gently. Add the whipped cream and fold in gently.

5 Spoon into a large serving dish or individual small cups. Chill in the refrigerator for 3–4 hours. Just before serving, dust with a little sifted cocoa powder and then serve.

INGREDIENTS
Serves 4–6

6 cardamom pods
125 ml/4 fl oz milk
3 bay leaves
200 g/7 oz white chocolate
300 ml/½ pint double cream
3 medium egg whites
1–2 tsp cocoa powder, sifted,
  for dusting

Tasty Tip

Chocolate and spices go together very well as this recipe demonstrates. White chocolate has an affinity with spices such as cardamom, while dark and milk chocolate go very well with cinnamon.

Steamed Chocolate Chip Pudding

1 Lightly oil a 1.1 litre/2 pint pudding basin and line the base with a small circle of nonstick baking parchment. Sift the flour and baking powder into a bowl, add the breadcrumbs, suet and sugar and mix well.

2 Stir in the eggs and vanilla essence with the chocolate chips and mix with sufficient cold milk to form a smooth dropping consistency.

3 Spoon the mixture into the prepared basin and cover the pudding with a double sheet of baking parchment and then either a double sheet of tinfoil or a pudding cloth, with a pleat in the centre to allow for expansion. Secure tightly with string.

4 Place in the top of a steamer, set over a saucepan of simmering water and steam for 1½–2 hours, or until the pudding is cooked and firm to the touch – replenish the water as necessary. Remove and leave to rest for 5 minutes before turning out onto a warmed serving plate.

5 Meanwhile, make the custard. Blend a little of the milk with the cornflour and cocoa powder to form a paste. Stir in the remaining milk with the sugar and vanilla essence. Pour into a saucepan and bring to the boil, stirring. Whisk in the egg yolk and cook for 1 minute. Decorate the pudding with grated chocolate and serve with the sauce.

INGREDIENTS
Serves 6

175 g/6 oz self-raising flour
½ tsp baking powder
75 g/3 oz fresh white
  breadcrumbs
125 g/4 oz shredded suet
125 g/4 oz golden caster sugar
2 medium eggs, lightly beaten
1 tsp vanilla essence
125 g/4 oz chocolate chips
150 ml/¼ pint cold milk
grated chocolate, to decorate

FOR THE CHOCOLATE CUSTARD:
300 ml/½ pint milk
1 tbsp cornflour
1 tbsp cocoa powder
1 tbsp caster sugar
½ tsp vanilla essence
1 medium egg yolk

Helpful Hint

The cornflour in the custard helps to stabilise it, so if, when you are cooking the custard it appears to begin curdling, remove it from the heat immediately and pour it into a clean bowl. Whisk the custard for 1–2 minutes, until it becomes smooth again.

Chocolate Fudge Sundae

1 To make the chocolate fudge sauce, place the chocolate and cream in a heavy-based saucepan and heat gently until the chocolate has melted into the cream. Stir until smooth. Mix the sugar with the flour and salt, then stir in sufficient chocolate mixture to make a smooth paste.

2 Gradually blend the remaining melted chocolate mixture into the paste, then pour into a clean saucepan. Cook over a low heat, stirring frequently until smooth and thick. Remove

from the heat and add the butter and vanilla essence. Stir until smooth, then cool slightly.

3 To make the sundae, crush the raspberries lightly with a fork and reserve. Spoon a little of the chocolate sauce into the bottom of 2 sundae glasses. Add a layer of crushed raspberries, then a scoop each of vanilla and chocolate ice cream.

4 Top each one with a scoop of the vanilla ice cream. Pour over the sauce, sprinkle over the almonds and serve with a wafer.

INGREDIENTS
Serves 2

FOR THE CHOCOLATE FUDGE SAUCE:
75 g/3 oz plain dark chocolate, broken into pieces
450ml/¾ pint double cream
175g/6 oz golden caster sugar
25 g/1 oz plain flour
pinch of salt
15 g/½ oz unsalted butter
1 tsp vanilla essence

FOR THE SUNDAE:
125g/4 oz raspberries, fresh or thawed if frozen
3 scoops vanilla ice cream
3 scoops homemade chocolate ice cream (see page 116)
2 tbsp toasted flaked almonds
a few wafers, to serve

Helpful Hint

Store any remaining fudge sauce in the refrigerator for 1–2 weeks, warming it just before serving. Ice cream will keep for up to 1 month in the freezer compartment of the refrigerator – or for 2 months in the freezer. It should be kept at a temperature at -18°C/0.4°F. If using homemade ice cream, allow to soften in the refrigerator for at least 30 minutes before using.

Chocolate Ice Cream

1 Set the freezer to rapid freeze, 2 hours before freezing. Place the single cream and chocolate in a heavy-based saucepan and heat gently until the chocolate has melted. Stir until smooth. Take care not to let the mixture boil. Remove from the heat.

2 Whisk the eggs, egg yolks and all but 1 tablespoon of the sugar together in a bowl until thick and pale.

3 Whisk the warmed single cream and chocolate mixture with the vanilla essence into the custard mixture. Place the bowl over a saucepan of simmering water and continue whisking until the mixture thickens and will coat the back of a spoon. To test, lift the spoon out of the mixture and draw a clean finger through the mixture coating the spoon, if it leaves a clean line, then it is ready.

4 Stand the bowl in cold water to cool. Sprinkle the surface with the reserved sugar

to prevent a skin forming while it is cooling. Whip the double cream until soft peaks form, then whisk into the cooled chocolate custard.

5 Turn the ice cream mixture into a rigid container and freeze for 1 hour. Beat the ice cream thoroughly with a wooden spoon to break up all the ice crystals, then return to the freezer.

6 Continue to freeze the ice cream for a further hour, then remove and beat again.

7 Repeat this process once or twice more, then leave the ice cream in the freezer until firm. Leave to soften in the refrigerator for at least 30 minutes before serving.

8 Remove from the refrigerator, then sprinkle over the chopped nuts and grated chocolate and serve with physalis. Turn the freezer back to its normal setting.

INGREDIENTS
Makes 1 litre/1¾ pints

450 ml/¾ pint single cream
200 g/7 oz plain dark chocolate
2 medium eggs
2 medium egg yolks
125 g/4 oz caster sugar
1 tsp vanilla essence
300 ml/½ pint double cream

TO SERVE:
chopped nuts
coarsely grated white and plain
   dark chocolate
a few physalis

Helpful hint

When beating the ice cream, expect it to melt a little. This is what should happen. Beating is necessary to break down any large ice crystals that have formed so that the finished ice cream is smooth rather than grainy or icy.

White Chocolate Trifle

1 Place the Swiss roll slices in the bottom of a trifle dish and pour over the brandy, Irish cream liqueur and a little of the reserved black cherry juice to moisten the Swiss roll. Arrange the black cherries on the top.

2 Pour 600 ml/1 pint of the cream into a saucepan and add the white chocolate. Heat gently to just below simmering point. Whisk together the egg yolks, caster sugar, cornflour and vanilla essence in a small bowl.

3 Gradually whisk the egg mixture into the hot cream, then strain into a clean saucepan and return to the heat.

4 Cook the custard gently, stirring throughout until thick and coats the back of a spoon.

5 Leave the custard to cool slightly, then pour over the trifle. Leave the trifle to chill in the refrigerator for at least 3–4 hours, or preferably overnight.

6 Before serving, lightly whip the remaining cream until soft peaks form, then spoon the cream over the set custard. Using the back of a spoon, swirl the cream in a decorative pattern. Sprinkle with grated plain and milk chocolate and serve.

INGREDIENTS
Serves 6

1 homemade or bought chocolate Swiss roll, sliced

4 tbsp brandy

2 tbsp Irish cream liqueur

425 g can black cherries, drained and pitted, with 3 tbsp of the juice reserved

900 ml/1½ pints double cream

125 g/4 oz white chocolate, broken into pieces

6 medium egg yolks

50 g/2 oz caster sugar

2 tsp cornflour

1 tsp vanilla essence

50 g/2 oz plain dark chocolate, grated

50 g/2 oz milk chocolate, grated

Helpful Hint

It is critical that the custard is not allowed to boil once the eggs have been added. Otherwise, the mixture turns to sweet scrambled eggs and is unusable. Cook over a very gentle heat, stirring constantly and testing the mixture often.

White Chocolate Eclairs

1 Preheat the oven to 190°C/ 375°F/Gas Mark 5, 10 minutes before baking. Lightly oil a baking sheet. Place the butter and 150 ml/¼ pint of water in a saucepan and heat until the butter has melted, then bring to the boil.

2 Remove the saucepan from the heat and immediately add the flour all at once, beating with a wooden spoon until the mixture forms a ball in the centre of the saucepan. Leave to cool for 3 minutes.

3 Add the eggs a little at a time, beating well after each addition until the paste is smooth, shiny and of a piping consistency.

4 Spoon the mixture into a piping bag fitted with a plain nozzle. Sprinkle the oiled baking sheet with water. Pipe the mixture onto the baking sheet in 7.5 cm/3 inch lengths, using a knife to cut each pastry length neatly.

5 Bake in the preheated oven for 18–20 minutes, or until well risen and golden. Make a slit along the side of each eclair, to let the steam escape.

6 Return the eclairs to the oven for a further 2 minutes to dry out. Transfer to a wire rack and leave to cool.

7 Halve the passion fruit, and using a small spoon, scoop the pulp of 4 of the fruits into a bowl. Add the cream, kirsch and icing sugar and whip until the cream holds it shape. Carefully spoon or pipe into the eclairs.

8 Melt the chocolate in a small heatproof bowl set over a saucepan of simmering water and stir until smooth.

9 Leave the chocolate to cool slightly, then spread over the top of the eclairs. Scoop the seeds and pulp out of the remaining passion fruit. Sieve. Use the juice to drizzle around the eclairs when serving.

INGREDIENTS
Serves 4–6

50 g/2 oz unsalted butter
60 g/2½ oz plain flour, sifted
2 medium eggs, lightly beaten
6 ripe passion fruit
300 ml/½ pint double cream
3 tbsp kirsch
1 tbsp icing sugar
125 g/4 oz white chocolate, broken into pieces

Helpful Hint

Passion fruit are readily available in supermarkets. They are small, round purplish fruits that should have quite wrinkled skins. Smooth passion fruit are not ripe and will have little juice or flavour.

Chocolate Roulade

1 Preheat the oven to 180°C/ 350°F/Gas Mark 4, 10 minutes before baking. Oil and line a 33 x 23 cm /13 x 9 inch Swiss roll tin with a single sheet of nonstick baking parchment. Dust a large sheet of baking parchment with 2 tablespoons of the caster sugar.

2 Place the egg yolks in a bowl with the remaining sugar, set over a saucepan of gently simmering water and whisk until pale and thick. Sift the cocoa powder into the mixture and carefully fold in.

3 Whisk the egg whites in a clean, grease-free bowl until soft peaks form. Gently add 1 tablespoon of the whisked egg whites into the chocolate mixture then fold in the remaining whites. Spoon the

mixture onto the prepared tin, smoothing the mixture into the corners. Bake in the preheated oven for 20–25 minutes, or until risen and springy to the touch.

4 Turn the cooked roulade out onto the sugar-dusted baking parchment and carefully peel off the lining paper. Cover with a clean damp tea towel and leave to cool.

5 To make the filling, pour the cream and whisky into a bowl and whisk until the cream holds its shape. Grate in the chilled creamed coconut, add the icing sugar and gently stir in. Uncover the roulade and spoon about three-quarters of coconut cream on the roulade and roll up. Spoon the remaining cream on the top and sprinkle with the coconut, then serve.

INGREDIENTS
Serves 8

150 g/5 oz golden caster sugar
5 medium eggs, separated
50 g/2 oz cocoa powder

FOR THE FILLING:
300 ml/½ pint double cream
3 tbsp whisky
50 g/2 oz creamed coconut, chilled
2 tbsp icing sugar
coarsely shredded coconut, toasted

Helpful Hint
Take care when rolling up the roulade in this recipe as it can break up quite easily.

Chocolate Pancakes

1 Preheat the oven to 200°C/400°F/Gas Mark 6, 15 minutes before cooking. To make the pancakes, sift the flour, cocoa powder, sugar and nutmeg into a bowl and make a well in the centre. Beat the eggs and milk together, then gradually beat into the flour mixture to form a batter. Stir in 50 g/2 oz of the melted butter and leave to stand for 1 hour.

2 Heat an 18 cm/7 inch nonstick frying pan and brush with a little melted butter. Add about 3 tablespoons of the batter and swirl to cover the base of the pan. Cook over a medium heat for 1–2 minutes, flip over and cook for a further 40 seconds. Repeat with the remaining batter. Stack the pancakes interleaving with greaseproof paper.

3 To make the sauce, place the mango, white wine and sugar in a saucepan and bring to the boil over a medium heat, then

simmer for 2–3 minutes, stirring constantly. When the mixture has thickened add the rum. Chill in the refrigerator.

4 For the filling, melt the chocolate and cream in a small heavy-based saucepan over a medium heat. Stir until smooth, then leave to cool. Beat the egg yolks with the caster sugar for 3–5 minutes, or until the mixture is pale and creamy, then beat in the chocolate mixture.

5 Beat the egg whites until stiff, then add a little to the chocolate mixture. Stir in the remainder. Spoon a little of the mixture onto a pancake. Fold in half, then fold in half again, forming a triangle. Repeat with the remaining pancakes.

6 Brush the pancakes with a little melted butter and bake in the preheated oven for 15–20 minutes or until the filling is set. Serve hot or cold with the mango sauce.

INGREDIENTS
Serves 6

FOR THE PANCAKES:
75 g/3 oz plain flour
1 tbsp cocoa powder
1 tsp caster sugar
½ tsp freshly grated nutmeg
2 medium eggs
175 ml/6 fl oz milk
75 g/3 oz unsalted butter, melted

FOR THE MANGO SAUCE:
1 ripe mango, peeled and diced
50 ml/2 fl oz white wine
2 tbsp golden caster sugar
2 tbsp rum

FOR THE FILLING:
225 g/8 oz plain dark chocolate
75 ml/3 fl oz double cream
3 eggs, separated
25 g/1 oz golden caster sugar

Chocolate Meringue
Nest with Fruity Filling

1 Preheat the oven to 110°C/ 225°F/Gas Mark ¼, 5 minutes before baking and line a baking sheet with nonstick baking parchment. Place the hazelnuts and 2 tablespoons of the caster sugar in a food processor and blend to a powder. Add the chocolate and blend again until the chocolate is roughly chopped.

2 In a clean, grease-free bowl, whisk the egg whites and salt until soft peaks form. Gradually whisk in the remaining sugar a teaspoonful at a time and continue to whisk until the meringue is stiff and shiny. Fold in the cornflour with the white wine vinegar with the chocolate and hazelnut mixture.

3 Spoon the mixture into 8 mounds, about 10 cm/ 4 inches in diameter, on the baking parchment. Do not worry if not perfect shapes. Make a hollow in each mound, then place in the preheated oven. Cook for 1½ hours, then switch the oven off and leave in the oven until cool.

4 To make the filling, whip the cream until soft peaks form. In another bowl, beat the mascarpone cheese until it is softened, then mix with the cream. Spoon the mixture into the meringue nests and top with the fresh fruits. Decorate with a few chocolate curls and serve.

INGREDIENTS
Serves 8

125 g/4 oz hazelnuts, toasted
125 g/4 oz golden caster sugar
75 g/3 oz plain dark chocolate,
  broken into pieces
2 medium egg whites
pinch of salt
1 tsp cornflour
½ tsp white wine vinegar
chocolate curls, to decorate

FOR THE FILLING:
150 ml/¼ pint double cream
150 g/5 oz mascarpone cheese
prepared summer fruits, such as
  strawberries, raspberries and
  redcurrants

Helpful Hint

To make chocolate curls, melt the chocolate over hot water then pour onto a cool surface, preferably marble if available. Leave until just set but not hard, then using a large cook's knife or a cheese parer, push the blade at an angle across the surface of the chocolate to form curls.

Triple Chocolate Cheesecake

1 Preheat the oven to 180°C/ 350°F/Gas Mark 4, 10 minutes before baking. Lightly oil a 23 x 7.5 cm/9 x 3 inch springform tin.

2 To make the base, mix together the crushed biscuits and melted butter. Press into the base of the tin and leave to set. Chill in the refrigerator.

3 Place the white chocolate and cream in a small heavy-based saucepan and heat gently until the chocolate has melted. Stir until smooth and reserve.

4 Beat the sugar and eggs together until light and creamy in colour, add the cream cheese and beat until the mixture is smooth and free from lumps.

5 Stir the reserved white chocolate cream together with the cornflour into the soft cream cheese mixture.

6 Add the dark and milk chocolate to the soft cream cheese mixture and mix lightly together until blended.

7 Spoon over the chilled base, place on a baking sheet and bake in the preheated oven for 1 hour.

8 Switch off the heat, open the oven door and leave the cheesecake to cool in the oven. Chill in the refrigerator for at least 6 hours before removing the cheesecake from the tin. Cut into slices and transfer to serving plates. Serve with fromage frais.

INGREDIENTS
Serves 6

FOR THE BASE:
150 g/5 oz digestive biscuits, crushed
50 g/2 oz butter, melted

FOR THE CHEESECAKE:
75 g/3 oz white chocolate, roughly chopped
300 ml/½ pint double cream
50 g/2 oz caster sugar
3 medium eggs, beaten
400 g/14 oz full fat soft cream cheese
2 tbsp cornflour
75 g/3 oz plain dark chocolate, roughly chopped
75 g/3 oz milk chocolate, roughly chopped
fromage frais, to serve

Helpful Hint

Leaving the cheesecake to cool in the oven helps to prevent cracks from forming on the top. However, do not worry if the top does crack – it will not affect the flavour of the cheesecake.

Fruity Chocolate Pudding with Sticky Chocolate Sauce

1 Lightly oil 4 x 200 ml/ 7 fl oz individual pudding basins and sprinkle with a little of the muscovado sugar. Place a few orange segments in each basin followed by a spoonful of the cranberries.

2 Cream the remaining muscovado sugar with the margarine until light and fluffy, then gradually beat in the eggs a little at a time, adding 1 tablespoon of the flour after each addition. Sift the remaining flour, baking powder and cocoa powder together, then stir into the creamed mixture with 1 tablespoon of cooled boiled water to give a soft dropping consistency. Spoon the mixture into the basins.

3 Cover each pudding with a double sheet of nonstick baking parchment with a pleat in the centre and secure tightly with string. Cover with a double sheet of tinfoil with a pleat in

the centre to allow for expansion and secure tightly with string. Place in the top of a steamer, set over a saucepan of gently simmering water and steam steadily for 45 minutes, or until firm to the touch. Remember to replenish the water if necessary. Remove the puddings from the steamer and leave to rest for about 5 minutes before running a knife around the edges of the puddings and turning out onto individual plates.

4 Meanwhile, make the chocolate sauce. Melt the chocolate and butter in a heatproof bowl set over a saucepan of gently simmering water. Add the sugar and golden syrup and stir until dissolved, then stir in the milk and continue to cook, stirring often, until the sauce thickens. Decorate the puddings with a few chocolate curls and serve with the sauce.

INGREDIENTS
Serves 4

125 g/4 oz dark muscovado sugar
1 orange, peeled and segmented
75 g/3 oz cranberries, fresh or
  thawed if frozen
125g/4 oz soft margarine
2 medium eggs
75 g/3 oz plain flour
½ tsp baking powder
3 tbsp cocoa powder
chocolate curls, to decorate

FOR THE STICKY CHOCOLATE SAUCE:
175 g/6 oz plain dark chocolate,
  broken into pieces
50 g/2 oz butter
50 g/2 oz caster sugar
2 tbsp golden syrup
200 ml/7 fl oz milk

Helpful Hint

To make ahead, cook, unmould, then reheat on High in the microwave.

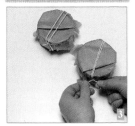

Chocolate Mallow Pie

1 Preheat the oven to 180°C/ 350°F/Gas Mark 4, 10 minutes before baking. Lightly oil an 18 cm/7 inch flan tin.

2 Place the biscuits in a polythene bag and finely crush with a rolling pin. Alternatively, place in a food processor and blend until fine crumbs are formed.

3 Melt the butter in a medium-sized sauce-pan, add the crushed biscuits and mix together. Press into the base of the prepared tin and leave to cool in the refrigerator.

4 Melt 125 g/4 oz of the chocolate with the marsh-mallows and 2 tablespoons of water in a saucepan over a gentle heat, stirring constantly. Leave to

cool slightly, then stir in the egg yolk, beat well, then return to the refrigerator until cool.

5 Whisk the egg white until stiff and standing in peaks, then fold into the chocolate mixture.

6 Lightly whip the cream and fold three-quarters of the cream into the chocolate mixture. Reserve the remainder. Spoon the chocolate cream into the flan case and chill in the refrigerator until set.

7 When ready to serve, spoon the remaining cream over the chocolate pie, swirling in a decorative pattern. Grate the remaining dark chocolate and sprinkle over the cream, then serve.

INGREDIENTS
Serves 6

200 g/7 oz digestive biscuits
75 g/3 oz butter, melted
175 g/6 oz plain dark chocolate
20 marshmallows
1 medium egg, separated
300 ml/½ pint double cream

Tasty Tip

Replace the digestive biscuits with an equal weight of chocolate-covered digestive biscuits to make a quick change to this recipe.

Chocolate Rice Pudding Brûlée

1 Preheat the oven to 150°C/ 300°F/Gas Mark 2, 10 minutes before cooking. Preheat the grill on high when ready to use. Gradually blend the cocoa powder with 3 tablespoons of boiling water to form a soft, smooth paste. Place the rice and milk, bay leaf, orange zest and the cocoa powder paste in a saucepan. Bring to the boil, stirring constantly.

2 Reduce the heat and simmer for 20 minutes, or until the rice is tender. Remove from the heat and discard the bay leaf, then add the white chocolate and stir until melted.

3 Whisk together the caster sugar and egg yolks until thick, then stir in the cream. Stir in the rice mixture together

with the vanilla essence. Pour into a buttered shallow dish. Stand the dish in a baking tin with sufficient hot water to come halfway up the sides of the dish.

4 Cook in the preheated oven for 1½ hours or until set. Stir occasionally during cooking, either removing the skin from the top or stirring the skin into the pudding. Remove from the tin and leave until cool.

5 When ready to serve, sprinkle the demerara sugar over the surface of the rice pudding. Place under the preheated grill and cook until the sugar melts and caramelises, turning the dish occasionally. Either serve immediately or chill in the refrigerator for 1 hour before serving.

INGREDIENTS
Serves 6

2 tbsp cocoa powder
75 g/3 oz short-grain rice
600 ml/1 pint milk
1 bay leaf
grated zest of 1 orange
50 g/2 oz white chocolate,
  roughly chopped
1 tbsp golden caster sugar
4 medium egg yolks
225 ml/8 fl oz double cream
½ tsp vanilla essence
4 tbsp demerara sugar

Tasty Tip

Short-grain rice is often labelled 'pudding rice'. The rice is short, quite fat and pearly in appearance. It has a great deal of starch, which comes out of the rice during the long cooking and helps to make the finished dish very creamy.

Baked Lemon & Sultana Cheesecake

1 Preheat the oven to 170°C/ 325°F/Gas Mark 3. Oil a 20.5 cm/8 inch loose-bottomed round cake tin with non-stick baking paper.

2 Beat 50 g/2 oz of the sugar and the butter together until light and creamy, then stir in the self-raising flour, baking powder and 1 egg.

3 Mix lightly together until well blended. Spoon into the prepared tin and spread the mixture over the base. Separate the 4 remaining eggs and reserve.

4 Blend the cheese in a food processor until soft. Gradually add the eggs yolks and sugar and blend until smooth. Turn into a bowl and stir in the rest of the flour, lemon rind and juice.

5 Mix lightly before adding the crème fraîche and sultanas, stirring well.

6 Whisk the egg whites until stiff, fold into the cheese mixture and pour into the tin. Tap lightly on the surface to remove any air bubbles. Bake in the preheated oven for about 1 hour, or until golden and firm.

7 Cover lightly if browning too much. Switch the oven off and leave in the oven to cool for 2–3 hours.

8 Remove the cheesecake from the oven and when completely cold remove from the tin. Sprinkle with the icing sugar, decorate with the blackcurrants or blueberries and mint leaves and serve.

INGREDIENTS
Cuts into 10 slices

275 g/10 oz caster sugar
50 g/2 oz butter
50 g/2 oz self-raising flour
½ level tsp baking powder
5 large eggs
450 g/1 lb cream cheese
40 g/1½ oz plain flour
grated rind of 1 lemon
3 tbsp fresh lemon juice
150 ml/¼ pint crème fraîche
75 g/3 oz sultanas

TO DECORATE:
1 tbsp icing sugar
fresh blackcurrants or blueberries
mint leaves

Tasty Tip

Vary the flavour by adding a little freshly grated nutmeg and ½ teaspoon of ground cinnamon to the base in step 2. Add a little of both spices to the icing sugar before sprinkling.

Crunchy Rhubarb Crumble

1 Preheat the oven to 180°C/ 350°F/Gas Mark 4. Place the flour in a large bowl and cut the butter into cubes. Add to the flour and rub in with the fingertips until the mixture looks like fine breadcrumbs, or blend for a few seconds in a food processor.

2 Stir in the rolled oats, demerara sugar, sesame seeds and cinnamon. Mix well and reserve.

3 Prepare the rhubarb by removing the thick ends of the stalks and cut diagonally into 2.5 cm/1 inch chunks. Wash thoroughly and pat dry with a clean tea towel. Place the rhubarb in a 1.1 litre/2 pint pie dish.

4 Sprinkle the caster sugar over the rhubarb and top with the reserved crumble mixture. Level the top of the crumble so that all the fruit is well covered and press down firmly. If liked, sprinkle the top with a little extra caster sugar.

5 Place on a baking sheet and bake in the preheated oven for 40–50 minutes, or until the fruit is soft and the topping is golden brown. Sprinkle the pudding with some more caster sugar and serve hot with custard or cream.

INGREDIENTS
Serves 6

125 g/4 oz plain flour
50 g/2 oz softened butter
50 g/2 oz rolled oats
50 g/2 oz demerara sugar
1 tbsp sesame seeds
½ tsp ground cinnamon
450 g/1 lb fresh rhubarb
50 g/2 oz caster sugar
custard or cream, to serve

Tasty Tip

To make homemade custard, pour 600 ml/1 pint of milk with a few drops of vanilla essence into a saucepan and bring to the boil. Remove from the heat and allow to cool. Meanwhile, whisk 5 egg yolks and 3 tablespoons of caster sugar together in a mixing bowl until thick and pale in colour. Add the milk, stir and strain into a heavy-based saucepan. Cook the custard on a low heat, stirring constantly until the consistency of double cream. Pour over the rhubarb crumble and serve.

Iced Bakewell Tart

1 Preheat the oven to 200°C/ 400°F/Gas Mark 6. Place the flour and salt in a bowl, rub in the butter and vegetable fat until the mixture resembles breadcrumbs. Alternatively, blend quickly, in short bursts in a food processor.

2 Add the eggs with sufficient water to make a soft, pliable dough. Knead lightly on a floured board then chill in the refrigerator for about 30 minutes. Roll out the pastry and use to line a 23 cm/9 inch loose-bottomed flan tin.

3 For the filling, mix together the melted butter, sugar, almonds and beaten eggs and add a few drops of almond essence. Spread the base of the

pastry case with the raspberry jam and spoon over the egg mixture.

4 Bake in the preheated oven for about 30 minutes, or until the filling is firm and golden brown. Remove from the oven and allow to cool completely.

5 When the tart is cold make the icing by mixing together the icing sugar and lemon juice, a little at a time, until the icing is smooth and of a spreadable consistency.

6 Spread the icing over the tart, leave to set for 2–3 minutes and sprinkle with the almonds. Chill in the refrigerator for about 10 minutes and serve.

INGREDIENTS
Cuts into 8 slices

FOR THE RICH PASTRY:
175 g/6 oz plain flour
pinch of salt
60 g/2½ oz butter, cut into
  small pieces
50 g/2 oz white vegetable fat,
  cut into small pieces
2 small egg yolks, beaten

FOR THE FILLING:
125 g/4 oz butter, melted
125 g/4 oz caster sugar
125 g/4 oz ground almonds
2 large eggs, beaten
few drops of almond essence
2 tbsp seedless raspberry jam

FOR THE ICING:
125 g/4 oz icing sugar, sifted
6–8 tsp fresh lemon juice
25 g/1 oz toasted flaked almonds

Tasty Tip

This tart is delicious when served with spoonfuls of thick Greek yogurt or traditional vanilla ice cream. It is not essential to use raspberry jam in this recipe. If there is none in the store cupboard use any seedless jam available. Blackcurrant jam would work particularly well.

Apricot & Almond Slice

1 Preheat the oven to 180°C/350°F/Gas Mark 4. Oil a 20.5 cm/8 inch square tin and line with non-stick baking paper.

2 Sprinkle the sugar and the flaked almonds over the paper, then arrange the apricot halves cut side down on top.

3 Cream the butter and sugar together in a large bowl until light and fluffy.

4 Gradually beat the eggs into the butter mixture, adding a spoonful of flour after each addition of egg.

5 When all the eggs have been added, stir in the remaining flour and ground almonds and mix thoroughly.

6 Add the almond essence and the apricots and stir well.

7 Spoon the mixture into the prepared tin, taking care not to dislodge the apricot halves. Bake in the preheated oven for 1 hour, or until golden and firm to touch.

8 Remove from the oven and allow to cool slightly for 15–20 minutes. Turn out carefully, discard the lining paper and transfer to a serving dish. Pour the honey over the top of the cake, sprinkle on the toasted almonds and serve.

INGREDIENTS
Cuts into 10 slices

2 tbsp demerara sugar
25 g/1 oz flaked almonds
400 g can apricot
  halves, drained
225 g/8 oz butter
225 g/8 oz caster sugar
4 medium eggs
200 g/7 oz self-raising flour
25 g/1 oz ground almonds
½ tsp almond essence
50 g/2 oz ready-to-eat dried
  apricots, chopped
3 tbsp clear honey
3 tbsp roughly chopped
  almonds, toasted

Helpful Hint

This cake should keep for about three to five days if stored correctly. Allow the cake to cool completely, then remove from the tin and discard the lining paper. Store in an airtight container lined with greaseproof paper or baking parchment and keep in a cool place.

Queen of Puddings

1 Preheat the oven to 170°C/ 325°F/Gas Mark 3. Oil a 900 ml/1½ pint ovenproof baking dish and reserve.

2 Mix the breadcrumbs and sugar together in a bowl.

3 Pour the milk into a small saucepan and heat gently with the butter and lemon rind until the butter has melted.

4 Allow the mixture to cool a little, then pour over the breadcrumbs. Stir well and leave to soak for 30 minutes.

5 Whisk the egg yolks into the cooled breadcrumb mixture and pour into the prepared dish.

6 Place the dish on a baking sheet and bake in the preheated oven for about 30 minutes, or until firm and set. Remove from the oven.

7 Allow to cool slightly, then spread the jam over the pudding. Whisk the egg whites until stiff and standing in peaks.

8 Gently fold in the caster sugar with a metal spoon or rubber spatula. Pile the meringue over the top of the pudding.

9 Return the dish to the oven for a further 25–30 minutes, or until the meringue is crisp and just slightly coloured. Serve hot or cold.

INGREDIENTS
Serves 4

*75 g/3 oz fresh
white breadcrumbs
25 g/1 oz granulated sugar
450 ml/¾ pint full-cream milk
25 g/1 oz butter
grated rind of 1 small lemon
2 medium eggs, separated
2 tbsp seedless raspberry jam
50 g/2 oz caster sugar*

Helpful Hint

When whisking egg whites it is imperative that the bowl is completely clean and free of any grease. To ensure that the meringue does not collapse, whisk the egg whites until stiff. Gradually add the sugar, a spoonful at a time, whisking well between each addition. Place in the oven immediately after all of the sugar has been added.

Crème Brûlée with Sugared Raspberries

1 Preheat the oven to 150°C/300°F/Gas Mark 2. Pour the cream into a bowl and place over a saucepan of gently simmering water. Heat gently but do not allow to boil.

2 Meanwhile, whisk together the egg yolks, 50 g/2 oz of the caster sugar and the vanilla essence. When the cream is warm, pour it over the egg mixture briskly whisking until it is mixed completely.

3 Pour into 6 individual ramekin dishes and place in a roasting tin.

4 Fill the tin with sufficient water to come halfway up the sides of the dishes.

5 Bake in the preheated oven for about 1 hour, or until the puddings are set. (To test if set, carefully insert a round bladed knife into the centre, if the knife comes out clean they are set.)

6 Remove the puddings from the roasting tin and allow to cool. Chill in the refrigerator, preferably overnight.

7 Sprinkle the sugar over the top of each dish and place the puddings under a preheated hot grill.

8 When the sugar has caramelised and turned deep brown, remove from the heat and cool. Chill the puddings in the refrigerator for 2–3 hours before serving.

9 Toss the raspberries in the remaining caster sugar and sprinkle over the top of each dish. Serve with a little extra cream if liked.

INGREDIENTS
Serves 6

600 ml/1 pint fresh whipping cream
4 medium egg yolks
75 g/3 oz caster sugar
½ tsp vanilla essence
25 g/1 oz demerara sugar
175 g/6 oz fresh raspberries

Helpful Hint

Most chefs use blow torches to brown the sugar in step 5, as this is the quickest way to caramelise the top of the dessert. Take great care if using a blow torch, especially when lighting. Otherwise use the grill, making sure that it is very hot and the dessert is thoroughly chilled before caramelising the sugar topping. This will prevent the custard underneath from melting.

Chocolate Sponge Pudding with Fudge Sauce

1 Preheat the oven to 170°C/ 325°F/Gas Mark 3. Oil a 900 ml/1½ pint pie dish.

2 Cream the butter and the sugar together in a large bowl until light and fluffy.

3 Stir in the melted chocolate, flour, drinking chocolate and egg and mix together.

4 Turn the mixture into the prepared dish and level the surface.

5 To make the fudge sauce, blend the brown sugar, cocoa powder and pecan nuts together and sprinkle evenly over the top of the pudding.

6 Stir the caster sugar into the hot black coffee until it has dissolved.

7 Carefully pour the coffee over the top of the pudding.

8 Bake in the preheated oven for 50–60 minutes, until the top is firm to touch. There will now be a rich sauce underneath the sponge.

9 Remove from the oven, dust with icing sugar and serve hot with crème fraîche.

INGREDIENTS
Serves 4

75 g/3 oz butter
75 g/3 oz caster sugar
50 g/2 oz plain dark
  chocolate, melted
50 g/2 oz self-raising flour
25 g/1 oz drinking chocolate
1 large egg
1 tbsp icing sugar, to dust
crème fraîche, to serve

FUDGE SAUCE:
50 g/2 oz soft light brown sugar
1 tbsp cocoa powder
40 g/1½ oz pecan nuts,
  roughly chopped
25 g/1 oz caster sugar
300 ml/½ pint hot, strong
  black coffee

Tasty Tip
Try placing 6 halved and stoned fresh red plums
in the base of the dish before adding the
prepared chocolate sponge.

Eve's Pudding

1 Preheat the oven to 180°C/ 350°F/Gas Mark 4. Oil a 1.1 litre/2 pint baking dish.

2 Peel, core and slice the apples and place a layer in the base of the prepared dish.

3 Sprinkle over some of the blackberries, a little demerara sugar and lemon zest.

4 Continue to layer the apple and blackberries in this way until all the ingredients have been used.

5 Cream the sugar and butter together until light and fluffy.

6 Beat in the vanilla essence and then the eggs a little at a time, adding a spoonful of flour after each addition. Fold in the extra flour with a metal spoon or rubber spatula and mix well.

7 Spread the sponge mixture over the top of the fruit and level with the back of a spoon.

8 Place the dish on a baking sheet and bake in the preheated oven for 35–40 minutes, or until well risen and golden brown. (To test if the pudding is cooked, press the cooked sponge lightly with a clean finger – if it springs back the sponge is cooked.)

9 Dust the pudding with a little icing sugar and serve immediately with the custard.

INGREDIENTS
Serves 6

450 g/1 lb cooking apples
175 g/6 oz blackberries
75 g/3 oz demerara sugar
grated rind of 1 lemon
125 g/4 oz caster sugar
125 g/4 oz butter
few drops of vanilla essence
2 medium eggs, beaten
125 g/4 oz self-raising flour
1 tbsp icing sugar
ready-made custard, to serve

Food Fact

Eve's pudding is a classic English pudding and has been popular since the early 20th century. At that time there were many different varieties of cooking apples grown throughout the country. Unfortunately, many of these apples have now disappeared.

Lemon & Apricot Pudding

1 Preheat the oven to 180°C/ 350°F/Gas Mark 4. Oil a 1.1 litre/2 pint pie dish.

2 Soak the apricots in the orange juice for 10–15 minutes or until most of the juice has been absorbed, then place in the base of the pie dish.

3 Cream the butter and sugar together with the lemon rind until light and fluffy.

4 Separate the eggs. Beat the egg yolks into the creamed mixture with a spoonful of flour after each addition. Add the remaining flour and beat well until smooth.

5 Stir the milk and lemon juice into the creamed mixture. Whisk the egg whites in a grease-free mixing bowl until stiff and standing in peaks. Fold into the mixture using a metal spoon or rubber spatula.

6 Pour into the prepared dish and place in a baking tray filled with enough cold water to come halfway up the sides of the dish.

7 Bake in the preheated oven for about 45 minutes, or until the sponge is firm and golden brown. Remove from the oven. Serve immediately with the custard or fresh cream.

INGREDIENTS
Serves 4

125 g/4 oz ready-to-eat dried apricots
3 tbsp orange juice, warmed
50 g/2 oz butter
125 g/4 oz caster sugar
juice and grated rind of 2 lemons
2 medium eggs
50 g/2 oz self-raising flour
300 ml/½ pint milk
custard or fresh cream, to serve

Helpful Hint

This pudding is cooked in a bain-marie to control the temperature around the dish – it needs to stay at just below point. Bain-maries are ideal when cooking custards, sauces and other egg dishes. When using one, ensure that the water is kept topped up.

Strawberry Flan

1 Preheat the oven to 200°C/400°F/Gas Mark 6. Place the flour, butter and vegetable fat in a food processor and blend until the mixture resembles fine breadcrumbs. Stir in the sugar, then with the machine running, add the egg yolk and enough water to make a fairly stiff dough. Knead lightly, cover and chill in the refrigerator for 30 minutes.

2 Roll out the pastry and use to line a 23 cm/9 inch loose-bottomed flan tin. Place a piece of greaseproof paper in the pastry case and cover with baking beans or rice. Bake in the preheated oven for 15–20 minutes, until just firm. Reserve until cool.

3 Make the filling by whisking the eggs and sugar together until thick and pale. Gradually stir in the flour and then the milk. Pour into a small saucepan and simmer for 3–4 minutes stirring throughout.

4 Add the vanilla essence to taste, then pour into a bowl and leave to cool. Cover with greaseproof paper to prevent a skin from forming.

5 When the filling is cold, whisk until smooth then pour on to the cooked flan case. Slice the strawberries and arrange on the top of the filling. Decorate with the mint leaves and serve.

INGREDIENTS
Serves 6

SWEET PASTRY:
175 g/6 oz plain flour
50 g/2 oz butter
50 g/2 oz white vegetable fat
2 tsp caster sugar
1 medium egg yolk, beaten

FOR THE FILLING:
1 medium egg, plus 1 extra
  egg yolk
50 g/2 oz caster sugar
25 g/1 oz plain flour
300 ml/½ pint milk
few drops of vanilla essence
450 g/1 lb strawberries, cleaned
  and hulled
mint leaves, to decorate

Tasty Tip
In the summer, when the choice of fruit is greater why not try topping the flan with a variety of mixed fruits. Arrange strawberries, raspberries, kiwi fruit and blueberries on top of the filling. If liked, heat 3 tablespoons of seedless raspberry jam with 2 teaspoons of lemon juice. Stir until smooth, then use to brush over the fruit. Allow to set before serving.

Rich Double-crust Plum Pie

1 Preheat the oven to 200°C/ 400°F/Gas Mark 6. Make the pastry by rubbing the butter and white vegetable fat into the flour until it resembles fine breadcrumbs or blend in a food processor. Add the egg yolks and enough water to make a soft dough. Knead lightly, then wrap and leave in the refrigerator for about 30 minutes.

2 Meanwhile, prepare the fruit. Rinse and dry the plums, then cut in half and remove the stones. Slice the plums into chunks and cook in a saucepan with 25 g/1 oz of the sugar and 2 tablespoons of water for 5–7 minutes, or until slightly softened. Remove from the heat and add the remaining sugar to taste and allow to cool.

3 Roll out half the chilled pastry on a lightly floured surface and use to line the base

and sides of a 1.1 litre/ 2 pint pie dish. Allow the pastry to hang over the edge of the dish. Spoon in the prepared plums.

4 Roll out the remaining pastry to use as the lid and brush the edge with a little water. Wrap the pastry around the rolling pin and place over the plums.

5 Press the edges together to seal and mark a decorative edge around the rim of the pastry by pinching with the thumb and forefinger or using the back of a fork.

6 Brush the lid with milk, and make a few slits in the top. Use any trimmings to decorate the top of the pie with pastry leaves. Place on a baking sheet and bake in the preheated oven for 30 minutes, or until golden brown. Sprinkle with a little caster sugar and serve hot or cold.

INGREDIENTS
Serves 6

FOR THE PASTRY:
75 g/3 oz butter
75 g/3 oz white vegetable fat
225 g/8 oz plain flour
2 medium egg yolks

FOR THE FILLING:
450 g/1 lb fresh plums,
  preferably Victoria
50 g/2 oz caster sugar
1 tbsp milk
a little extra caster sugar

Helpful Hint

As Victoria plums have only a short season, from August to September, it is best to use other varieties that have been imported. Alternatively buy English plums in season. Halve, store and freeze them then use as required.

Baked Apple Dumplings

1 Preheat the oven to 200°C/ 400°F/Gas Mark 6. Lightly oil a baking tray. Place the flour and salt in a bowl and stir in the suet.

2 Add just enough water to the mixture to mix to a soft but not sticky dough, using the fingertips.

3 Turn the dough on to a lightly floured board and knead lightly into a ball.

4 Divide the dough into 4 pieces and roll out each piece into a thin square, large enough to encase the apples.

5 Peel and core the apples and place 1 apple in the centre of each square of pastry.

6 Fill the centre of the apple with mincemeat, brush the edges of each pastry square with water and draw the corners up to meet over each apple.

7 Press the edges of the pastry firmly together and decorate with pastry leaves and shapes made from the extra pastry trimmings.

8 Place the apples on the prepared baking tray, brush with the egg white and sprinkle with the sugar.

9 Bake in the preheated oven for 30 minutes or until golden and the pastry and apples are cooked. Serve the dumplings hot with the custard or vanilla sauce.

INGREDIENTS
Serves 4

225 g/8 oz self-raising flour
¼ tsp salt
125 g/4 oz shredded suet
4 medium cooking apples
4–6 tsp luxury mincemeat
1 medium egg white, beaten
2 tsp caster sugar
custard or vanilla sauce, to serve

Tasty Tip

To make vanilla sauce, blend 1½ tablespoons of cornflour with 3 tablespoons of milk to a smooth paste. Bring just under 300 ml/½ pint of milk to just below boiling point. Stir in the cornflour paste and cook over a gentle heat, stirring throughout until thickened and smooth. Remove from the heat and add 1 tablespoon of caster sugar, a knob of butter and ½ teaspoon of vanilla essence. Stir until the sugar and butter have melted, then serve.

Tasty Tip

For a homemade mincemeat, mix together 125 g/4 oz of mixed fruit and 1 tablespoon of toasted flaked almonds. Add 25 g/1 oz of butter, 2 tablespoons of light muscovado sugar and 1 teaspoon of mixed spice. Warm on a low heat, stirring. Place a spoonful into the centre of the apple and continue with the recipe.

Jam Roly Poly

1 Preheat the oven to 200°C/ 400°F/Gas Mark 6. Make the pastry by sifting the flour and salt into a large bowl.

2 Add the suet and mix lightly, then add the water a little at a time and mix to form a soft and pliable dough. (Take care not to make the dough too wet.)

3 Turn the dough out on to a lightly floured board and knead gently until smooth.

4 Roll the dough out into a 23 cm/9 inch x 28 cm/11 inch rectangle.

5 Spread the jam over the pastry leaving a border of 1 cm/½ inch all round. Fold the border over the jam and brush the edges with water.

6 Lightly roll the rectangle up from one of the short sides, seal the top edge and press the ends together. (Do not roll the pudding up too tightly.)

7 Turn the pudding upside down on to a large piece of greaseproof paper large enough to come halfway up the sides. (If using non-stick paper, then oil lightly.)

8 Tie the ends of the paper, to make a boat-shaped paper case for the pudding to sit in and to leave plenty of room for the roly poly to expand.

9 Brush the pudding lightly with milk and sprinkle with the sugar. Bake in the preheated oven for 30–40 minutes, or until well risen and golden. Serve immediately with the jam sauce.

INGREDIENTS
Serves 6

225 g/8 oz self-raising flour
¼ tsp salt
125 g/4 oz shredded suet
about 150 ml/¼ pint water
3 tbsp strawberry jam
1 tbsp milk, to glaze
1 tsp caster sugar
ready-made jam sauce, to serve

Tasty Tip

To make jam sauce, warm 4 tablespoons of jam such as seedless raspberry jam with 150 ml/¼ pint of water or orange juice. Stir until smooth. Blend 2 teaspoons of arrowroot with 1 tablespoon of water or juice to a smooth paste. Bring the jam mixture to almost boiling point, then stir in the blended arrowroot. Cook, stirring until the mixture thickens slightly and clears, then serve.

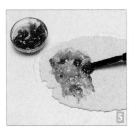

Egg Custard Tart

1 Preheat the oven to 200°C/ 400°F/Gas Mark 6. Oil a 20.5 cm/8 inch flan tin or dish.

2 Make the pastry by cutting the butter and vegetable fat into small cubes. Add to the flour in a large bowl and rub in, until the mixture resembles fine breadcrumbs.

3 Add the egg, sugar and enough water to form a soft and pliable dough. Turn on to a lightly floured board and knead. Wrap and chill in the refrigerator for 30 minutes.

4 Roll the pastry out on to a lightly floured surface or pastry board and use to line the oiled flan tin. Place in the refrigerator to reserve.

5 Warm the milk in a small saucepan. Briskly whisk together the eggs, egg yolk and caster sugar.

6 Pour the milk into the egg mixture and whisk until blended.

7 Strain through a sieve into the pastry case. Place the flan tin on a baking sheet.

8 Sprinkle the top of the tart with nutmeg and bake in the preheated oven for about 15 minutes.

9 Turn the oven down to 170°C/ 325°F/Gas Mark 3 and bake for a further 30 minutes, or until the custard has set. Serve hot or cold.

INGREDIENTS
Serves 6

SWEET PASTRY:
50 g/2 oz butter
50 g/2 oz white vegetable fat
175 g/6 oz plain flour
1 medium egg yolk, beaten
2 tsp caster sugar

FOR THE FILLING:
300 ml/½ pint milk
2 medium eggs, plus
 1 medium egg yolk
25 g/1 oz caster sugar
½ tsp freshly grated nutmeg

Helpful Hint

Nowadays eggs are normally date stamped so it is possible to ensure that they are eaten when they are at their best. Another way to test if an egg is fresh is to place an uncooked egg in a bowl of water – if it lies at the bottom it is fresh; if it tilts it is older (use for frying or scrambling); if it floats, discard.

Golden Castle Pudding

1 Preheat the oven to 180°C 350°F/Gas Mark 4. Lightly oil 4–6 individual pudding bowls and place a small circle of lightly oiled non-stick baking or greaseproof paper in the base of each one.

2 Place the butter and caster sugar in a large bowl, then beat together until the mixture is pale and creamy. Stir in the vanilla essence and gradually add the beaten eggs, a little at a time. Add a tablespoon of flour after each addition of egg and beat well.

3 When the mixture is smooth, add the remaining flour and fold in gently. Add a tablespoon of water and mix

to form a soft mixture that will drop easily off a spoon.

4 Spoon enough mixture into each basin to come halfway up the tin, allowing enough space for the puddings to rise. Place on a baking sheet and bake in the preheated oven for about 25 minutes until firm and golden brown.

5 Allow the puddings to stand for 5 minutes. Discard the paper circle and turn out on to individual serving plates.

6 Warm the golden syrup in a small saucepan and pour a little over each pudding. Serve hot with the crème fraîche or custard.

INGREDIENTS
Serves 4–6

125 g/4 oz butter
125 g/4 oz caster sugar
a few drops of vanilla essence
2 medium eggs, beaten
125 g/4 oz self-raising flour
4 tbsp golden syrup
crème fraîche or ready-made
*   custard, to serve*

Helpful Hint

For a change, make the traditional Castle Pudding by placing a spoonful of jam in the base of each basin. Top with the sponge and bake.

College Pudding

1 Preheat the oven to 180°C/
350°F/Gas Mark 4. Lightly
oil an ovenproof 900 ml/1½
pint ovenproof pudding basin
and place a small circle of
greaseproof paper in the base.

2 Mix the shredded suet and
breadcrumbs together and
rub lightly together with the
fingertips to remove any lumps.

3 Stir in the dried fruit,
spices, sugar and baking
powder. Add the eggs and beat
lightly together until the mixture
is well blended and the fruit is
evenly distributed.

4 Spoon the mixture into
the prepared pudding basin
and level the surface. Place on a
baking tray and cover lightly
with some greaseproof paper.

5 Bake in the preheated
oven for 20 minutes, then
remove the paper and continue
to bake for a further 10–15
minutes, or until the top is firm.

6 When the pudding is
cooked, remove from the
oven and carefully turn out on
to a warmed serving dish.
Decorate with the orange zest
and serve immediately.

INGREDIENTS
Serves 4

125 g/4 oz shredded suet
125 g/4 oz fresh
 white breadcrumbs
50 g/2 oz sultanas
50 g/2 oz seedless raisins
½ tsp ground cinnamon
¼ tsp freshly grated nutmeg
¼ tsp mixed spice
50 g/2 oz caster sugar
½ tsp baking powder
2 medium eggs, beaten
orange zest, to garnish

Tasty Tip

Like many other suet puddings this recipe is relatively
cheap to make. For extra fruitiness add some apple purée
to the mixture. To make, peel, core and chop 1 cooking
apple. Place in a saucepan with 25 g/1 oz of sugar and
4 tablespoons of water. Simmer until softened but not
falling apart, then roughly mash. Add the purée to the
mixture in step 3 and continue as before.

Cherry Batter Pudding

1 Preheat the oven to 220°C/ 425°F/Gas Mark 7. Lightly oil a 900 ml/1½ pint shallow baking dish.

2 Rinse the cherries, drain well and remove the stones (using a cherry stoner if possible). If using canned cherries, drain well, discard the juice and place in the prepared dish.

3 Sift the flour and salt into a large bowl. Stir in 2 tablespoons of the caster sugar and make a well in the centre. Beat the eggs, then pour into the well of the dry ingredients.

4 Warm the milk and slowly pour into the well, beating throughout and gradually drawing in the flour from the sides of the bowl. Continue until a smooth batter has formed.

5 Melt the butter in a small saucepan over a low heat, then stir into the batter with the rum. Reserve for 15 minutes, then beat again until smooth and easy to pour.

6 Pour into the prepared baking dish and bake in the preheated oven for 30–35 minutes, or until golden brown and set.

7 Remove the pudding from the oven, sprinkle with the remaining sugar and serve hot with plenty of fresh cream.

INGREDIENTS
Serves 4

450 g/1 lb fresh cherries (or 425 g can pitted cherries)
50 g/2 oz plain flour
pinch of salt
3 tbsp caster sugar
2 medium eggs
300 ml/½ pint milk
40 g/1½ oz butter
1 tbsp rum
extra caster sugar, to dredge
fresh cream, to serve

Food Fact

The traditional name of this French speciality is *Clafoutis*. For that extra hit of cherry flavour why not replace the rum used in this recipe with *kirsch* – an eau-de-vie rather than a liqueur which is made from pine kernels and cherry fruit juice to produce a brandy. It is made in Alsace as well as in the Blackforest region in Germany.

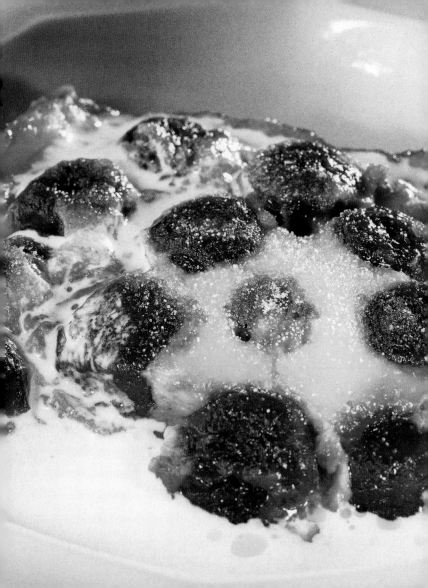

Apple & Cinnamon Brown Betty

1 Preheat the oven to 180°C/ 350°F/Gas Mark 4. Lightly oil a 900 ml/1½ pint ovenproof dish. Peel, core and slice the apples and place in a saucepan with the caster sugar, lemon rind and 2 tablespoons of water. Simmer for 10–15 minutes or until tender.

2 Mix the breadcrumbs with the sugar and the cinnamon. Place half the sweetened apples in the base of the prepared dish and spoon over half of the crumb mixture. Place the remaining apples on top and cover with the rest of the crumb mixture.

3 Melt the butter and pour over the surface of the pudding. Cover the dish with non-stick baking paper and bake

in the preheated oven for 20 minutes. Remove the paper and bake for a further 10–15 minutes, or until golden.

4 Meanwhile, make the custard by whisking the egg yolks and sugar together until creamy. Mix 1 tablespoon of the milk with the cornflour, until a paste forms and reserve.

5 Warm the rest of the milk until nearly boiling and pour over the egg mixture with the paste and vanilla essence.

6 Place the bowl over a sauce pan of gently simmering water. Stir over the heat until thickened and can coat the back of a spoon. Strain into a jug and serve hot over the pudding.

INGREDIENTS
Serves 4

450 g/1 lb cooking apples
50 g/2 oz caster sugar
finely grated rind of 1 lemon
125 g/4 oz fresh white
 breadcrumbs
125 g/4 oz demerara sugar
½ tsp ground cinnamon
25 g/1 oz butter

FOR THE CUSTARD:
3 medium egg yolks
1 tbsp caster sugar
500 ml/1 pint milk
1 tbsp cornflour
few drops of vanilla essence

Tasty Tip

For a richer, more luxurious custard, substitute the
milk in this recipe for double cream and increase
the number of eggs yolks used to 4.

Lattice Treacle Tart

1 Preheat the oven to 190°C/ 375°F/Gas Mark 5. Make the pastry by placing the flour, butter and white vegetable fat in a food processor. Blend in short sharp bursts until the mixture resembles fine breadcrumbs. Remove from the processor and place on a pastry board or in a large bowl.

2 Stir in enough cold water to make a dough and knead in a large bowl or on a floured surface until smooth and pliable.

3 Roll out the pastry and use to line a 20.5 cm/ 8 inch loose-bottomed fluted flan dish or tin. Reserve the pastry trimmings for decoration. Chill for 30 minutes.

4 Meanwhile, to make the filling, place the golden syrup in a saucepan and warm gently with the lemon rind and juice. Tip the breadcrumbs into the pastry case and pour the syrup mixture over the top.

5 Roll the pastry trimmings out on a lightly floured surface and cut into 6–8 thin strips. Lightly dampen the pastry edge of the tart, then place the strips across the filling in a lattice pattern. Brush the ends of the strips with water and seal to the edge of the tart. Brush a little beaten egg over the pastry and bake in the preheated oven for a 25 minutes, or until the filling is just set. Serve hot or cold.

INGREDIENTS
Serves 4

FOR THE PASTRY:
175 g/6 oz plain flour
40 g/1½ oz butter
40 g/1½ oz white vegetable fat

FOR THE FILLING:
225 g/8 oz golden syrup
finely grated rind and juice
* of 1 lemon*
75 g/3 oz fresh white
* breadcrumbs*
1 small egg, beaten

Tasty Tip
Why not replace the breadcrumbs with the
same amount of desiccated coconut?

Osborne Pudding

1 Preheat the oven to 170°C/ 325°F/Gas Mark 3. Lightly oil a 1.1 litre/2 pint baking dish.

2 Remove the crusts from the bread and spread thickly with butter and marmalade. Cut the bread into small triangles.

3 Place half the bread in the base of the dish and sprinkle over the dried mixed fruit, 1 tablespoon of the orange juice and half the caster sugar.

4 Top with the remaining bread and marmalade, buttered side up and pour over the remaining orange juice. Sprinkle over the remaining caster sugar.

5 Whisk the eggs with the milk and cream and pour over the pudding. Reserve for

about 30 minutes to allow the bread to absorb the liquid.

6 Place in a roasting tin and pour in enough boiling water to come halfway up the sides of the dish. Bake in the preheated oven for 50–60 minutes, or until the pudding is set and the top is crisp and golden.

7 Meanwhile, make the marmalade sauce. Heat the orange zest and juice with the marmalade and brandy if using.

8 Mix 1 tablespoon of water with the cornflour and mix together well.

9 Add to the saucepan and cook on a low heat, stirring until warmed through and thickened. Serve the pudding hot with the marmalade sauce.

INGREDIENTS
Serves 4

8 slices of white bread
50 g/2 oz butter
2 tbsp marmalade
50 g/2 oz luxury mixed dried fruit
2 tbsp fresh orange juice
40 g/1½ oz caster sugar
2 large eggs
450 ml/¾ pint milk
150 ml/¼ pint whipping cream

MARMALADE SAUCE:
zest and juice of 1 orange
2 tbsp thick-cut orange marmalade
1 tbsp brandy (optional)
2 tsp cornflour

Tasty Tip

To make an orange sauce instead, omit the marmalade and add the juice of another 3 oranges and a squeeze of lemon juice to make 250 ml/9 fl oz. Follow the recipe as before but increase the cornflour to 1½ tablespoons.

Chocolate, Orange & Pine Nut Tart

1 Preheat the oven to 200°C/ 400°F/Gas Mark 6, 15 minutes before baking. Place the flour, salt and sugar in a food processor with the butter and blend briefly. Add the egg yolks, 2 tablespoons of iced water and the vanilla essence and blend until a soft dough is formed. Remove and knead until smooth, wrap in clingfilm and chill in the refrigerator for 1 hour.

2 Lightly oil a 23 cm/9 inch loose-based flan tin. Roll the dough out on a lightly floured surface to a 28 cm/11 inch round and use to line the tin. Press into the sides of the flan tin, crimp the edges, prick the base with a fork and chill in the refrigerator for 1 hour. Bake blind in the preheated oven for

10 minutes. Remove and place on a baking sheet. Reduce the oven temperature to 190°C/375°F/Gas Mark 5.

3 To make the filling, sprinkle the chocolate and the pine nuts evenly over the base of the pastry case. Beat the eggs, orange zest, Cointreau and cream in a bowl until well blended, then pour over the chocolate and pine nuts.

4 Bake in the oven for 30 minutes, or until the pastry is golden and the custard mixture is just set. Transfer to a wire rack to cool slightly. Heat the marmalade with 1 tablespoon of water and brush over the tart. Serve warm or at room temperature.

INGREDIENTS
Cuts into 8–10 slices

FOR THE SWEET SHORTCRUST PASTRY:
150 g/5 oz plain flour
½ tsp salt
3–4 tbsp icing sugar
125 g/4 oz unsalted butter, diced
2 medium egg yolks, beaten
½ tsp vanilla essence

FOR THE FILLING:
125 g/4 oz plain dark chocolate, chopped
60 g/2½ oz pine nuts, lightly toasted
2 large eggs
grated zest of 1 orange
1 tbsp Cointreau
225 ml/8 fl oz whipping cream
2 tbsp orange marmalade

Food Fact
Cointreau is an orange-flavoured liqueur and is used in many recipes. You could substitute Grand Marnier or any other orange liqueur, if you prefer.

Chocolate Pecan Pie

1 Preheat the oven to 180°C/ 350°F/Gas Mark 4, 10 minutes before baking. Roll the prepared pastry out on a lightly floured surface and use to line a 25.5 cm/10 inch pie plate. Roll the trimmings out and use to make a decorative edge around the pie, then chill in the refrigerator for 1 hour.

2 Reserve about 60 perfect pecan halves, or enough to cover the top of the pie, then coarsely chop the remainder and reserve. Melt the chocolate and butter in a small saucepan over a low heat or in the microwave and reserve.

3 Beat the eggs and brush the base and sides of the pastry with a little of the beaten egg. Beat the sugar, golden syrup and vanilla essence into the beaten eggs. Add the pecans, then beat in the chocolate mixture.

4 Pour the filling into the pastry case and arrange the reserved pecan halves in concentric circles over the top. Bake in the preheated oven for 45–55 minutes, or until the filling is well risen and just set. If the pastry edge begins to brown too quickly, cover with strips of tinfoil. Remove from the oven and serve with ice cream.

INGREDIENTS
Cuts into 8–10 slices

225 g/8 oz prepared shortcrust pastry (see page 136)
200 g/7 oz pecan halves
125 g/4 oz plain dark chocolate, chopped
25 g/1 oz butter, diced
3 medium eggs
125 g/4 oz light brown sugar
175 ml/6 fl oz golden syrup
2 tsp vanilla essence
vanilla ice cream, to serve

Helpful Hint

Store chocolate in a cool, dark, dry place. The best temperature to store it is 20°C/68°F – if warmer the chocolate will sweat.

Helpful Hint

The pastry case in this recipe is not baked blind, but the pie does not become soggy because of the long cooking time, which allows the pastry to become crisp.

Pear & Chocolate Custard Tart

1 Preheat the oven to 190°C/375°F/Gas Mark 5, 10 minutes before baking. To make the pastry, put the butter, sugar and vanilla essence into a food processor and blend until creamy. Add the flour and cocoa powder and process until a soft dough forms. Remove the dough, wrap in clingfilm and chill in the refrigerator for at least 1 hour.

2 Roll out the dough between 2 sheets of clingfilm to a 28 cm/11 inch round. Peel off the top sheet of clingfilm and invert the pastry round into a lightly oiled 23 cm/9 inch loose-based flan tin, easing the dough into the base and sides. Prick the base with a fork, then chill in the refrigerator for 1 hour.

3 Place a sheet of nonstick baking parchment and baking beans in the case and bake blind in the preheated oven for 10 minutes. Remove the parchment and beans and bake for a further 5 minutes. Remove and cool.

4 To make the filling, heat the chocolate, cream and half the sugar in a medium saucepan over a low heat, stirring until melted and smooth. Remove from the heat and cool slightly before beating in the egg, egg yolk and crème de cacao. Spread evenly over the pastry case base.

5 Peel the pears, then cut each pear in half and carefully remove the core. Cut each half crossways into thin slices and arrange over the custard, gently fanning the slices towards the centre and pressing into the chocolate custard. Bake in the oven for 10 minutes.

6 Reduce the oven temperature to 180°C/350°F/Gas Mark 4 and sprinkle the surface evenly with the remaining sugar. Bake in the oven for 20–25 minutes, or until the custard is set and the pears are tender and glazed. Remove from the oven and leave to cool slightly. Cut into slices, then serve with spoonfuls of whipped cream.

INGREDIENTS
Cuts into 6–8 slices

*FOR THE CHOCOLATE
  PASTRY:*
*125 g/4 oz unsalted butter,
  softened*
60 g/2½ oz caster sugar
2 tsp vanilla essence
175 g/6 oz plain flour, sifted
40 g/1½ oz cocoa powder
whipped cream, to serve

FOR THE FILLING:
*125 g/4 oz plain dark chocolate,
  chopped*
225 ml/8 fl oz whipping cream
50 g/2 oz caster sugar
1 large egg
1 large egg yolk
1 tbsp crème de cacao
3 ripe pears

Helpful Hint

The chocolate pastry is very soft so rolling it between sheets of cling filmwill make it much easier to handle without having to add a lot of extra flour.

Double Chocolate Truffle Slice

1 Preheat the oven to 200°C/ 400°F/Gas Mark 6, 15 minutes before baking. Prepare the chocolate pastry and chill in the refrigerator, according to instructions.

2 Roll the dough out to a rectangle about 38 x 15 cm/15 x 6 inches and use to line a rectangular loose-based flan tin, trim then chill in the refrigerator for 1 hour.

3 Place a sheet of nonstick baking parchment and baking beans in the pastry case, then bake blind in the preheated oven for 20 minutes. Remove the baking parchment and beans and bake for 10 minutes more. Leave to cool completely.

4 Bring the cream to the boil. Remove from the heat and add the chocolate all at once, stirring until melted and smooth. Beat in the butter, then stir in the brandy liqueur. Leave to cool slightly, then pour into the cooked pastry shell. Refrigerate until set.

5 Cut out 2.5 cm/1 inch strips of nonstick baking parchment. Place over the tart in a crisscross pattern and dust with icing sugar or cocoa.

6 Arrange chocolate leaves, caraque or curls around the edges of the tart. Refrigerate until ready to serve. Leave to soften at room temperature for 15 minutes before serving.

INGREDIENTS
Cuts into 12–14 slices

1 quantity Chocolate Pastry (see page 314)
300 ml/½ pint double cream
300 g/11 oz plain dark chocolate, chopped
25–40 g/1–1½ oz unsalted butter, diced
50 ml/2 fl oz brandy or liqueur
icing sugar or cocoa powder for dusting

Tasty Tip

Liqueurs that would work very well in this recipe include Tia Maria, Kahlua, Cointreau, Grand Marnier, Amaretto and Crème de Menthe.

Double Chocolate Banoffee Tart

1 Preheat the oven to 190°C/ 375°F/Gas Mark 5, 10 minutes before baking. Place the condensed milk in a heavy-based saucepan and place over a gentle heat. Bring to the boil, stirring constantly. Boil gently for about 3–5 minutes or until golden. Remove from the heat and leave to cool.

2 To make the crust, place the biscuits with the melted butter, sugar and ginger in a food processor and blend together. Press into the sides and base of 23 cm/9 inch loose-based flan tin with the back of a spoon. Chill in the refrigerator for 15–20 minutes, then bake in the preheated oven for 5–6 minutes. Remove from the oven and leave to cool.

3 Melt the dark chocolate in a medium-sized saucepan with 150 ml/¼ pint of the whipping cream, the golden syrup and the butter over a low heat. Stir until smooth. Carefully pour into the crumb crust, tilting the tin to

distribute the chocolate layer evenly. Chill in the refrigerator for at least 1 hour or until set.

4 Heat 150 ml/¼ pint of the remaining cream until hot, then add all the white chocolate and stir until melted and smooth. Stir in the vanilla essence and strain into a bowl. Leave to cool to room temperature.

5 Scrape the cooked condensed milk into a bowl and whisk until smooth, adding a little of the remaining cream if too thick. Spread over the chocolate layer, then slice the bananas and arrange evenly over the top.

6 Whisk the remaining cream until soft peaks form. Stir a spoonful of the cream into the white chocolate mixture, then fold in the remaining cream. Spread over the bananas, swirling to the edge. Dust with cocoa powder and chill in the refrigerator until ready to serve.

INGREDIENTS
Cuts into 8 slices

2 x 400 g cans sweetened
  condensed milk
175 g/6 oz plain dark chocolate,
  chopped
600 ml/1 pint whipping cream
1 tbsp golden syrup
25 g/1 oz butter, diced
150 g/5 oz white chocolate,
  grated or finely chopped
1 tsp vanilla essence
2–3 ripe bananas
cocoa powder, for dusting

FOR THE GINGER
  CRUMB CRUST:
24–26 gingernut biscuits, roughly
  crushed
100 g/3½ oz butter, melted
1–2 tbsp sugar, or to taste
½ tsp ground ginger

Tasty Tip

Do not assemble the tart more than 2–3 hours before serving as it will go too soft.

Chocolate Apricot Linzer Torte

1 Preheat the oven to 375°C/ 190°F/Gas Mark 5, 10 minutes before baking. Lightly oil a 28 cm/11 inch flan tin. Place the almonds and half the sugar into a food processor and blend until finely ground. Add the remaining sugar, flour, cocoa powder, cinnamon, salt and orange zest and blend again. Add the diced butter and blend in short bursts to form coarse crumbs. Add the water 1 tablespoon at a time until the mixture starts to come together.

2 Turn onto a lightly floured surface and knead lightly, roll out, then using your finger-tips, press half the dough onto the base and sides of the tin. Prick the base with a fork and chill in the refrigerator. Roll out the remaining dough between 2 pieces of clingfilm to a 28–30.5 cm/11–12 inch round. Slide the round onto a baking sheet and chill in the refrigerator for 30 minutes.

3 For the filling, spread the apricot jam evenly over the chilled pastry base and sprinkle with the chopped chocolate.

4 Slide the dough round onto a lightly floured surface and peel off the top layer of clingfilm. Using a straight edge, cut the round into 1 cm/½ inch strips; allow to soften until slightly flexible. Place half the strips, about 1 cm/½ inch apart, to create a lattice pattern. Press down on each side of each crossing to accentuate the effect. Press the ends of the strips to the edge, cutting off any excess. Bake in the preheated oven for 35 minutes, or until cooked. Leave to cool before dusting with icing sugar and serve cut into slices.

INGREDIENTS
Cuts into 10–12 slices

FOR THE CHOCOLATE ALMOND PASTRY:

75 g/3 oz whole blanched almonds
125 g/4 oz caster sugar
215 g/7½ oz plain flour
2 tbsp cocoa powder
1 tsp ground cinnamon
½ tsp salt
grated zest of 1 orange
225 g/8 oz unsalted butter, diced
2–3 tbsp iced water

FOR THE FILLING:

350 g/12 oz apricot jam
75 g/3 oz milk chocolate, chopped
icing sugar, for dusting

Tasty Tip

When making the pastry do not allow the dough to form into a ball or it will be tough.

Chocolate Peanut Butter Pie

1 Place the wafers or cookies with the melted butter, sugar and vanilla essence in a food processor and blend together. Press into the base of 23 cm/9 inch pie plate or flat tin. Chill in the refrigerator for 15–20 minutes.

2 Place 3 tablespoons of cold water in a bowl and sprinkle over the powdered gelatine, leave until softened.

3 Blend half the sugar with the cornflour and salt in a heavy-based saucepan and gradually whisk in the milk. Bring to the boil, then reduce the heat and boil gently for 1–2 minutes, or until thickened and smooth, stirring constantly.

4 Beat all the egg yolks together then whisk in half the hot milk mixture and whisk until blended. Whisk in the remaining milk mixture, return to a clean saucepan and cook gently until the mixture comes to the boil and thickens.

Boil, stirring vigorously, for 1 minute, then pour a quarter of the custard into a bowl. Add the chopped chocolate and rum or vanilla essence and stir until the chocolate has melted and the mixture is smooth. Pour into the chocolate crust and chill in the refrigerator until set.

5 Whisk the softened gelatine into the remaining custard and whisk until thoroughly dissolved. Whisk in the peanut butter until melted and smooth. Whisk the egg whites until stiff, then whisk in the remaining sugar, 1 tablespoon at a time.

6 Whip the cream until soft peaks form. Fold 125 ml/4 fl oz of the cream into the custard, then fold in the egg whites. Spread the peanut butter cream mixture over the chocolate layer. Spread or pipe over the surface with the remaining cream, forming decorative swirls. Decorate with chocolate curls and chill in the refrigerator until ready to serve.

INGREDIENTS
Cuts into 8 slices

22–24 chocolate wafers or peanut butter cookies
100 g/3½ oz butter, melted
1–2 tbsp sugar
1 tsp vanilla essence
1½ tbsp gelatine
100 g/3½ oz caster sugar
1 tbsp cornflour
½ tsp salt
225 ml/8 fl oz milk
2 large eggs, separated
2 large egg yolks
100 g/3½ oz plain dark chocolate, chopped
2 tbsp rum or 2 tsp vanilla essence
125 g/4 oz smooth peanut butter
300 ml/½ pint whipping cream
chocolate curls, to decorate

Mini Pistachio & Chocolate Strudels

1 Preheat the oven to 170°C/ 325°F/Gas Mark 3, 10 minutes before baking. Lightly oil 2 large baking sheets. For the filling, mix the finely chopped pistachio nuts, the sugar and dark chocolate in a bowl. Sprinkle with the rosewater and stir lightly together and reserve.

2 Cut each filo pastry sheet into 4 to make 23 x 18 cm/ 9 x 7 inch rectangles. Place 1 rectangle on the work surface and brush with a little melted butter. Place another rectangle on top and brush with a little more butter. Sprinkle with a little caster sugar and spread about 1 dessertspoon of the filling along one short end. Fold the short end over the filling, then fold in the long edges and roll up. Place on the baking sheet seam-side down. Continue with the remaining pastry sheets and filling until both are used.

3 Brush each strudel with the remaining melted butter and sprinkle with a little caster sugar. Bake in the preheated oven for 20 minutes, or until golden brown and the pastry is crisp.

4 Remove from the oven and leave on the baking sheet for 2 minutes, then transfer to a wire rack. Dust with icing sugar. Place the melted white chocolate in a small piping bag fitted with a plain writing pipe and pipe squiggles over the strudel. Leave to set before serving.

INGREDIENTS
Makes 24

5 large sheets filo pastry
50 g/2 oz butter, melted
1–2 tbsp caster sugar for
  sprinkling
50 g/2 oz white chocolate,
  melted, to decorate

FOR THE FILLING:
125 g/4 oz unsalted pistachios,
  finely chopped
3 tbsp caster sugar
50 g/2 oz plain dark chocolate,
  finely chopped
1–2 tsp rosewater
1 tbsp icing sugar for dusting

Tasty Tip
Keep the unused filo pastry covered with a clean damp tea towel to prevent it from drying out.

'Mars' Bar Mousse in Filo Cups

1 Preheat the oven to 180°C/ 350°F/Gas Mark 4, 10 minutes before baking. Lightly oil 6 x 150 ml/¼ pint ramekins. Cut the filo pastry into 15 cm/6 inch squares, place 1 square on the work surface, then brush with a little of the melted butter, sprinkle with a little caster sugar. Butter a second square and lay it over the first at an angle, sprinkle with a little more caster sugar and repeat with 2 more pastry squares.

2 Press the assembled filo pastry into the oiled ramekin, pressing into the base to make a flat bottom and keeping the edges pointing up. Continue making the cups in this way, then place on a baking sheet and bake in the preheated oven for 10–15 minutes or until crisp and golden. Remove and leave to cool before removing the filo cups from the ramekins. Leave until cold.

3 Melt the 'Mars' bars and milk in a small saucepan,

stirring constantly until melted and smooth. Leave to cool for 10 minutes, stirring occasionally.

4 Whisk the cream until thick and stir a spoonful into the melted 'Mars' bar mixture, then fold in the remaining cream. Whisk the egg white until stiff and fold into the 'Mars' bar mixture together with the cocoa powder. Chill the mousse in the refrigerator for 2–3 hours.

5 For the topping, boil 125 ml/ 4 fl oz of the whipping cream, add the grated white chocolate and vanilla essence and stir until smooth, then strain into a bowl and leave to cool. Whisk the remaining cream until thick, then fold into the white chocolate cream mixture.

6 Spoon the mousse into the filo cups, cover with the cream mixture and sprinkle with grated chocolate. Chill in the refrigerator before serving with chocolate sauce, if liked.

INGREDIENTS
Serves 6

6 large sheets filo pastry, thawed
if frozen
40 g/1½ oz unsalted butter,
melted
1 tbsp caster sugar
3 x 60 g/2½ oz 'Mars' bars,
coarsely chopped
1½ tbsp milk
300 ml/½ pint double cream
1 large egg white
1 tsp cocoa powder
1 tbsp plain dark grated chocolate
chocolate sauce (see page 332), to
serve (optional)

FOR TOPPING:
300 ml/½ pint whipping cream
125 g/4 oz white chocolate,
grated
1 tsp vanilla essence

Tasty Tip

When working with filo pastry, keep the dough that you are not using wrapped so it does not dry out.

Raspberry Chocolate Ganache & Berry Tartlets

1 Preheat the oven to 200°C/400°F/Gas Mark 6, 15 minutes before cooking. Make the chocolate pastry and use to line 8 x 7.5 cm/3 inch tartlet tins. Bake blind in the preheated oven for 12 minutes.

2 Place 400 ml/14 fl oz of the cream and half of the raspberry jam in a saucepan and bring to the boil, whisking constantly to dissolve the jam. Remove from the heat and add the chocolate all at once, stirring until the chocolate has melted.

3 Pour into the pastry-lined tartlet tins, shaking gently to distribute the ganache evenly. Chill in the refrigerator for 1 hour or until set.

4 Place the berries in a large shallow bowl. Heat the remaining raspberry jam with half the framboise liqueur over a medium heat until melted and bubbling. Drizzle over the berries and toss gently to coat.

5 Divide the berries among the tartlets, piling them up if necessary. Chill in the refrigerator until ready to serve.

6 Remove the tartlets from the refrigerator for at least 30 minutes before serving. Using an electric whisk, whisk the remaining cream with the caster sugar and the remaining framboise liqueur until it is thick and softly peaking. Serve with the tartlets and crème fraîche.

INGREDIENTS
Serves 8

1 quantity Chocolate Pastry (see page 314)
600 ml/1 pint whipping cream
275 g/10 oz seedless raspberry jam
225 g/8 oz plain dark chocolate, chopped
700 g/1½ lb raspberries or other summer berries
50 ml/2 fl oz framboise liqueur
1 tbsp caster sugar
crème fraîche, to serve

Tasty Tip
Try substituting an equal quantity of white chocolate for the plain chocolate in this recipe, as raspberries go very well with it.

White Chocolate & Macadamia Tartlets

1 Preheat the oven to 200°C/400°F/Gas Mark 6, 15 minutes before baking. Roll the pastry out on a lightly floured surface and use to line 10 x 7.5–9 cm/3–3½ inch tartlet tins. Line each tin with a small piece of tinfoil and fill with baking beans. Arrange on a baking sheet and bake blind in the preheated oven for 10 minutes. Remove the tinfoil and baking beans and leave to cool.

2 Beat the eggs with the sugar until light and creamy, then beat in the golden syrup, the butter, cream and vanilla or almond essence. Stir in the macadamia nuts. Sprinkle 100 g/3½ oz of the chopped white chocolate equally over the bases of the tartlet cases and divide the mixture evenly among them.

3 Reduce the oven temperature to 180°C/350°F/Gas Mark 4 and bake the tartlets for 20 minutes, or until the tops are puffy and golden and the filling is set. Remove from the oven and leave to cool on a wire rack.

4 Carefully remove the tartlets from their tins and arrange closely together on the wire rack. Melt the remaining white chocolate and, using a teaspoon or a small paper piping bag, drizzle the melted chocolate over the surface of the tartlets in a zig-zag pattern. Serve slightly warm or at room temperature.

INGREDIENTS
Makes 10

1 quantity Sweet Shortcrust Pastry (see page 310)
2 medium eggs
50 g/2 oz caster sugar
250 ml/9 fl oz golden syrup
40 g/1½ oz butter, melted
50 ml/2 fl oz whipping cream
1 tsp vanilla or almond essence
225 g/8 oz unsalted macadamia nuts, coarsely chopped
150 g/5 oz white chocolate, coarsely chopped

Food Fact

Macadamia nuts come from Hawaii and are large, crisp, buttery flavoured nuts. They are readily available from supermarkets.

Chocolaty Puffs

1 Preheat the oven to 220°C/ 425°F/Gas Mark 7, 15 minutes before baking. Lightly oil a large baking sheet. To make the choux pastry, sift the flour and cocoa powder together. Place 250 ml/9 fl oz of water, the salt, sugar and butter in a saucepan and bring to the boil. Remove from the heat and add the flour mixture all at once, beating vigorously with a wooden spoon until the mixture forms a ball in the centre of the saucepan. Return to the heat and cook for 1 minute stirring, then cool slightly.

2 Using an electric mixer, beat in 4 of the eggs, 1 at a time, beating well after each addition. Beat the last egg and add a little at a time until the dough is thick and shiny and just falls from a spoon when tapped lightly on the side of the saucepan.

3 Pipe or spoon 12 large puffs onto the prepared baking sheet, leaving space

between them. Cook in the preheated oven for 30–35 minutes, or until puffy and golden. Remove from the oven, slice off the top third of each bun and return to the oven for 5 minutes to dry out. Remove and leave to cool.

4 For the filling, heat the chocolate with 125 ml/ 4 fl oz of the double cream and 1 tablespoon of caster sugar, if using, stirring until smooth, then leave to cool. Whisk the remaining cream until soft peaks form and stir in the crème de cacao, if using. Quickly fold the cream into the chocolate, then spoon or pipe into the choux buns and place the lids on top.

5 Place all the ingredients for the sauce in a small saucepan and heat gently, stirring until smooth. Remove from the heat and leave to cool, stirring occasionally until thickened. Pour over the puffs and serve immediately.

INGREDIENTS
Makes 12 large puffs

FOR THE CHOUX PASTRY:
150 g/5 oz plain flour
2 tbsp cocoa powder
½ tsp salt
1 tbsp sugar
125 g/4 oz butter, cut into pieces
5 large eggs

FOR THE CHOCOLATE CREAM FILLING:
225 g/8 oz plain dark chocolate, chopped
600 ml/1 pint double cream
1 tbsp caster sugar (optional)
2 tbsp crème de cacao (optional)

FOR THE CHOCOLATE SAUCE:
225 g/8 oz plain dark chocolate
300 ml/½ pint whipping cream
50 g/2 oz butter, diced
1–2 tbsp golden syrup
1 tsp vanilla essence

Rice Pudding & Chocolate Tart

1 Preheat the oven to 200°C/ 400°F/Gas Mark 6, 15 minutes before baking. Roll the chocolate pastry out and use to line a 23 cm/9 inch flan tin. Place a sheet of nonstick baking parchment and baking beans in the tin and bake blind in the preheated oven for 15 minutes.

2 For the ganache, place the cream and golden syrup in a heavy-based saucepan and bring to the boil. Remove from the heat and add the chocolate all at once, stirring until smooth. Beat in the butter and vanilla essence, pour into the baked pastry case and reserve.

3 For the rice pudding, bring the milk and salt to the boil in a medium-sized saucepan. Split the vanilla pod and scrape

the seeds into the milk and add the vanilla pod. Sprinkle in the rice, then bring to the boil. Reduce the heat and simmer until the rice is tender and the milk is creamy. Remove from the heat.

4 Blend the cornflour and sugar together, then stir in 2 table-spoons of water to make a paste. Stir a little of the hot rice mixture into the cornflour mixture, then stir the cornflour mixture into the rice. Bring to the boil and cook, stirring constantly until thickened. Set the base of the saucepan into a bowl of iced water and stir until cooled and thickened. Spoon the rice pudding into the tart, smoothing the surface. Leave to set. Dust with cocoa powder, decorate with a few blueberries and fresh mint to serve.

INGREDIENTS
Serves 8

1 quantity Chocolate Pastry
  (see page 314)
1 tsp cocoa powder for dusting

FOR THE CHOCOLATE GANACHE:
200 ml/7 fl oz double cream
1 tbsp golden syrup
175 g/6 oz plain dark chocolate,
  chopped
1 tbsp butter
1 tsp vanilla essence

FOR THE RICE PUDDING:
1 litre/1¾ pints milk
½ tsp salt
1 vanilla pod
100 g/3½ oz long-grain white
  rice
1 tbsp cornflour
2 tbsp sugar

TO DECORATE:
few fresh blueberries
sprigs of fresh mint

Helpful Hint

Baking beans are usually made of ceramic, which hold the heat well and help to cook the pastry case. If you don't have ceramic baking beans, you can use rice or dried pulses instead.

Chocolate Fruit Pizza

1 Preheat the oven to 200°C/ 400°F/Gas Mark 6, 15 minutes before baking. Lightly oil a large baking sheet. Roll the prepared pastry out to a 23 cm/ 9 inch round and place the pastry round onto the baking sheet, and crimp the edges. Using a fork, prick the base all over and chill in the refrigerator for 30 minutes.

2 Line the pastry with tinfoil and weigh down with an ovenproof flat dinner plate or base of a large flan tin and bake blind in the preheated oven until the edges begin to colour. Remove from the oven and discard the weight and tinfoil.

3 Carefully spread the chocolate spread over the pizza base and arrange the peach and nectarine slices around the outside edge in overlapping circles. Toss the berries with the plain chocolate and arrange in the centre. Drizzle with the melted butter and sprinkle with the sugar.

4 Bake in the preheated oven for 10–12 minutes, or until the fruit begins to soften. Transfer the pizza to a wire rack.

5 Sprinkle the white chocolate and hazelnuts over the surface and return to the oven for 1 minute or until the chocolate begins to soften. If the pastry starts to darken too much, cover the edge with strips of tinfoil. Remove to a wire rack and leave to cool. Decorate with sprigs of fresh mint and serve warm.

INGREDIENTS
Serves 8

1 quantity Sweet Shortcrust Pastry (see page 310)
2 tbsp chocolate spread
1 small peach, very thinly sliced
1 small nectarine, very thinly sliced
150 g/5 oz strawberries, halved or quartered
75 g/3 oz raspberries
75 g/3 oz blueberries
75 g/3 oz plain dark chocolate, coarsely chopped
1 tbsp butter, melted
2 tbsp sugar
75 g/3 oz white chocolate, chopped
1 tbsp hazelnuts, toasted and chopped
sprigs of fresh mint, to decorate

Helpful Hint

Alternatively, preheat the grill and grill the pizza until the fruits begin to caramelise and the white chocolate begins to melt, do not overheat as the white chocolate could split and become gritty.

Chocolate Lemon Tartlets

1 Preheat the oven to 200°C/ 400°F/Gas Mark 6, 15 minutes before baking. Roll the prepared pastry out on a lightly floured surface and use to line 10 x 7.5 cm/3 inch tartlet tins. Place a small piece of crumpled tinfoil in each and bake blind in the preheated oven for 12 minutes. Remove from the oven and leave to cool.

2 Bring the cream to the boil, then remove from the heat and add the chocolate all at once. Stir until smooth and melted. Beat in the butter and vanilla essence and pour into the tartlets and leave to cool.

3 Beat the lemon curd until soft and spoon a thick layer over the chocolate in each tartlet, spreading gently to the edges. Do not chill in the refrigerator or the chocolate will be too firm.

4 Place the prepared custard sauce into a large bowl and gradually whisk in the cream and almond essence until the custard is smooth and runny.

5 To serve, spoon a little custard onto a plate and place a tartlet in the centre. Sprinkle with grated chocolate and almonds, then serve.

INGREDIENTS
Makes 10

1 quantity Sweet Shortcrust Pastry (see page 310)
175 ml/6 fl oz double cream
175 g/6 oz plain dark chocolate, chopped
2 tbsp butter, diced
1 tsp vanilla essence
350 g/12 oz lemon curd
225 ml/8 fl oz prepared custard sauce
225 ml/8 fl oz single cream
½–1 tsp almond essence

TO DECORATE:
grated chocolate
toasted flaked almonds

Tasty Tip

Lemon curd is very easy to make. In a medium-sized heatproof bowl, mix together 175 g/6 oz of caster sugar, the grated rind and juice of 2 large lemons and 4 large eggs. Add 125 g/4 oz cubed unsalted butter and place the bowl over a saucepan of gently simmering water. Stir often until thickened, about 20 minutes. Leave to cool and use as above.

Fudgy Mocha Pie
with Espresso Custard Sauce

1 Preheat the oven to 180°C/
350°F/Gas Mark 4, 10
minutes before serving. Line
with tinfoil or lightly oil a deep
23 cm/9 inch pie plate. Melt the
chocolate and butter in a small
saucepan over a low heat and
stir until smooth, then reserve.
Dissolve the instant espresso
powder in 1–2 tablespoons of
hot water and reserve.

2 Beat the eggs with the
golden syrup, the sugar, the
dissolved espresso powder, the
cinnamon and milk until blended.
Add the melted chocolate mixture
and whisk until blended. Pour
into the pie plate.

3 Bake the pie in the
preheated oven for about
20–25 minutes, or until the
edge has set but the centre is
still very soft. Leave to cool,
remove from plate then dust
lightly with icing sugar.

4 To make the custard
sauce, dissolve the instant
espresso powder with 2–3
tablespoons of hot water, then
whisk into the prepared custard
sauce. Slowly add the single
cream, whisking constantly,
then stir in the coffee-flavoured
liqueur, if using. Serve slices of
the pie in a pool of espresso
custard with strawberries.

INGREDIENTS
Cuts into 10 slices

125 g/4 oz plain dark chocolate,
chopped
125 g/4 oz butter, diced
1 tbsp instant espresso powder
4 large eggs
1 tbsp golden syrup
125 g/4 oz sugar
1 tsp ground cinnamon
3 tbsp milk
icing sugar, for dusting
few fresh strawberries, to serve

ESPRESSO CUSTARD SAUCE:

2–3 tbsp instant espresso
powder, or to taste
225 ml/8 fl oz prepared custard
sauce
225 ml/8 fl oz single cream
2 tbsp coffee-flavoured liqueur
(optional)

Helpful Hint

There are many brands of ready-made custard
available, including brands in tins, but many supermarkets
are now selling fresh custard in tubs that can usually be
found with the dairy products.

Chocolate Pecan Angel Pie

1 Preheat the oven to 110°C/ 225°F/Gas Mark ¼. 5 minutes before baking. Lightly oil a 23 cm/9 inch pie plate.

2 Using an electric mixer, whisk the egg whites and cream of tartar on a low speed until foamy, then increase the speed and beat until soft peaks form.

3 Gradually beat in the sugar, 1 tablespoon at a time, beating well after each addition, until stiff glossy peaks form and the sugar is completely dissolved. (Test by rubbing a bit of meringue between your fingers – if gritty, continue beating.) This will take about 15 minutes.

4 Beat in 2 teaspoons of the vanilla essence, then fold in the nuts and the chocolate chips.

5 Spread the meringue evenly in the pie plate, making a shallow well in the centre and slightly building up the sides.

6 Bake in the preheated oven for 1–1¼ hours or until a golden creamy colour. Lower the oven temperature if the meringue colours too quickly. Turn the oven off, but do not remove the meringue. Leave the oven door ajar (about 5 cm/2 inches) for about 1 hour. Transfer to a wire rack until cold.

7 Pour the double cream into a small saucepan and bring to the boil. Remove from the heat, add the grated white chocolate and stir until melted. Add the remaining vanilla essence and leave to cool, then whip until thick.

8 Spoon the white chocolate whipped cream into the pie shell, piling it high and swirling decoratively. Decorate with fresh raspberries and chocolate curls. Chill in the refrigerator for 2 hours before serving. When ready to serve, add sprigs of mint on the top and cut into slices.

INGREDIENTS
Cuts into 8–10 slices

4 large egg whites
¼ tsp cream of tartar
225 g/8 oz caster sugar
3 tsp vanilla essence
100 g/3½ oz pecans, lightly
  toasted and chopped
75 g/3 oz dark chocolate chips
150 ml/¼ pint double cream
150 g/5 oz white chocolate,
  grated

TO DECORATE:
fresh raspberries
dark chocolate curls
few sprigs of fresh mint

Helpful Hint

The meringue needs to be cooked gently at a low temperature and then allowed to cool in the oven so that it can become crisp and dry without cracking too much.

Frozen Mississippi Mud Pie

1 Prepare the crumb crust and use to line a 23 cm/9 inch loose-based flan tin and freeze for 30 minutes.

2 Soften the ice creams at room temperature for about 25 minutes. Spoon the chocolate ice cream into the crumb crust, spreading it evenly over the base, then spoon the coffee ice cream over the chocolate ice cream, mounding it slightly in the centre. Return to the freezer to refreeze the ice cream.

3 For the topping, heat the dark chocolate with the cream, golden syrup and vanilla essence in a saucepan. Stir until the chocolate has melted and is smooth. Pour into a bowl and chill in the refrigerator, stirring occasionally, until cold but not set.

4 Spread the cooled chocolate mixture over the top of the frozen pie. Sprinkle with the chocolate and return to the freezer for 1½ hours or until firm. Serve at room temperature.

INGREDIENTS
Cuts 6–8 slices

1 quantity Ginger Crumb Crust
(see page 318)
600 ml/1 pint chocolate ice cream
600 ml/1 pint coffee-flavoured
ice cream

FOR THE CHOCOLATE TOPPING:
175 g/6 oz plain dark chocolate,
chopped
50 ml/2 fl oz single cream
1 tbsp golden syrup
1 tsp vanilla essence
50 g/2 oz coarsely grated white
and milk chocolate

Helpful Hint

Use the best-quality ice cream that is available for this recipe. Look for chocolate ice cream with added ingredients such as chocolate chips, pieces of toffee or rippled chocolate. If preferred you can add some raspberries, chopped nuts or small pieces of chopped white chocolate to both the chocolate and coffee ice cream.

Tasty Tip

As an alternative, slice the frozen pie and serve with the chocolate topping while it is still hot.

White Chocolate Mousse & Strawberry Tart

1 Preheat the oven to 200°C/ 400°F/Gas Mark 6, 15 minutes before baking. Roll the prepared pastry out on a lightly floured surface and use to line a 25.5 cm/10 inch flan tin.

2 Line with either tinfoil or nonstick baking parchment and baking beans then bake blind in the preheated oven for 15–20 minutes. Remove the tinfoil or baking parchment and return to the oven for a further 5 minutes.

3 To make the mousse, place the white chocolate with 2 tablespoons of water and 125 ml/4 fl oz of the cream in a saucepan and heat gently, stirring until the chocolate has melted and is smooth. Remove from the heat, stir in the kirsch or framboise liqueur and cool.

4 Whip the remaining cream until soft peaks form. Fold a spoonful of the cream into the

cooled white chocolate mixture, then fold in the remaining cream. If using, whisk the egg whites until stiff and gently fold into the white chocolate cream mixture to make a softer, lighter mousse. Chill in the refrigerator for 15–20 minutes.

5 Heat the strawberry jam with the kirsch or framboise liqueur and brush or spread half the mixture onto the pastry base. Leave to cool.

6 Spread the chilled chocolate mousse over the jam and arrange the sliced strawberries in concentric circles over the mousse. If necessary, reheat the strawberry jam and glaze the strawberries lightly.

7 Chill the tart in the refrigerator for about 3–4 hours, or until the chocolate mousse has set. Cut into slices and serve.

INGREDIENTS
Cuts into 10 slices

1 quantity Sweet Shortcrust Pastry (see page 310)
60 g/2½ oz strawberry jam
1–2 tbsp kirsch or framboise liqueur
450–700 g/1–1½ lb ripe strawberries, sliced lengthways

FOR THE WHITE CHOCOLATE MOUSSE:
250 g/9 oz white chocolate, chopped
350 ml/12 oz double cream
3 tbsp kirsch or framboise liqueur
1–2 large egg whites (optional)

Helpful Hint

This recipe contains raw egg whites, which should be eaten with caution by vulnerable groups including the elderly, young and pregnant women. If you are worried, omit them from the recipe.

Chocolate Raspberry Mille Feuille

1 Preheat the oven to 200°C/400°F/Gas Mark 6, 15 minutes before baking. Lightly oil a large baking sheet and sprinkle with a little water. Roll out the pastry on a lightly floured surface to a rectangle about 43 x 28 cm/17 x 11 inches. Cut into 3 long strips. Mark each strip crossways at 6.5 cm/2½ inch intervals using a sharp knife; this will make cutting the baked pastry easier and neater. Carefully transfer to the baking sheet, keeping the edges as straight as possible.

2 Bake in the preheated oven for 20 minutes or until well risen and golden brown. Place on a wire rack and leave to cool. Carefully transfer each rectangle to a work surface and using a sharp knife, trim the long edges straight. Cut along the knife marks to make 18 rectangles.

3 Place all the ingredients for the raspberry sauce in a food processor and blend until smooth. If the purée is too thick, add a little water. Taste and adjust the sweetness if necessary. Strain into a bowl, cover and chill in the refrigerator.

4 Place 1 pastry rectangle on the work surface flat-side down, spread with a little chocolate ganache and sprinkle with a few fresh raspberries. Spread a second rectangle with a little ganache, place over the first, pressing gently, then sprinkle with a few raspberries. Place a third rectangle on top, flat-side up, and spread with a little chocolate ganache.

5 Arrange some raspberries on top and dust lightly with a little icing sugar. Repeat with the remaining pastry rectangles, chocolate ganache and fresh raspberries.

6 Chill in the refrigerator until required and serve with the raspberry sauce and any remaining fresh raspberries.

INGREDIENTS
Serves 6

450 g/1 lb puff pastry, thawed if frozen
1 quantity Chocolate Raspberry Ganache (see page 328), chilled
700 g/1½ lbs fresh raspberries, plus extra for decorating
icing sugar for dusting

FOR THE RASPBERRY SAUCE:
225 g/8 oz fresh raspberries
2 tbsp seedless raspberry jam
1–2 tbsp caster sugar, or to taste
2 tbsp lemon juice or framboise liqueur

Helpful Hint

If you prefer, make 1 big *mille feuille* by leaving the 3 strips whole in step 2. Slice the finished *mille feuille* with a sharp serrated knife.

Lemon & Ginger Buns

1 Preheat the oven to 220°C/ 425°F/Gas Mark 7 15 minutes before baking. Cut the butter or margarine into small pieces and place in a large bowl.

2 Sift the flour, baking powder, ginger and salt together and add to the butter with the lemon rind.

3 Using the fingertips rub the butter into the flour and spice mixture until it resembles coarse breadcrumbs.

4 Stir in the sugar, sultanas, chopped mixed peel and stem ginger.

5 Add the egg and lemon juice to the mixture, then using a round bladed knife stir well to mix. (The mixture should be quite stiff and just holding together.)

6 Place heaped tablespoons of the mixture on to a lightly oiled baking tray, making sure that the dollops of mixture are well apart.

7 Using a fork rough up the edges of the buns and bake in the preheated oven for 12–15 minutes.

8 Leave the buns to cool for 5 minutes before transferring to a wire rack until cold, then serve. Otherwise store the buns in an airtight tin and eat within 3–5 days.

INGREDIENTS
Makes 15

175 g/6 oz butter or margarine
350 g/12 oz plain flour
2 tsp baking powder
½ tsp ground ginger
pinch of salt
finely grated rind of 1 lemon
175 g/6 oz soft light brown sugar
125 g/4 oz sultanas
75 g/3 oz chopped mixed peel
25 g/1 oz stem ginger,
  finely chopped
1 medium egg
juice of 1 lemon

Tasty Tip

For a gooey, sticky treat, brush the buns with a little syrup from the jar of stem ginger and scatter with some extra finely chopped stem ginger, as soon as they have been removed from the oven.

Apple & Cinnamon Crumble-top Cake

1 Preheat the oven to 180°C/ 350°F/Gas Mark 4 10 minutes before baking. Lightly oil and line the base of a 20.5 cm/8 inch deep round cake tin with greaseproof or baking paper.

2 Finely chop the apples and mix with the lemon juice. Reserve while making the cake.

3 For the crumble topping, sift the flour and cinnamon together into a large bowl.

4 Rub the butter or margarine into the flour and cinnamon until the mixture resembles coarse breadcrumbs.

5 Stir the sugar into the breadcrumbs and reserve.

6 For the base, cream the butter or margarine and sugar together until light and fluffy. Gradually beat the eggs into the sugar and butter mixture a little at a time until all the egg has been added.

7 Sift the flour and gently fold in with a metal spoon or rubber spatula.

8 Spoon into the base of the prepared cake tin. Arrange the apple pieces on top, then lightly stir the milk into the crumble mixture.

9 Scatter the crumble mixture over the apples and bake in the preheated oven for 1½ hours. Serve cold with cream or custard.

INGREDIENTS
Cuts into 8 slices

FOR THE TOPPING:
350 g/12 oz eating apples, peeled
1 tbsp lemon juice
125 g/4 oz self-raising flour
1 tsp ground cinnamon
75 g/3 oz butter or margarine
75 g/3 oz demerara sugar
1 tbsp milk

FOR THE BASE:
125 g/4 oz butter or margarine
125 g/4 oz caster sugar
2 medium eggs
150 g/5 oz self-raising flour
Cream or freshly made custard,
 to serve.

Tasty Tip
For a crunchier-textured topping, stir in 50 g/2 oz of chopped mixed nuts and seeds to the crumble mixture in step 5.

Chocolate & Coconut Cake

1 Preheat the oven to 180°C/ 350°F/Gas Mark 4 10 minutes before baking. Melt the chocolate in a small bowl placed over a saucepan of gently simmering water, ensuring that the base of the bowl does not touch the water. When the chocolate has melted, stir until smooth and allow to cool.

2 Lightly oil and line the bases of 2 x 18 cm/7 inch sandwich tins with greaseproof or baking paper. In a large bowl beat the butter or margarine and sugar together with a wooden spoon until light and creamy. Beat in the eggs a little at a time, then stir in the melted chocolate.

3 Sift the flour and cocoa powder together and gently fold into the chocolate mixture

with a metal spoon or rubber spatula. Add the desiccated coconut and mix lightly. Divide between the 2 prepared tins and smooth the tops.

4 Bake in the preheated oven for 25–30 minutes, or until a skewer comes out clean when inserted into the centre of the cake. Allow to cool in the tin for 5 minutes, then turn out, discard the lining paper and leave on a wire rack until cold.

5 Beat together the butter or margarine and creamed coconut until light. Add the icing sugar and mix well. Spread half of the icing on 1 cake and press the cakes together. Spread the remaining icing over the top, sprinkle with the coconut and serve.

INGREDIENTS
Cuts into 8 slices

125 g/4 oz plain dark chocolate, roughly chopped
175 g/6 oz butter or margarine
175 g/6 oz caster sugar
3 medium eggs, beaten
15 g/6 oz self-raising flour
1 tbsp cocoa powder
50 g/2 oz desiccated coconut

FOR THE ICING:
125 g/4 oz butter or margarine
2 tbsp creamed coconut
225 g/8 oz icing sugar
25 g/1 oz desiccated coconut, lightly toasted

Tasty Tip

Why not experiment with the chocolate in this recipe? For a different taste, try using orange-flavoured dark chocolate or add 1–2 tablespoons of rum when melting the chocolate.

Citrus Cake

1 Preheat the oven to 325°C/ 170°F/ Gas Mark 3 10 minutes before baking. Lightly oil and line the base of a round 20.5 cm/8 inch deep cake tin with baking paper.

2 In a large bowl, cream the sugar and butter or margarine together until light and fluffy. Whisk the eggs together and beat into the creamed mixture a little at a time.

3 Beat in the orange juice with 1 tablespoon of the flour. Sift the remaining flour on to a large plate several times, then with a metal spoon or rubber spatula, fold into the creamed mixture.

4 Spoon into the prepared cake tin. Stir the finely grated orange rind into the lemon curd and dot randomly across the top of the mixture.

5 Using a fine skewer swirl the lemon curd through the cake mixture. Bake in the preheated oven for 35 minutes, until risen and golden. Allow to cool for 5 minutes in the tin, then turn out carefully on to a wire rack.

6 Sift the icing sugar into a bowl, add the grated lemon rind and juice and stir well to mix. When the cake is cold cover the top with the icing and serve.

INGREDIENTS
Cuts into 6 slices

175 g/6 oz golden caster sugar
175 g/6 oz butter or margarine
3 medium eggs
2 tbsp orange juice
175 g/6 oz self-raising flour
finely grated rind of 2 oranges
5 tbsp lemon curd
125 g/4 oz icing sugar
finely grated rind of 1 lemon
1 tbsp freshly squeezed
   lemon juice

Food Fact

Repeated sifting as in step 3 removes impurities from the flour while adding air to it. Using golden caster sugar gives a richer sweeter taste than normal caster sugar and contrasts particularly well with the citrus flavours in this cake.

Victoria Sponge with Mango & Mascarpone

1 Preheat the oven to 190°C/ 375°F/Gas Mark 5 10 minutes before baking. Lightly oil 2 x 18 cm/7 inch sandwich tins and lightly dust with caster sugar and flour, tapping the tins to remove any excess.

2 In a large bowl cream the butter or margarine and sugar together with a wooden spoon until light and creamy.

3 In another bowl mix the eggs and vanilla essence together. Sift the flour several times on to a plate.

4 Beat a little egg into the butter and sugar, then a little flour and beat well.

5 Continue adding the flour and eggs alternately, beating between each addition, until the mixture is well mixed and smooth. Divide the mixture between the 2 prepared cake tins, level the surface, then using the back of a large spoon, make a slight dip in the centre of each cake.

6 Bake in the preheated oven for 25–30 minutes, until the centre of the cake springs back when gently pressed with a clean finger. Turn out on to a wire rack and leave the cakes until cold.

7 Beat the icing sugar and mascarpone cheese together, then chop the mango into small cubes.

8 Use half the mascarpone and mango to sandwich the cakes together. Spread the rest of the mascarpone on top, decorate with the remaining mango and serve. Otherwise lightly cover and store in the refrigerator. Use within 3–4 days.

INGREDIENTS
Cuts into 8 slices

175 g/6 oz caster sugar, plus extra for dusting
175 g/6 oz self-raising flour, plus extra for dusting
175 g/6 oz butter or margarine
3 large eggs
1 tsp vanilla essence
25 g/1 oz icing sugar
250 g/9 oz mascarpone cheese
1 large ripe mango, peeled

Tasty Tip

Mango has been used in this recipe, but 125 g/4 oz of mashed strawberries could be used instead. Reserve a few whole strawberries, slice and use to decorate the cake.

Almond Cake

1 Preheat the oven to 150°C/300°F/Gas Mark 2. Lightly oil and line the base of a 20.5 cm/8 inch deep round cake tin with greaseproof or baking paper.

2 Cream together the butter or margarine and sugar with a wooden spoon until light and fluffy.

3 Beat the eggs and essences together. Gradually add to the sugar and butter mixture and mix well between each addition.

4 Sift the flour and mix with the ground almonds. Beat into the egg mixture until mixed well and smooth. Pour into the prepared cake tin.

5 Roughly chop the whole almonds and scatter over the cake before baking in the preheated oven.

6 Bake in the preheated oven for 45 minutes, or until golden and risen and a skewer inserted into the centre of the cake comes out clean.

7 Remove from the tin and leave to cool on a wire rack. Melt the chocolate in a small bowl placed over a saucepan of gently simmering water, stirring until smooth and free of lumps.

8 Drizzle the melted chocolate over the cooled cake and serve once the chocolate has set.

INGREDIENTS
Cuts into 8 slices

225 g/8 oz butter or margarine
225 g/8 oz caster sugar
3 large eggs
1 tsp vanilla essence
1 tsp almond essence
125 g/4 oz self-raising flour
175 g/6 oz ground almonds
50 g/2 oz whole
  almonds, blanched
25 g/1 oz plain dark chocolate

Tasty Tip

Baking with ground almonds helps to keep the cake moist as well as adding a slight nutty flavour to the cake. 1–2 tablespoons orange water can be added with the zest of 1 orange in step 4 if a fragrant citrus flavour is desired, but do omit the vanilla essence.

Lemon Drizzle Cake

1 Preheat the oven to 180°C/ 350°F/Gas Mark 4 10 minutes before baking. Lightly oil and line the base of an 18 cm/7 inch square cake tin with baking paper.

2 In a large bowl, cream the butter or margarine and sugar together until soft and fluffy.

3 Beat the eggs, then gradually add a little of the egg to the creamed mixture, adding 1 tablespoon of flour after each addition.

4 Finely grate the rind from 1 of the lemons and stir into the creamed mixture, beating well until smooth. Squeeze the juice from the lemon, strain, then stir into the mixture.

5 Spoon into the prepared tin, level the surface and

bake in the preheated oven for 25–30 minutes. Using a zester remove the peel from the last lemon and mix with 25 g/1 oz of the granulated sugar and reserve.

6 Squeeze the juice into a small saucepan. Add the rest of the granulated sugar to the lemon juice in the saucepan and heat gently, stirring occasionally.

7 When the sugar has dissolved simmer gently for 3–4 minutes until syrupy.

8 With a cocktail stick or fine skewer prick the cake all over.

9 Sprinkle the lemon zest and sugar over the top of the cake, drizzle over the syrup and leave to cool in the tin. Cut the cake into squares and serve.

INGREDIENTS
Cuts into 16 squares

125 g/4 oz butter or margarine
175 g/6 oz caster sugar
2 large eggs
175 g/6 oz self-raising flour
2 lemons, preferably unwaxed
50 g/2 oz granulated sugar

Food Fact

This classic cake is a favourite in many kitchens. The buttery sponge is perfectly complimented by the lemon syrup, which soaks into the cake giving it a gooeyness which is even better the next day!

Double Chocolate Cake with Cinnamon

1 Preheat the oven to 190°C/ 375°F/Gas Mark 5 10 minutes before baking. Lightly oil and line the base of 2 x 20.5 cm/8 inch sandwich tins with greaseproof or baking paper. Sift the cocoa powder, cinnamon and flour together and reserve.

2 In a large bowl cream the butter or margarine and sugar, until light and fluffy. Beat in the eggs a little at a time until they are all incorporated and the mixture is smooth. (If it looks curdled at any point beat in 1 tablespoon of the sifted flour.)

3 Using a rubber spatula or metal spoon, fold the sifted flour and cocoa powder into the egg mixture until mixed well.

4 Divide between the 2 prepared cake tins, and level the surface. Bake in the preheated oven for 25–30 minutes, until springy to the touch and a skewer inserted into the centre of the cake comes out clean. Turn out on to a wire rack to cool.

5 To make the filling, coarsely break the white chocolate and heat the cream very gently in a small saucepan. Add the broken chocolate, stirring until melted. Leave to cool, then using half of the cooled white chocolate sandwich the cakes together.

6 Top the cake with the remaining cooled white chocolate. Coarsely grate the dark chocolate over the top and serve.

INGREDIENTS
Cuts into 10 slices

50 g/2 oz cocoa powder
1 tsp ground cinnamon
225 g/8 oz self-raising flour
225 g/8 oz unsalted butter
  or margarine
225 g/8 oz caster sugar
4 large eggs

FOR THE FILLING:

125 g/4 oz white chocolate
50 ml/2 fl oz double cream
25 g/1 oz plain dark chocolate

Helpful Hint

Adding some sifted flour can help to prevent the mixture from curdling (see step 2). Removing the eggs from the refrigerator and allowing them to return to room temperature before use also helps. Remember to add just a little egg at a time!

Swiss Roll

1 Preheat the oven to 220°C/ 425°F/Gas Mark 7 15 minutes before baking. Lightly oil and line the base of a 23 x 33 cm/9 x 13 inch Swiss roll tin with a single sheet of greaseproof or baking paper.

2 Sift the flour several times, then reserve on top of the oven to warm a little.

3 Place a mixing bowl with the eggs, vanilla essence and sugar over a saucepan of hot water, ensuring that the base of the bowl is not touching the water.

4 With the saucepan off the heat whisk with an electric hand whisk until the egg mixture becomes pale and mousse-like and has increased in volume.

5 Remove the basin from the saucepan and continue to whisk for a further 2–3 minutes. Sift in the flour and very gently fold in using a metal spoon or rubber spatula, trying not to knock out the air whisked in already. Pour into the prepared tin tilting to ensure that the mixture is evenly distributed.

6 Bake in the preheated oven for 10–12 minutes, or until well risen, golden brown and the top springs back when touched lightly with a clean finger.

7 Sprinkle the toasted, chopped hazelnuts over a large sheet of greaseproof paper.

8 When the cake has cooked turn out on to the hazelnut covered paper and trim the edges of the cake. Holding an edge of the paper with the short side of the cake nearest you, roll the cake up.

9 When fully cold carefully unroll and spread with the jam and then the cream. Roll back up and serve. Otherwise, store in the refrigerator and eat within 2 days.

INGREDIENTS
Cuts into 8 slices

75 g/3 oz self-raising flour
3 large eggs
1 tsp vanilla essence
90 g/3½ oz caster sugar
25 g/1 oz hazelnuts, toasted and
  finely chopped
3 tbsp apricot conserve
300 ml/½ pint double cream,
  lightly whipped

Tasty Tip

Any flavour of jam can be used in this recipe. While apricot jam is delicious, traditional raspberry or blackcurrant jam also works very well. In place of the cream why not try butter cream icing or beaten mascarpone as a filling.

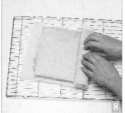

Toffee Apple Cake

1 Preheat the oven to 180°C/ 350°F/Gas Mark 4 10 minutes before baking time. Lightly oil and line the bases of 2 x 20.5 cm/8 inch sandwich tins with greaseproof or baking paper.

2 Thinly slice the apples and toss in the brown sugar until well coated. Arrange them over the base of the prepared tins and reserve.

3 Cream together the butter or margarine and caster sugar until light and fluffy.

4 Beat the eggs together in a small bowl and gradually beat them into the creamed mixture, beating well between each addition.

5 Sift the flour into the mixture and using a metal spoon or rubber spatula, fold in.

6 Divide the mixture between the 2 cake tins and level the surface.

7 Bake in the preheated oven for 25–30 minutes, until golden and well risen. Leave in the tins to cool.

8 Lightly whip the cream with 1 tablespoon of the icing sugar and vanilla essence.

9 Sandwich the cakes together with the cream. Mix the remaining icing sugar and ground cinnamon together, sprinkle over the top of the cake and serve.

INGREDIENTS
Cuts into 8 slices

2 small eating apples, peeled
4 tbsp soft dark brown sugar
175 g/6 oz butter or margarine
175 g/6 oz caster sugar
3 medium eggs
175 g/6 oz self-raising flour
150 ml/¼ pint double cream
2 tbsp icing sugar
½ tsp vanilla essence
½ tsp ground cinnamon

Tasty Tip

The dark brown sugar used in this recipe could be replaced with a dark muscovado sugar to give a deliciously rich toffee flavour to the apples. When baked the sugar will melt slightly into a caramel consistency.

Cappuccino Cakes

1 Preheat the oven to 190°C/ 375°F/Gas Mark 5 10 minutes before baking. Place 6 large paper muffin cases into a muffin tin or alternatively place on to a baking sheet.

2 Cream the butter or margarine and sugar together until light and fluffy. Break the eggs into a small bowl and beat lightly with a fork.

3 Using a wooden spoon beat the eggs into the butter and sugar mixture a little at a time, until they are all incorporated.

4 If the mixture looks curdled beat in a spoonful of the flour to return the mixture to a smooth consistency. Finally beat in the black coffee.

5 Sift the flour into the mixture, then with a metal spoon or rubber spatula gently fold in the flour.

6 Place spoonfuls of the mixture into the muffin cases.

7 Bake in the preheated oven for 20–25 minutes, or until risen and springy to the touch. Cool on a wire rack.

8 In a small bowl beat together the mascarpone cheese, icing sugar and vanilla essence.

9 When the cakes are cold, spoon the vanilla mascarpone on to the top of each one. Dust with cocoa powder and serve. Eat within 24 hours and store in the refrigerator.

INGREDIENTS
Makes 6

125 g/4 oz butter or margarine
125 g/4 oz caster sugar
2 medium eggs
1 tbsp strong black coffee
150 g/5 oz self-raising flour
125 g/4 oz mascarpone cheese
1 tbsp icing sugar, sifted
1 tsp vanilla essence
sifted cocoa powder, to dust

Tasty Tip

The combination of coffee with the vanilla-flavoured mascarpone is heavenly! Make sure, however, that you use a good-quality coffee in this recipe. Colombian coffee is generally good and at its best possesses a smooth rounded flavour.

Honey Cake

1 Preheat the oven to 180°C/350°F/Gas Mark 4 10 minutes before baking. Lightly oil and line the base of an 18 cm/7 inch deep round cake tin with lightly oiled greaseproof or baking paper.

2 In a saucepan gently heat the butter, sugar and honey until the butter has just melted.

3 Sift the flour, bicarbonate of soda and mixed spice together into a bowl.

4 Beat the egg and the milk until mixed thoroughly.

5 Make a well in the centre of the sifted flour and pour in the melted butter and honey.

6 Using a wooden spoon, beat well, gradually drawing in the flour from the sides of the bowl.

7 When all the flour has been beaten in, add the egg mixture and mix thoroughly. Pour into the prepared tin and sprinkle with the flaked almonds.

8 Bake in the preheated oven for 30–35 minutes, or until well risen and golden brown and a skewer inserted into the centre of the cake comes out clean.

9 Remove from the oven, cool for a few minutes in the tin before turning out and leaving to cool on a wire rack. Drizzle with the remaining tablespoon of honey and serve.

INGREDIENTS
Makes into 6 slices

50 g/2 oz butter
25 g/1 oz caster sugar
125 g/4 oz clear honey
175 g/6 oz plain flour
½ tsp bicarbonate of soda
½ tsp mixed spice
1 medium egg
2 tbsp milk
25 g/1 oz flaked almonds
1 tbsp clear honey, to drizzle

Tasty Tip

Serve a slice of this cake with a large spoonful of Greek yogurt on the side. The tart taste of the yogurt compliments the sweetness of the honey and spice perfectly – ideal for an afternoon treat.

Fruit Cake

1 Preheat the oven to 150°C/ 300°C/Gas Mark 2 10 minutes before baking. Lightly oil and line a 23 cm/9 inch deep round cake tin with a double thickness of greaseproof paper.

2 In a large bowl cream together the butter or margarine, sugar and orange rind, until light and fluffy, then beat in the treacle.

3 Beat in the eggs a little at a time, beating well between each addition.

4 Reserve 1 tablespoon of the flour. Sift the remaining flour, the spices and bicarbonate of soda into the mixture.

5 Mix all the fruits and the reserved flour together, then stir into the cake mixture.

6 Turn into the prepared tin and smooth the top, making a small hollow in the centre of the cake mixture.

7 Bake in the preheated oven for 1 hour, then reduce the heat to 140°C/275°F/Gas Mark 1.

8 Bake for a further 1½ hours, or until cooked and a skewer inserted into the centre comes out clean. Leave to cool in the tin, then turn the cake out and serve. Otherwise, when cold store in an airtight tin.

INGREDIENTS
Cuts into 10 slices

225 g/8 oz butter or margarine
200 g/7 oz soft brown sugar
finely grated rind of 1 orange
1 tbsp black treacle
3 large eggs, beaten
275 g/10 oz plain flour
¼ tsp ground cinnamon
½ tsp mixed spice
pinch of freshly grated nutmeg
¼ tsp bicarbonate of soda
75 g/3 oz mixed peel
50 g/2 oz glacé cherries
125 g/4 oz raisins
125 g/4 oz sultanas
125 g/4 oz ready-to-eat dried
  apricots, chopped

Tasty Tip

For a fruit cake with a kick, remove the cake from the oven when cooked and leave to cool. When the cake has cooled, turn out and make holes in the base of the cake with a skewer. Dribble over 4–5 tablespoons of your favourite alcohol such as whisky, brandy or Drambuie.

Banana Cake

1 Preheat the oven to 190°C/375°F/Gas Mark 5 10 minutes before baking. Lightly oil and line the base of an 18 cm/7 inch deep round cake tin with greaseproof or baking paper.

2 Mash 2 of the bananas in a small bowl, sprinkle with the lemon juice and a heaped tablespoon of the sugar. Mix together lightly and reserve.

3 Gently heat the remaining sugar and butter or margarine in a small saucepan until the butter has just melted.

4 Pour into a small bowl, then allow to cool slightly. Sift the flour and cinnamon into a large bowl and make a well in the centre.

5 Beat the eggs into the cooled sugar mixture, pour into the well of flour, and mix thoroughly.

6 Gently stir in the mashed banana mixture. Pour half of the mixture into the prepared tin. Thinly slice the remaining banana and arrange over the cake mixture.

7 Sprinkle over the chopped walnuts, then cover with the remaining cake mixture.

8 Bake in the preheated oven for 50–55 minutes, or until well risen and golden brown. Allow to cool in the tin, turn out and sprinkle with the ground cinnamon and caster sugar. Serve hot or cold with a jug of fresh cream for pouring.

INGREDIENTS
Cuts into 8 slices

3 medium-sized ripe bananas
1 tsp lemon juice
150 g/5 oz soft brown sugar
75 g/3 oz butter or margarine
250 g/9 oz self-raising flour
1 tsp ground cinnamon
3 medium eggs
50 g/2 oz walnuts, chopped
1 tsp each ground cinnamon and caster sugar, to decorate
fresh cream, to serve

Helpful Hint

The riper the bananas used in this recipe the better! Look out for reductions in supermarkets and fruit shops as ripe bananas are often sold very cheaply. This cake tastes really delicious the day after it has been made – the sponge solidifies slightly yet does not lose any moisture. Eat within 3–4 days.

Coffee & Pecan Cake

1 Preheat the oven to 190°C/ 375°F/Gas Mark 5 10 minutes before baking. Lightly oil and line the bases of 2 x 18 cm/7 inch sandwich tins with greaseproof or baking paper. Sift the flour and reserve.

2 Beat the butter or margarine and sugar together until light and creamy. Dissolve the coffee in 2 tablespoons of hot water and allow to cool.

3 Lightly mix the eggs with the coffee liquid. Gradually beat into the creamed butter and sugar, adding a little of the sifted flour with each addition.

4 Fold in the pecans, then divide the mixture between the prepared tins and bake in the preheated oven for 20–25 minutes, or until well risen and firm to the touch.

5 Leave to cool in the tins for 5 minutes before turning out and cooling on a wire rack.

6 To make the icing, blend together the coffee and cocoa powder with enough boiling water to make a stiff paste. Beat into the butter and icing sugar.

7 Sandwich the 2 cakes together using half of the icing. Spread the remaining icing over the top of the cake and decorate with the whole pecans to serve. Store in an airtight tin.

INGREDIENTS
Cuts into 8 slices

175 g/6 oz self-raising flour
125 g/4 oz butter or margarine
175 g/6 oz golden caster sugar
1 tbsp instant coffee powder or granules
2 large eggs
50 g/2 oz pecans, roughly chopped

FOR THE ICING:
1 tsp instant coffee powder or granules
1 tsp cocoa powder
75 g/3 oz unsalted butter, softened
175 g/6 oz icing sugar, sifted
whole pecans, to decorate

Helpful Hint

To enjoy this cake whenever you want without actually having to make it all the time, simply bake in bulk. Follow the recipe up to step 5, then when the cakes have cooled wrap in greaseproof paper or tinfoil and freeze. When desired, remove from the freezer, loosen the wrappings and allow to defrost slowly at room temperature. Serve with or without icing.

Gingerbread

1 Preheat the oven to 150°C/
300°C/Gas Mark 2 10
minutes before baking. Lightly
oil and line the base of a 20.5
cm/8 inch deep round cake tin
with greaseproof or baking paper.

2 In a saucepan gently heat
the butter or margarine,
black treacle and sugar, stirring
occasionally until the butter
melts. Leave to cool slightly.

3 Sift the flour and ground
ginger into a large bowl.

4 Make a well in the centre,
then pour in the treacle
mixture. Reserve 1 tablespoon
of the milk, then pour the rest
into the treacle mixture. Stir
together lightly until mixed.

5 Beat the eggs together,
then stir into the mixture.

6 Dissolve the bicarbonate
of soda in the remaining 1
tablespoon of warmed milk and
add to the mixture.

7 Beat the mixture until well
mixed and free of lumps.

8 Pour into the prepared tin
and bake in the preheated
oven for 1 hour, or until well
risen and a skewer inserted into
the centre comes out clean.

9 Cool in the tin, then
remove. Slice the stem ginger into thin slivers and sprinkle
over the cake. Drizzle with
the syrup and serve.

INGREDIENTS
Cuts into 8 slices

175 g/6 oz butter or margarine
225 g/8 oz black treacle
50 g/2 oz dark muscovado sugar
350 g/12 oz plain flour
2 tsp ground ginger
150 ml/¼ pint milk, warmed
2 medium eggs
1 tsp bicarbonate of soda
1 piece of stem ginger in syrup
1 tbsp stem ginger syrup

Food Fact

There are many different types of gingerbread, ranging in
colour from a deep rich dark brown to a light golden. This is
due to the type of treacle and the amount of bicarbonate of
soda used. One well-known gingerbread from Yorkshire is
Parkin which uses both golden syrup and black treacle.

Carrot Cake

1 Preheat the oven to 150°C/ 300°F/Gas Mark 2 10 minutes before baking. Lightly oil and line the base of a 15 cm/ 6 inch deep square cake tin with greaseproof or baking paper.

2 Sift the flour, spices, baking powder and bicarbonate of soda together into a large bowl.

3 Stir in the dark muscovado sugar and mix together.

4 Lightly whisk the oil and eggs together, then gradually stir into the flour and sugar mixture. Stir well.

5 Add the carrots and walnuts. Mix thoroughly, then pour into the prepared cake tin. Bake

in the preheated oven for 1¼ hours, or until light and springy to the touch and a skewer inserted into the centre of the cake comes out clean.

6 Remove from the oven and allow to cool in the tin for 5 minutes before turning out on to a wire rack. Reserve until cold.

7 To make the icing, beat together the cream cheese, orange rind, orange juice and vanilla essence. Sift the icing sugar and stir into the cream cheese mixture.

8 When cold, discard the lining paper, spread the cream cheese icing over the top and serve cut into squares.

INGREDIENTS
Cuts into 8 slices

200 g/7 oz plain flour
½ tsp ground cinnamon
½ tsp freshly grated nutmeg
1 tsp baking powder
1 tsp bicarbonate of soda
150 g/5 oz dark
  muscovado sugar
200 ml/7 fl oz vegetable oil
3 medium eggs
225 g/8 oz carrots, peeled and
  roughly grated
50 g/2 oz chopped walnuts

FOR THE ICING:
175 g/6 oz cream cheese
finely grated rind of 1 orange
1 tbsp orange juice
1 tsp vanilla essence
125 g/4 oz icing sugar

Tasty Tip

For a fruitier cake, add 1 grated apple and 50 g/2 oz of dried sultanas in step 5. To plump up the dried sultanas, soak for an hour, or overnight in 300 ml/½ pint of cold tea.

Jammy Buns

1 Preheat the oven to 190°C/
375°F/Gas Mark 5 10
minutes before baking. Lightly
oil a large baking sheet.

2 Sift the flours and baking
powder together into a large
bowl, then tip in the grains
remaining in the sieve.

3 Cut the butter or margarine
into small pieces. (It is easier
to do this when the butter is in
the flour as it helps stop the butter
from sticking to the knife.)

4 Rub the butter into the
flours until it resembles
coarse breadcrumbs. Stir in the
sugar and cranberries.

5 Using a round bladed knife
stir in the beaten egg and
milk. Mix to form a firm dough.
Divide the mixture into 12 and
roll into balls.

6 Place the dough balls on the
baking tray, leaving enough
space for expansion. Press the
thumb into the centre of each
ball making a small hollow.

7 Spoon a little of the jam
in each hollow. Pinch lightly
to seal the tops.

8 Bake in the preheated oven
for 20–25 minutes, or until
golden brown. Cool on a wire
rack and serve.

INGREDIENTS
Makes 12

175 g/6 oz plain flour
175 g/6 oz wholemeal flour
2 tsp baking powder
150 g/5 oz butter or margarine
125 g/4 oz golden caster sugar
50 g/2 oz dried cranberries
1 large egg, beaten
1 tbsp milk
4–5 tbsp seedless raspberry jam

Tasty Tip

In this recipe any type of jam can be used. However, look for
one with a high-fruit content. Alternatively replace the jam
with a fruit compote. Simply boil some fruit with a little sugar
and water, then leave to cool before placing inside the buns.

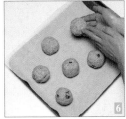

Whisked Sponge Cake

1 Preheat the oven to 200°C/400°F/Gas Mark 6 15 minutes before baking. Mix 1 teaspoon of the flour and 1 teaspoon of the sugar together. Lightly oil 2 x 18 cm/7 inch sandwich tins and dust lightly with the sugar and flour.

2 Place the eggs in a large heatproof bowl. Add the sugar, then place over a saucepan of gently simmering water ensuring that the base of the bowl does not touch the hot water. Using an electric whisk beat the sugar and eggs until they become light and fluffy. (The whisk should leave a trail in the mixture when it is lifted out.)

3 Remove the bowl from the saucepan of water, add the vanilla essence and continue beating for 2–3 minutes. Sift the flour gently into the egg mixture and using a metal spoon or rubber spatula carefully fold in, taking care not to over mix and remove all the air that has been whisked in.

4 Divide the mixture between the 2 prepared cake tins. Tap lightly on the work surface to remove any air bubbles. Bake in the preheated oven for 20–25 minutes, or until golden. Test that the cake is ready by gently pressing the centre with a clean finger – it should spring back.

5 Leave to cool in the tins for 5 minutes, then turn out on to a wire rack. Blend the jam and the crushed raspberries together. When the cakes are cold spread over the jam mixture and sandwich together. Dredge the top with icing sugar and serve.

INGREDIENTS
Cuts into 6 slices

125 g/4 oz plain flour, plus 1 tsp
175 g/6 oz caster sugar, plus 1 tsp
3 medium eggs
1 tsp vanilla essence
4 tbsp raspberry jam
50 g/2 oz fresh raspberries, crushed
icing sugar, to dredge

Tasty Tip

For a creamier low-fat filling mix the crushed raspberries or strawberries with 4 tablespoons each of low-fat Greek yogurt and low-fat crème fraîche.

Marble Cake

1 Preheat the oven to 190°C/ 375°F/Gas Mark 5 10 minutes before baking. Lightly oil and line the base of an 20.5 cm/8 inch deep round cake tin with greaseproof or baking paper.

2 In a large bowl, cream the butter or margarine and sugar together until light and fluffy.

3 Beat the eggs together. Beat into the creamed mixture a little at a time, beating well between each addition. When all the egg has been added, fold in the flour with a metal spoon or rubber spatula.

4 Divide the mixture equally between 2 bowls. Beat the grated orange rind into one of the bowls with a little of the orange juice. Mix the cocoa powder with the remaining orange juice until smooth, then add to the other bowl and beat well.

5 Spoon the mixture into the prepared tin, in alternate spoonfuls. When all the cake mixture is in the tin, take a skewer and swirl it in the 2 mixtures.

6 Tap the base of the tin on the work surface to level the mixture. Bake in the preheated oven for 50 minutes, or until cooked and a skewer inserted into the centre of the cake comes out clean.

7 Remove from the oven and leave in the tin for a few minutes before cooling on a wire rack. Discard the lining paper.

8 For the topping, place the orange zest and juice with the granulated sugar in a small saucepan and heat gently until the sugar has dissolved.

9 Bring to the boil and simmer gently for 3–4 minutes, until the juice is syrupy. Pour over the cooled cake and serve when cool. Otherwise, store in an airtight tin.

INGREDIENTS
Cuts into 8 slices

225 g/8 oz butter or margarine
225 g/8 oz caster sugar
4 medium eggs
225 g/8 oz self-raising
 flour, sifted
finely grated rind and juice of
 1 orange
25 g/1 oz cocoa powder, sifted

FOR THE TOPPING:
zest and juice of 1 orange
1 tbsp granulated sugar

Helpful Hint

This cake has a wonderful combination of rich chocolate and orangey sponge. It is important, not to swirl too much in step 2, as the desired effect is to have blocks of different coloured sponge.

Chocolate Creams

1 Break the chocolate into small pieces, then place in a heatproof bowl set over a saucepan of gently simmering water. Add the brandy and heat gently, stirring occasionally until the chocolate has melted and is smooth. Remove from the heat and leave to cool slightly, then beat in the egg yolks, 1 at a time, beating well after each addition. Reserve.

2 Whisk the egg whites until stiff but not dry, then stir 1 tablespoon into the chocolate mixture. Add the remainder and stir in gently. Chill in the refrigerator while preparing the cream.

3 Whip the cream until just beginning to thicken, then stir in the sugar, orange rind and Cointreau and continue to whisk together until soft peaks form. Spoon the chocolate mousse into the cream mixture and using a metal spoon, fold the 2 mixtures together to create a marbled effect. Alternatively, continue folding the 2 mixtures together until mixed thoroughly. Spoon into 4 individual glass dishes, cover each dessert with clingfilm and chill in the refrigerator for 2 hours.

4 Using a potato peeler, shave the white chocolate into curls. Uncover the desserts and scatter over the shavings. Peel the husks back from the physalis berries and pinch together for decoration. Top each dessert with 2 berries and chill in the refrigerator until ready to serve.

INGREDIENTS
Serves 4

125 g/4 oz plain dark chocolate
1 tbsp brandy
4 medium eggs, separated
200 ml/7 fl oz pint double cream
1 tbsp caster sugar
grated rind of 1 orange
2 tbsp Cointreau
25 g/1 oz white chocolate
8 physalis, to decorate

Food Fact

Physalis are also known as cape gooseberries. They are small, shiny, orange fruits that come in papery husks. Simply peel back the papery husks to reveal the fruit and use to decorate all sorts of desserts and fruit salads.

Chocolate & Saffron Cheesecake

1 Preheat the oven to 200°C/ 400°F/Gas Mark 6, 15 minutes before baking. Lightly oil a 20.5 cm/8 inch fluted flan tin. Soak the saffron threads in 1 tablespoon of hot water for 20 minutes. Sift the flour and salt into a bowl. Cut the butter into small dice, then add to the flour and using your fingertips, rub in the butter until the mixture resembles breadcrumbs. Stir in the sugar.

2 Beat the egg yolk with 1 tablespoon of cold water, add to the mixture and mix together until a smooth and pliable dough is formed. Add a little extra water if necessary. Knead on a lightly floured surface until free from cracks, then wrap in clingfilm and chill in the refrigerator for 30 minutes.

3 Roll the pastry out on a lightly floured surface and use to line the flan tin. Prick the pastry base and sides with a fork and line with nonstick baking parchment and baking beans. Bake blind in the preheated oven for 12 minutes. Remove the beans and baking parchment and continue to bake blind for 5 minutes.

4 Beat together the curd cheese and granulated sugar, then beat in the melted chocolate, saffron liquid, the milk and eggs, mix until blended thoroughly. Pour the mixture into the cooked flan case and place on a baking sheet.

5 Reduce the oven temperature to 190°C/375°F/Gas Mark 5 and bake for 15 minutes, then reduce the oven temperature to 180°C/350°F/Gas Mark 4 and continue to bake for 20–30 minutes or until set.

6 Remove the cheesecake from the oven and leave for 10 minutes before removing from the flan tin, if serving warm. If serving cold, leave in the flan tin to cool before removing and placing on a serving platter. Sprinkle with icing sugar before serving.

INGREDIENTS
Serves 6

¼ tsp saffron threads
175 g/6 oz plain flour
pinch of salt
75 g/3 oz butter
1 tbsp caster sugar
1 medium egg yolk
350 g/12 oz curd cheese
75 g/3 oz golden granulated
 sugar
125 g/4 oz plain dark chocolate,
 melted and cooled
6 tbsp milk
3 medium eggs
1 tbsp icing sugar, sifted,
 to decorate

Food Fact

Saffron is the stamen of a particular type of crocus. It must be picked by hand and the yield is very small, making it very expensive. However, it is always used very sparingly and keeps very well.

Caramelised Chocolate Tartlets

1 Preheat the oven to 200°C/ 400°F/Gas Mark 6, 15 minutes before baking. Lightly oil 6 individual tartlet tins. Roll out the ready-made pastry on a lightly floured surface and use to line the oiled tins. Prick the bases and sides with a fork and line with nonstick baking parchment and baking beans. Bake blind for 10 minutes in the preheated oven, then remove from the oven and discard the baking beans and the baking parchment.

2 Reduce the oven temperature to 180°C/ 350°F/Gas Mark 4. Heat the coconut milk and 15 g/½ oz of the sugar in a heavy-based saucepan, stirring constantly until the sugar has dissolved. Remove the saucepan from the heat and leave to cool.

3 Stir the melted chocolate, the beaten egg and the vanilla essence into the cooled coconut milk. Stir until well mixed, then strain into the cooked pastry cases. Place on a baking sheet and bake in the oven for 25 minutes or until set. Remove and leave to cool, then chill in the refrigerator.

4 Preheat the grill, then arrange the fruits in a decorative pattern on the top of each tartlet. Sprinkle with the remaining demerara sugar and place the tartlets in the grill pan. Grill for 2 minutes or until the sugar bubbles and browns. Turn the tartlets, if necessary and take care not to burn the sugar. Remove from the grill and leave to cool before serving.

INGREDIENTS
Serves 6

350 g/12 oz ready-made shortcrust pastry, thawed if frozen
150 ml/¼ pint coconut milk
40 g/1½ oz demerara sugar
50 g/2 oz plain dark chocolate, melted
1 medium egg, beaten
few drops vanilla essence
1 small mango, peeled, stoned and sliced
1 small papaya, peeled, deseeded and chopped
1 star fruit, sliced
1 kiwi, peeled and sliced, or use fruits of your choice

Helpful Hint

Before grilling, you may find it useful to cover the edges of the pastry with tinfoil to prevent it burning under the hot grill.

Hazelnut Meringues with Chocolate Sauce

1 Preheat the oven to 150°C/ 300°F/Gas Mark 2, 10 minutes before baking. Line 2 baking sheets with nonstick baking parchment. Whisk the egg whites in a large grease-free bowl until stiff, then add the caster sugar, 1 teaspoonful at a time, whisking well after each addition. Continue to whisk until the mixture is stiff and dry, then using a metal spoon, fold in the ground hazelnuts.

2 Using 2 dessertspoons, spoon the mixture into 12 quenelle shapes onto the baking parchment. Sprinkle over the ground hazelnuts and bake in the preheated oven for

1½–2 hours or until dry and crisp. Switch the oven off and leave to cool in the oven.

3 To make the chocolate sauce, place the chocolate with the butter and 4 tablespoons of the cream and the golden syrup in a heavy-based saucepan and heat, stirring occasionally, until the chocolate has melted and the mixture is blended. Do not boil. Whip the remaining cream until soft peaks form.

4 Sandwich the meringues together with the whipped cream and place on serving plates. Spoon over the sauce and serve with a fresh berries.

INGREDIENTS
Serves 6

4 medium egg whites
225 g/8 oz caster sugar
125 g/4 oz ground hazelnuts
50 g/2 oz toasted hazelnuts, sliced
fresh berries, such as raspberries, strawberries and blueberries, to serve

FOR THE CHOCOLATE SAUCE:
225 g/8 oz plain dark chocolate, broken into pieces
50 g/2 oz butter
300 ml/½ pint double cream
1 tbsp golden syrup

Helpful Hint

It is important to add the sugar gradually when making meringues because if the sugar is not fully dissolved into the egg white it might leach out during cooking, making the meringues 'sweat'.

Iced Chocolate & Raspberry Mousse

1 Break the sponge finger biscuits into small pieces and divide between 4 individual glass dishes. Blend together the orange juice and Grand Marnier, then drizzle evenly over the sponge fingers. Cover with clingfilm and chill in the refrigerator for 30 minutes.

2 Meanwhile, place the cream in a small heavy-based saucepan and heat gently, stirring occasionally until boiling. Remove the saucepan from the heat then add the pieces of dark chocolate and leave to stand, untouched for about 7 minutes. Using a whisk, whisk the chocolate and cream together,

until the chocolate has melted and is well blended and completely smooth. Leave to cool slightly.

3 Place the frozen raspberries and icing sugar into a food processor or liquidizer and blend until roughly crushed.

4 Fold the crushed raspberries into the cream and chocolate mixture and mix lightly until well blended. Spoon over the chilled sponge finger biscuits. Lightly dust with a little cocoa powder and decorate with whole raspberries, mint leaves and grated white chocolate. Serve immediately.

INGREDIENTS
Serves 4

12 sponge finger biscuits
juice of 2 oranges
2 tbsp Grand Marnier
300 ml/½ pint double cream
175 g/6 oz plain dark chocolate, broken into small pieces
225 g/8 oz frozen raspberries
6 tbsp icing sugar, sifted
cocoa powder, for dusting

TO DECORATE:
few fresh whole raspberries
few mint leaves
grated white chocolate

Helpful Hint

Remove the raspberries from the freezer about 20 minutes before you need to purée them. This will soften them slightly but they will still be frozen.

White Chocolate Terrine with Red Fruit Compote

1 Set the freezer to rapid freeze at least 2 hours before required. Lightly oil and line a 450 g/1 lb loaf tin with clingfilm, taking care to keep the clingfilm as wrinkle free as possible. Break the white chocolate into small pieces and place in a heatproof bowl set over a saucepan of gently simmering water. Leave for 20 minutes or until melted, then remove from the heat and stir until smooth. Leave to cool.

2 Whip the cream until soft peaks form. Beat the cream cheese until soft and creamy, then beat in the grated orange rind and 50 g/2 oz of the caster sugar. Mix well, then fold in the whipped cream and then the cooled melted white chocolate.

3 Spoon the mixture into the prepared loaf tin and level the surface. Place in the freezer and freeze for at least 4 hours or until frozen. Once frozen, remember to return the freezer to its normal setting.

4 Place the fruits with the remaining sugar in a heavy-based saucepan and heat gently, stirring occasionally, until the sugar has dissolved and the juices from the fruits are just beginning to run. Add the Cointreau.

5 Dip the loaf tin into hot water for 30 seconds and invert onto a serving plate. Carefully remove the tin and clingfilm. Decorate with sprigs of mint and serve sliced with the prepared red fruit compote.

INGREDIENTS
Serves 8

225 g/8 oz white chocolate
300 ml/½ pint double cream
225 g/8 oz full fat soft cream cheese
2 tbsp finely grated orange rind
125 g/4 oz caster sugar
350 g/12 oz mixed summer fruits, such as strawberries, blueberries and raspberries
1 tbsp Cointreau
sprigs of fresh mint, to decorate

Helpful Hint

Pour some boiled water into a tall jug and dip your knife into it for a few seconds. Dry the knife and use to slice the terrine, repeating the dipping when necessary.

Orange Chocolate Cheesecake

1 Lightly oil and line a 20.5 cm/8 inch round loose-based cake tin with non-stick baking parchment. Place the biscuits in a polythene bag and crush using a rolling pin. Alternatively, use a food processor. Melt the butter in a medium-sized heavy-based saucepan, add the crushed biscuits and mix well. Press the biscuit mixture into the base of the lined tin, then chill in the refrigerator for 20 minutes.

2 For the filling, remove the cream cheese from the refrigerator, at least 20 minutes before using, to allow the cheese to come to room temperature. Place the cream cheese in a bowl and beat until smooth, reserve.

3 Pour 4 tablespoons of water into a small bowl and sprinkle over the gelatine. Leave to stand for 5 minutes until spongy. Place the bowl over a saucepan of simmering water and allow to dissolve, stirring occasionally. Leave to cool slightly.

4 Melt the orange chocolate in a heatproof bowl set over a saucepan of simmering water, then leave to cool slightly.

5 Whip the cream until soft peaks form. Beat the gelatine and chocolate into cream cheese. Fold in the cream. Spoon into the tin and level the surface. Chill in the refrigerator for 4 hours until set.

6 Remove the cheesecake from the tin and place on a serving plate. Top with the fruits, dust with icing sugar and decorate with sprigs of mint.

INGREDIENTS
Serves 8

225 g/8 oz plain chocolate coated digestive biscuits
50 g/2 oz butter
450 g/1 lb mixed fruits, such as blueberries and raspberries
1 tbsp icing sugar, sifted
few sprigs of fresh mint, to decorate

FOR THE FILLING:

450 g/1 lb soft cream cheese
1 tbsp gelatine
350 g/12 oz orange chocolate, broken into segments
600 ml/1 pint double cream

Helpful Hint

Always add gelatine to the mixture you are working with and whisk well to evenly distribute it. Never add the mixture to the gelatine or it will tend to set in a lump.

Chocolate Rice Pudding

1 Preheat the oven to 170°C/ 325°F/Gas Mark 3, 10 minutes before cooking. Lightly butter a large ovenproof dish. Rinse the pudding rice, then place in the base of the buttered dish and sprinkle over the caster sugar.

2 Pour the evaporated milk and milk into a heavy-based saucepan and bring slowly to the boil over a low heat, stirring occasionally to avoid sticking. Pour the milk over the rice and sugar and stir well until well mixed and the sugar has dissolved.

3 Grate a little nutmeg over the top, then sprinkle with the ground cinnamon, if liked. Cover tightly with tinfoil and bake in the preheated oven for 30 minutes.

4 Remove the pudding from the oven and stir well to break up any lumps that may have formed. Cover with tinfoil and return to the oven for a further 30 minutes. Remove the pudding from the oven once again and stir to break up any more lumps.

5 Stir the chocolate chips into the rice pudding and then dot with the butter. Continue to bake, uncovered, in the oven for a further 45 minutes–1 hour, or until the rice is tender and the skin is golden brown. Serve warm, with or without the skin, according to personal preference. Serve with a few sliced strawberries and a spoonful of crème fraîche.

INGREDIENTS
Serves 4

60 g/2½ oz pudding rice
75 g/3 oz caster sugar
1 x 410 g can evaporated milk
600 ml/1 pint milk
pinch of freshly grated nutmeg
¼ tsp ground cinnamon, optional
50 g/2 oz plain chocolate chips
25 g/1 oz butter
freshly sliced strawberries, to decorate
crème fraîche, to serve

Tasty Tip

If chocolate chips are unavailable, use a piece of plain chocolate and chop it into small pieces instead.

Topsy Turvy Pudding

1 Preheat the oven to 180°C/ 350°F/Gas Mark 4, 10 minutes before baking. Lightly oil a 20.5 cm/8 inch deep round loose-based cake tin. Place the demerara sugar and 3 tablespoons of water in a small heavy-based saucepan and heat gently until the sugar has dissolved. Swirl the saucepan or stir with a clean wooden spoon to ensure the sugar has dissolved, then bring to the boil and boil rapidly until a golden caramel is formed. Pour into the base of the tin and leave to cool.

2 For the sponge, cream the butter and sugar together until light and fluffy. Gradually beat in the eggs a little at a time, beating well between each addition. Add a spoonful of flour after each addition to prevent the mixture curdling. Add the melted chocolate and

then stir well. Fold in the orange rind, self-raising flour and sifted cocoa powder and mix well.

3 Remove the peel from both oranges taking care to remove as much of the pith as possible. Thinly slice the peel into strips and then slice the oranges. Arrange the peel and then the orange slices over the caramel. Top with the sponge mixture and level the top.

4 Place the tin on a baking sheet and bake in the pre-heated oven for 40–45 minutes or until well risen, golden brown and an inserted skewer comes out clean. Remove from the oven, leave for about 5 minutes, invert onto a serving plate and sprinkle with cocoa powder. Serve with either custard or soured cream.

INGREDIENTS
Serves 6

FOR THE TOPPING:
175 g/6 oz demerara sugar
2 oranges

FOR THE SPONGE:
175 g/6 oz butter, softened
175 g/6 oz caster sugar
3 medium eggs, beaten
175 g/6 oz self-raising flour,
  sifted
50 g/2 oz plain dark chocolate,
  melted
grated rind of 1 orange
25 g/1 oz cocoa powder, sifted
custard or soured cream, to serve

Helpful Hint

When making the caramel in step 1, make sure the sugar has completely dissolved and that no sugar remains clinging to the side of the pan, otherwise the caramel will crystallise.

Chocolate Fruit Tiramisu

1 Cut the passion fruit and scoop out the seeds and reserve. Plunge the nectarines or peaches into boiling water and leave for 2–3 minutes.

2 Carefully remove the nectarines from the water, cut in half and remove the stones. Peel off the skin, chop the flesh finely and reserve.

3 Break the sponge finger biscuits and amaretti biscuits in half. Place the amaretti liqueur and prepared black coffee into a shallow dish and stir well. Place half the sponge fingers and amaretti biscuits into the amaretti and coffee mixture and soak for 30 seconds.

4 Lift out both biscuits from the liquor and arrange in the bases of 4 deep individual glass dishes.

5 Cream the mascarpone cheese until soft and creamy, then slowly beat in the fresh custard and mix well together.

6 Spoon half the mascarpone mixture over the biscuits in the dishes and sprinkle with 125 g/4 oz of the finely chopped or grated dark chocolate.

7 Arrange half the passion fruit seeds and the chopped nectarine or peaches over the chocolate and sprinkle with half the sifted cocoa powder.

8 Place the remaining biscuits in the remaining coffee liqueur mixture and soak for 30 seconds, then arrange on top of the fruit and cocoa powder. Top with the remaining chopped or grated chocolate, nectarine or peach and the mascarpone cheese mixture, piling the mascarpone high in the dishes.

9 Chill in the refrigerator for 1½ hours, then spoon the remaining passion fruit seeds and cocoa powder over the desserts. Chill in the refrigerator for 30 minutes and serve.

INGREDIENTS
Serves 4

2 ripe passion fruit
2 fresh nectarines or peaches
75 g/3 oz sponge finger biscuits
125 g/4 oz amaretti biscuits
5 tbsp amaretti liqueur
6 tbsp prepared black coffee
250 g/9 oz mascarpone cheese
450 ml/¾ pint fresh custard
200 g/7 oz plain dark chocolate, finely chopped or grated
2 tbsp cocoa powder, sifted

Food Fact

Mascarpone cheese is an Italian full fat cream cheese with a very thick, creamy texture and flavour. It is a classic ingredient of tiramisu. Here, it is mixed with some ready-made custard, which gives it a lighter texture.

Fruity Chocolate Bread Pudding

1 Preheat the oven to 180°C/ 350°F/Gas Mark 4, 10 minutes before cooking. Lightly butter a shallow ovenproof dish. Break the chocolate into small pieces, then place in a heatproof bowl set over a saucepan of gently simmering water. Heat gently, stirring frequently, until the chocolate has melted and is smooth. Remove from the heat and leave for about 10 minutes or until the chocolate begins to thicken slightly.

2 Cut the fruit loaf into medium to thick slices, then spread with the melted chocolate. Leave until almost set, then cut each slice in half to form a triangle. Layer the chocolate-coated bread slices and the chopped apricots in the buttered ovenproof dish.

3 Stir the cream and the milk together, then stir in the caster sugar. Beat the eggs, then gradually beat in the cream and milk mixture. Beat thoroughly until well blended. Carefully pour over the bread slices and apricots and leave to stand for 30 minutes.

4 Sprinkle with the demerara sugar and place in a roasting tin half filled with boiling water. Cook in the preheated oven for 45 minutes, or until golden and the custard is lightly set. Serve immediately.

INGREDIENTS
Serves 4

175 g/6 oz plain dark chocolate
1 small fruit loaf
125 g/4 oz ready-to-eat dried
  apricots, roughly chopped
450 ml/¾ pint single cream
300 ml/½ pint milk
1 tbsp caster sugar
3 medium eggs
3 tbsp demerara sugar, for
  sprinkling

Helpful Hint

It is important to leave the pudding to stand for at least 30 minutes, as described in step 3. This allows the custard to soak into the bread – otherwise it sets around the bread as it cooks, making the pudding seem stodgy.

Chocolate & Fruit Crumble

1 Preheat the oven to 190°C/375°F/Gas Mark 5, 10 minutes before baking. Lightly oil an ovenproof dish.

2 For the crumble, sift the flour into a large bowl. Cut the butter into small dice and add to the flour. Rub the butter into the flour until the mixture resembles fine breadcrumbs.

3 Stir the sugar, porridge oats and the chopped hazelnuts into the mixture and reserve.

4 For the filling, peel the apples, core and slice thickly. Place in a large heavy-based saucepan with the lemon juice and 3 tablespoons of water. Add the sultanas, raisins and the soft brown sugar. Bring slowly to the boil, cover and simmer over a gentle heat for 8–10 minutes, stirring occasionally, or until the apples are slightly softened.

5 Remove the saucepan from the heat and leave to cool slightly before stirring in the pears, ground cinnamon and the chopped chocolate.

6 Spoon into the prepared ovenproof dish. Sprinkle the crumble evenly over the top then bake in the preheated oven for 35–40 minutes or until the top is golden. Remove from the oven, sprinkle with the caster sugar and serve immediately.

INGREDIENTS
Serves 4

FOR THE CRUMBLE:
125 g/4 oz plain flour
125 g/4 oz butter
75 g/3 oz light soft brown sugar
50 g/2 oz rolled porridge oats
50 g/2 oz hazelnuts, chopped

FOR THE FILLING:
450 g/1 lb Bramley apples
1 tbsp lemon juice
50 g/2 oz sultanas
50 g/2 oz seedless raisins
50 g/2 oz light soft brown sugar
350 g/12 oz pears, peeled, cored
  and chopped
1 tsp ground cinnamon
125 g/4 oz plain dark chocolate,
  very roughly chopped
2 tsp caster sugar for sprinkling

Tasty Tip

Bramley apples have a sharp flavour and may need more sugar than other apples. Their advantage is that they are ideal for cooking and will form a purée very easily. If you prefer, use a dessert apple such as Golden Delicious or Granny Smith, but reduce the sugar accordingly.

Brandied Raisin Chocolate Mousse

1 Place the raisins in a bowl together with the sugar, then pour over the brandy. Stir well and cover with clingfilm. Leave to marinate overnight or until the raisins have absorbed most, or all of the brandy. Stir occasionally during marinating.

2 Break the chocolate into small pieces and place in a small heatproof bowl set over a saucepan of gently simmering water. Heat gently, stirring occasionally, until the chocolate has melted and is smooth. Remove the bowl from the heat and leave to stand for about 10 minutes, or until the chocolate cools and begins to thicken. Using a metal spoon or rubber spatula, carefully fold in the prepared custard.

3 Whip the cream until soft peaks form and fold into the chocolate custard mixture together with the coffee. Gently stir in the brandy-soaked raisins with any remaining brandy left in the bowl.

4 Whisk the egg white in a clean, grease-free bowl, until stiff but not dry, then fold 1 tablespoon into the chocolate mixture and mix together lightly. Add the remaining egg white and stir lightly until well mixed. Spoon into 4 tall glasses and chill in the refrigerator for up to 2 hours.

5 Just before serving, pipe a swirl of whipped cream on the top of each mousse and decorate with the chocolate curls, then serve.

INGREDIENTS
Serves 4

125 g/4 oz raisins
1 tsp soft brown sugar
3 tbsp brandy
200 g/7 oz plain dark chocolate
150 ml/¼ pint ready-made custard
300 ml/½ pint double cream
1 tbsp strong black coffee
1 medium egg white
50 ml/2 fl oz freshly whipped cream
chocolate curls, to decorate

Tasty Tip

Look for Lexia raisins, which are particularly large and plump.
They will soak up the alcohol really well.

Poached Pears with Chocolate Sauce

1 Pour the red wine with 150 ml/¼ pint of water into a heavy-based saucepan and stir in the sugar, the orange rind and juice with the ginger. Place over a gentle heat and bring slowly to the boil, stirring occasionally until the sugar has dissolved. Once the sugar has dissolved, boil steadily for 5 minutes, then remove from the heat.

2 Using a potato peeler, carefully peel the pears, leaving the stalks intact. If preferred, gently remove the cores from the base of each pear. (You can, if you prefer, leave the cores intact for a neater finish.) If necessary, cut a very thin slice off the base of each pear so they sit upright.

3 Carefully stand the pears in the hot syrup, return to the heat, cover with a lid and simmer gently for 20 minutes or until tender, turning the pears occasionally. Remove from the heat and leave to cool in the syrup, turning occasionally. Using a slotted spoon, transfer the pears to a large dish.

4 Strain the syrup, then bring back to the boil and boil rapidly until reduced and syrupy. Add the chocolate, cream and sugar to the saucepan and bring very slowly to the boil, stirring constantly until the chocolate has melted. Arrange the pears on serving plates and carefully spoon over the chocolate sauce. Serve immediately.

INGREDIENTS
Serves 4

300 ml/½ pint red wine
125 g/4 oz caster sugar
grated rind and juice of 1 small orange
2 cm/1 inch piece fresh root ginger, peeled and chopped
4 firm pears, such as Williams or Conference
175 g/6 oz plain dark chocolate
150 ml/¼ pint double cream
25 g/1 oz golden granulated sugar

Tasty Tip

Look for pears that are ripe but not soft. You can use unripe pears. Conference pears have a green skin even when ripe and an elongated shape that makes them look very elegant.

Chocolate Brûlée

1 Hull and clean the raspberries. Rinse lightly, then leave to dry on absorbent kitchen paper. Once dry, divide the raspberries evenly between 6 x 150 ml/¼ pint ramekins or individual dishes.

2 Whisk the caster sugar and egg yolks in a large bowl until very thick. Pour the cream into a heavy-based saucepan, place over a medium-high heat and bring to the boil. Remove from the heat and gradually whisk into the egg mixture, then whisk in the vanilla essence.

3 Place the bowl over a saucepan of simmering water and cook for about 15–20 minutes, stirring frequently, or until thick and the custard coats the back of a wooden spoon.

4 Remove the bowl from the heat, add the chopped white chocolate and stir until melted and well blended. Pour over the raspberries in the ramekins and leave to cool. Cover with cling-film and chill in the refrigerator for 6 hours or until firm.

5 Preheat the grill. Remove the ramekins from the refrigerator and sprinkle 1 tablespoon of the demerara sugar over each, ensuring that the custard is completely covered.

6 Cook under the preheated grill for 5–6 minutes, or until the sugar has melted and begun to caramelise. Remove from the grill, leave to cool slightly, then chill again in the refrigerator for at least 1 hour. Serve immediately.

INGREDIENTS
Serves 6

175 g/6 oz fresh raspberries
125 g/4 oz caster sugar
5 medium egg yolks
600 ml/1 pint double cream
1 tsp vanilla essence
175 g/6 oz white chocolate, chopped
6 tbsp demerara sugar

Helpful Hint

If your grill does not get hot enough, you could try using a small blowtorch to caramelise the sugar. Keep the flame moving slowly over the sugar until it is melted and bubbling. Leave to cool as above.

Chocolate Trifle

1 Slice the chocolate Swiss roll thickly and spread each slice with a little strawberry jam. Place the Swiss roll slices in the base of a trifle dish or glass bowl. Sprinkle over the sherry and brandy and leave to stand for 10 minutes to let the sherry and brandy soak into the Swiss roll. Slice half the strawberries and scatter evenly over the Swiss roll with half the diced mangos.

2 Break the chocolate into small pieces and place in a small heatproof bowl set over a saucepan of gently simmering water. Heat gently, stirring occasionally until the chocolate has melted and is smooth and free from lumps.

3 Blend the custard powder, sugar and milk to a smooth paste in a bowl, then pour into a heavy-based saucepan. Place over a gentle heat and cook, stirring constantly, until the custard is smooth and thick. Add the melted chocolate and stir until smooth and blended. Remove from the heat and leave to cool. Stir in the mascarpone cheese.

4 Spoon the custard mixture over the fruit and chill in the refrigerator for 1 hour. Whip the cream until soft peaks form and pile over the top of the set custard. Sprinkle over the toasted flaked almonds and decorate with the remaining whole strawberries and diced mango.

INGREDIENTS
Serves 4

1½ homemade or bought chocolate
  Swiss rolls
4 tbsp strawberry jam
3 tbsp medium sherry
3 tbsp brandy
350 g/12 oz fresh strawberries
2 small mangos, peeled, stoned
  and diced
200 g/7 oz plain dark chocolate
2 tbsp custard powder
2 tbsp granulated sugar
300 ml/½ pint full fat milk
250 g/9 oz mascarpone cheese
300 ml/½ pint double cream
15 g/½ oz toasted flaked almonds

Tasty Tip

If you prefer, use fresh custard. Heat gently, then stir in the chocolate and mascarpone cheese. Omit the custard powder, sugar and milk.

Chocolate Profiteroles

1 Preheat the oven to 220°C/ 425°F/Gas Mark 7, 15 minutes before cooking. Lightly oil 2 baking sheets. For the pastry, place the water and the butter in a heavy-based saucepan and bring to the boil. Remove from the heat and beat in the flour. Return to the heat and cook for 1 minute or until the mixture forms a ball in the centre of the saucepan.

2 Remove from the heat and leave to cool slightly, then gradually beat in the eggs a little at a time, beating well after each addition. Once all the eggs have been added, beat until the paste is smooth and glossy. Pipe or spoon 20 small balls onto the baking sheets, allowing plenty of room for expansion.

3 Bake in the preheated oven for 25 minutes or until well risen and golden brown. Reduce

the oven temperature to 180°C/ 350°F/Gas Mark 4. Make a hole in each ball and continue to bake for a further 5 minutes. Remove from the oven and leave to cool.

4 For the custard, place the milk and nutmeg in a heavy-based saucepan and bring to the boil. In another saucepan, whisk together the egg yolks, sugar and the flours, then beat in the hot milk. Bring to the boil and simmer, whisking constantly for 2 minutes. Cover and leave to cool.

5 Spoon the custard into the profiteroles and arrange on a large serving dish. Place all the sauce ingredients in a small saucepan and bring to the boil, then simmer for 10 minutes. Remove from the heat and cool slightly before serving with the chocolate profiteroles.

INGREDIENTS
Serves 4

FOR THE PASTRY:
150 ml/¼ pint water
50 g/2 oz butter
65 g/2½ oz plain flour, sifted
2 medium eggs, lightly beaten

FOR THE CUSTARD:
300 ml/½ pint milk
pinch of freshly grated nutmeg
3 medium egg yolks
50 g/2 oz caster sugar
2 tbsp plain flour, sifted
2 tbsp cornflour, sifted

FOR THE SAUCE:
175 g/6 oz soft brown sugar
150 ml/¼ pint boiling water
1 tsp instant coffee
1 tbsp cocoa powder
1 tbsp brandy
75 g/3 oz butter
1 tbsp golden syrup

Chocolate Chip Ice Cream

1 Set the freezer to rapid freeze. Simmer the raspberries with the sugar and lemon juice for 5 minutes. Leave to cool, then purée in a food processor. Press through a fine sieve to remove the pips. Reserve the coulis.

2 Pour the milk into a heavy-based saucepan and add the vanilla pod. Bring slowly to the boil, then remove from the heat and leave to infuse for 30 minutes. Remove the pod.

3 Whisk the egg yolks and caster sugar together until pale and creamy, then gradually whisk in the infused milk. Strain the mixture into a clean saucepan, place over a gentle heat and bring slowly to the boil. Cook over a gentle heat, stirring constantly, until the mixture thickens and coats the back of a wooden spoon. Do not let the mixture boil otherwise it will curdle. Once thickened, cover with clingfilm and leave the custard to cool completely.

4 Break half the chocolate into small pieces and place in a heatproof bowl set over a saucepan of gently simmering water. Heat gently, stirring frequently, until the chocolate has melted and smooth. Remove from the heat and leave to cool.

5 Whip the cream until soft peaks form and fold into the cooled custard. Roughly chop the remaining chocolate and stir into the custard mixture together with the melted chocolate. Spoon into a suitable container and freeze for 1 hour.

6 Remove from the freezer and beat well to break up all the ice crystals. Repeat the beating and freezing process twice more, then freeze for 4 hours or until the ice cream is solid. Allow to soften in the refrigerator for 30 minutes before serving with fresh fruit and the raspberry coulis. Remember to return the freezer to its normal setting.

INGREDIENTS
Serves 4

350 g/12 oz fresh raspberries, or thawed if frozen
25 g/1 oz icing sugar, or to taste
2 tbsp lemon juice
600 ml/1 pint milk
1 vanilla pod, seeds removed
6 medium egg yolks
125 g/4 oz caster sugar
450 g/1 lb plain dark chocolate
150 ml/¼ pint double cream
fresh fruit of your choice, to serve

Helpful Hint

If you prefer, you can use a food processor to beat the ice cream as described in step 6.

Rich Chocolate &
Orange Mousse Dessert

1 Oil and line a 900 g/2 lb loaf tin with clingfilm, taking care to keep the clingfilm as wrinkle free as possible. Arrange the sponge finger biscuits around the edge of the loaf tin, trimming the biscuits to fit if necessary.

2 Place the chocolate, butter and orange flower water in a heavy-based saucepan and heat gently, stirring occasionally, until the chocolate has melted and is smooth. Remove the saucepan from the heat, add the cocoa powder and 50 g/2 oz of the icing sugar. Stir until smooth, then beat in the egg yolks.

3 In a clean grease-free bowl whisk the egg whites until stiff but not dry. Sift in the remaining icing sugar and whisk until stiff and glossy. Fold the egg white mixture into the chocolate mixture and, using a metal spoon or rubber spatula, stir until well blended.

4 Spoon the mousse mixture into the prepared loaf tin and level the surface. Cover and chill in the refrigerator until set.

5 Meanwhile, place the caster sugar with 150 ml/¼ pint of water in a heavy-based saucepan and heat until the sugar has dissolved. Bring to the boil and boil for 5 minutes. Add the orange slices and simmer for about 2–4 minutes or until the slices become opaque. Drain on absorbent kitchen paper, reserve.

6 Trim the top of the biscuits to the same level as the mousse. Invert onto a plate and remove the tin and clingfilm.

7 Whip the cream until soft peaks form and spoon into a piping bag fitted with a star-shaped nozzle. Pipe swirls on top of the mousse and decorate with the orange slices. Chill in the refrigerator before serving.

INGREDIENTS
Serves 8

8–12 sponge finger biscuits
225 g/8 oz plain dark chocolate, broken into pieces
225 g/8 oz unsalted butter
2 tbsp orange flower water
40 g/1½ oz cocoa powder, sifted
125 g/4 oz icing sugar, sifted
5 medium eggs, separated
50 g/2 oz caster sugar
1 orange, thinly sliced
300 ml/½ pint double cream

Helpful Hint

When filling a piping bag, try to avoid air pockets, which will making piping quite difficult.

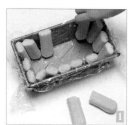

Chocolate & Rum Truffles

1 For the chocolate truffles, break the chocolate into pieces and place in a heatproof bowl set over a saucepan of gently simmering water. Leave for 20 minutes or until the chocolate has melted. Stir until the chocolate is smooth and remove from the heat. Leave to stand for about 6 minutes.

2 Beat the butter, the egg yolks, the brandy or kirsch and double cream together until smooth. Stir the melted chocolate into the butter and egg yolk mixture and stir until thick. Cover and leave to cool for about 30 minutes. Chill in the refrigerator for 1½ hours or until firm.

3 Divide the truffle mixture into 24 pieces and mould around the drained cherries. Roll in the cocoa powder until evenly coated. Place the truffles in petit four paper cases and chill in the refrigerator for 2 hours before serving.

4 To make the rum truffles, break the chocolate into small pieces and place in a heavy-based saucepan with the cream and rum. Heat gently until the chocolate has melted, then stir until smooth. Stir in the ground almonds and pour into a small bowl and chill in the refrigerator for at least 6 hours or until the mixture is thick.

5 Remove the truffle from the refrigerator and shape small spoonfuls, about the size of a cherry, into balls. Roll in the sifted icing sugar and place in petit four paper cases. Store the truffles in the refrigerator until ready to serve.

INGREDIENTS
Makes 44

FOR THE CHOCOLATE TRUFFLES:
225 g/8 oz plain chocolate
25 g/1 oz butter, softened
2 medium egg yolks
2 tsp brandy or kirsch
2 tsp double cream
24 maraschino cherries, drained
2 tbsp cocoa powder, sifted

FOR THE RUM TRUFFLES:
125 g/4 oz plain dark chocolate
2 tbsp rum
125 ml/4 fl oz double cream
50 g/2 oz ground almonds
2 tbsp icing sugar, sifted

Tasty Tip

These truffles are so easy to make, they are great to give as gifts. Roll some in icing sugar, as above, and roll others in cocoa powder. Arrange in a gift box in a chequerboard pattern.

Apricot & Almond Layer Cake

1 Preheat the oven to 180°C/ 350°F/Gas Mark 4, 10 minutes before baking. Lightly oil and line 2 x 23 cm/9 inch round cake tins. Cream the butter and sugar together until light and fluffy, then beat in the egg yolks, one at a time, beating well after each addition. Stir in the cooled chocolate with 1 tablespoon of cooled boiled water, then fold in the flour and ground almonds.

2 Whisk the egg whites until stiff, then gradually whisk in the icing sugar beating well after each addition. Whisk until the egg whites are stiff and glossy, then fold the egg whites into the chocolate mixture in 2 batches.

3 Divide the mixture evenly between the prepared tins and bake in the preheated oven

for 30–40 minutes or until firm. Leave for 5 minutes before turning out onto wire racks. Leave to cool completely.

4 Split the cakes in half. Gently heat the jam, pass through a sieve and stir in the amaretto liqueur. Place 1 cake layer onto a serving plate. Spread with a little of the jam, then sandwich with the next layer. Repeat with all the layers and use any remaining jam to brush over the entire cake. Leave until the jam sets.

5 Meanwhile, beat the butter and chocolate together until smooth, then cool at room temperature until thick enough to spread. Cover the top and sides of the cake with the chocolate icing and leave to set before slicing and serving.

INGREDIENTS
Cuts into 8–10 slices

150 g/5 oz unsalted butter, softened

125 g/4 oz caster sugar

5 medium eggs, separated

150 g/5 oz plain dark chocolate, melted and cooled

150 g/5 oz self-raising flour, sifted

50 g/2 oz ground almonds

75 g/3 oz icing sugar, sifted

300 g/11 oz apricot jam

1 tbsp amaretto liqueur

125 g/4 oz unsalted butter, melted

125 g/4 oz plain dark chocolate, melted

Helpful Hint

Use a very good-quality apricot jam as it is a major flavour in the finished cake.

Black & White Torte

1 Preheat the oven to 180°C/ 350°F/Gas Mark 4, 10 minutes before baking. Lightly oil and line a 23 cm/9 inch round cake tin. Beat the eggs and sugar in a large bowl until thick and creamy. Sift together the cornflour, plain flour and self-raising flour 3 times, then lightly fold into the egg mixture.

2 Spoon the mixture into the prepared tin and bake in the preheated oven for 35–40 minutes or until firm. Turn the cake out onto a wire rack and leave to cool.

3 Place 300 ml/½ pint of the double cream in a saucepan and bring to the boil. Immediately remove from the heat and add the plain chocolate and a further tablespoon of the liqueur. Stir until smooth. Repeat using the remaining cream, white chocolate and liqueur. Chill in

the refrigerator for 2 hours, then whisk each mixture until thick and creamy.

4 Place the dark chocolate mixture in a piping bag fitted with a plain nozzle and place half the white chocolate mixture in a separate piping bag fitted with a plain nozzle. Reserve the remaining white chocolate mixture.

5 Split the cold cake horizontally into 2 layers. Brush or drizzle the remaining liqueur over the cakes. Put 1 layer onto a serving plate. Pipe alternating rings of white and dark chocolate mixture to cover the first layer of cake. Use the reserved white chocolate mixture to cover the top and sides of the cake. Dust with cocoa powder, cut into slices and serve. Store in the refrigerator.

INGREDIENTS
Cuts into 8–10 slices

4 medium eggs
150 g/5 oz caster sugar
50 g/2 oz cornflour
50 g/2 oz plain flour
50 g/2 oz self-raising flour
900 ml/1½ pints double cream
150 g/5 oz plain dark chocolate, chopped
300 g/11 oz white chocolate, chopped
6 tbsp Grand Marnier, or other orange liqueur
cocoa powder for dusting

Mocha Truffle Cake

1 Preheat the oven to 180°C/350°F/Gas Mark 4, 10 minutes before cooking. Lightly oil and line a deep 23 cm/9 inch round cake tin. Beat the eggs and sugar in a bowl until thick and creamy.

2 Sift together the cornflour, self-raising flour and cocoa powder and fold lightly into the egg mixture. Spoon into the prepared tin and bake in the preheated oven for 30 minutes or until firm. Turn out onto a wire rack and leave until cold. Split the cold cake horizontally into 2 layers. Mix together the milk and coffee liqueur and brush onto the cake layers.

3 Stir the cooled white chocolate into one bowl and the cooled plain dark chocolate into another one.

Whip the cream until soft peaks form, then divide between the 2 bowls and stir. Place 1 layer of cake in a 23 cm/9 inch spring-form tin. Spread with half the white chocolate cream. Top with the dark chocolate cream, then the remaining white chocolate cream, finally place the remaining cake layer on top. Chill in the refrigerator for 4 hours or overnight until set.

4 When ready to serve, melt the milk chocolate and butter in a heatproof bowl set over a saucepan of simmering water and stir until smooth. Remove from the heat and leave until thick enough to spread, then use to cover the top and sides of the cake. Leave to set at room temperature, then chill in the refrigerator. Cut the cake into slices and serve.

INGREDIENTS
Cuts into 8–10 slices

3 medium eggs
125 g/4 oz caster sugar
40 g/1½ oz cornflour
40 g/1½ oz self-raising flour
2 tbsp cocoa powder
2 tbsp milk
2 tbsp coffee liqueur
100 g/3½ oz white chocolate, melted and cooled
200 g/7 oz plain dark chocolate, melted and cooled
600 ml/1 pint double cream
200 g/7 oz milk chocolate
100 g/3½ oz unsalted butter

Helpful Hint

Unless you are going to make a lot of chocolate or coffee desserts, liqueurs are very expensive to buy. Look for supermarket own label brands or miniatures.

Double Marble Cake

1 Preheat the oven to 180°C/ 350°F/Gas Mark 4, 10 minutes before baking. Lightly oil and line the base of a 20.5 cm/8 inch cake tin. Break the white and dark chocolate into small pieces, then place in 2 separate bowls placed over 2 pans of simmering water, ensuring that the bowls are not touching the water. Heat the chocolate until melted and smooth.

2 In a large bowl cream the sugar and butter together until light and fluffy. Beat in the egg yolks, 1 at a time and add a spoonful of flour after each addition. Stir in the ground almonds. In another bowl whisk the egg whites until stiff. Gently fold in the egg whites and the remaining sifted flour alternately into the almond mixture until all the flour and egg whites have been incorporated. Divide the mixture between 2 bowls. Gently stir the white chocolate into 1 bowl, then add the dark chocolate to the other bowl.

3 Place alternating spoonfuls of the chocolate mixtures in the prepared cake tin. Using a skewer, swirl the mixtures together to get a marbled effect, then tap the tin on the work surface to level the mixture. Bake in the preheated oven for 40 minutes, or until cooked through, then leave to cool for 5 minutes in the tin, before turning out onto a wire rack to cool completely.

4 Melt the chocolate with the cream and butter and stir until smooth. Cool, then whisk until thick and swirl over the top of the cake.

INGREDIENTS
Cuts into 8–10 slices

75 g/3 oz white chocolate
75 g/3 oz plain dark chocolate
175 g/6 oz caster sugar
175 g/6 oz butter
4 medium eggs, separated
125 g/4 oz plain flour, sifted
75 g/3 oz ground almonds

FOR THE TOPPING:

50 g/2 oz white chocolate, chopped
75 g/3 oz plain dark chocolate, chopped
50 ml/2 fl oz double cream
100 g/3½ oz unsalted butter

Helpful Hint

Place a folded tea towel under the mixing bowl when creaming or mixing by hand. This stops the bowl slipping around and makes the whole operation quicker and easier.

Chocolate Buttermilk Cake

1 Preheat the oven to 180°C/ 350°F/Gas Mark 4, 10 minutes before baking. Lightly oil and line a deep 23 cm/9 inch round cake tin. Cream together the butter, vanilla essence and sugar until light and fluffy, then beat in the egg yolks, 1 at a time.

2 Sift together the flour and cocoa powder and fold into the egg mixture together with the buttermilk. Whisk the egg whites until soft peaks form and fold carefully into the chocolate mixture in 2 batches. Spoon the mixture into the prepared tin and bake in the preheated oven for 1 hour or until firm. Cool slightly, then turn out onto a wire rack and leave until completely cold.

3 Place the chocolate and butter together in a heat-proof bowl set over a saucepan of simmering water and heat until melted. Stir until smooth, then leave at room temperature until the chocolate is thick enough to spread.

4 Split the cake horizontally in half. Use some of the chocolate mixture to sandwich the 2 halves together. Spread and decorate the top of the cake with the remaining chocolate mixture. Finally, whip the cream until soft peaks form and use to spread around the sides of the cake. Chill in the refrigerator until required. Serve cut into slices. Store in the refrigerator.

INGREDIENTS
Cuts into 8–10 slices

175 g/6 oz butter
1 tsp vanilla essence
350 g/12 oz caster sugar
4 medium eggs, separated
100 g/3½ oz self-raising flour
40 g/1½ oz cocoa powder
175 ml/6 fl oz buttermilk
200 g/7 oz plain dark chocolate
100 g/3½ oz butter
300 ml/½ pint double cream

Tasty Tip

If buttermilk is unavailable, measure 175 ml/6 fl oz of full fat milk and add 2 teaspoons of lemon juice or white wine vinegar. Leave to stand for 1 hour at room temperature and then use as above.

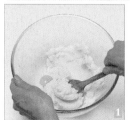

Peach & White Chocolate Gateau

1 Preheat the oven to 170°C/ 325°F/Gas Mark 3, 10 minutes before baking. Lightly oil and line a deep 23 cm/9 inch round cake tin. Cream the butter, orange rind and sugar together until light and fluffy. Add the eggs, 1 at a time, beating well after each addition, then beat in the cooled white chocolate.

2 Add the flour and 175 ml/ 6 fl oz of water in 2 batches. Spoon into the prepared tin and bake in the preheated oven for 1½ hours or until firm. Leave to stand for at least 5 minutes before turning out onto a wire rack to cool completely.

3 To make the filling, place the peaches in a bowl and pour over the liqueur. Leave to

stand for 30 minutes. Whip the cream with the icing sugar until soft peaks form, then fold in the peach mixture.

4 Split the cold cake in to 3 layers, place 1 layer on a serving plate and spread with half the peach filling. Top with a second sponge layer and spread with the remaining peach filling. Top with the remaining cake.

5 Whip the cream and icing sugar together until soft peaks form. Spread over the top and sides of the cake, piping some onto the top if liked. Press the hazelnuts into the side of cake and if liked sprinkle a few on top. Chill in the refrigerator until required. Serve cut into slices. Store the cake in the refrigerator.

INGREDIENTS
Cuts into 8–10 slices

175 g/6 oz unsalted butter, softened
2 tsp grated orange rind
175 g/6 oz caster sugar
3 medium eggs
100 g/3½ oz white chocolate, melted and cooled
225 g/8 oz self-raising flour, sifted
300 ml/½ pint double cream
40 g/1½ oz icing sugar
125 g/4 oz hazelnuts, toasted and chopped

FOR THE PEACH FILLING:

2 ripe peaches, peeled and chopped
2 tbsp peach or orange liqueur
300 ml/½ pint double cream
40 g/1½ oz icing sugar

Tasty Tip
When fresh peaches are out of season, use drained and chopped canned peaches instead.

Dark Chocolate Layered Torte

1 Preheat the oven to 150°C/ 300°F/Gas Mark 2, 10 minutes before baking. Lightly oil and line a 23 cm/9 inch square cake tin. Melt the butter in a saucepan, remove from the heat and stir in the coffee granules and 225 ml/8 fl oz hot water. Add the plain dark chocolate and sugar and stir until smooth, then pour into a bowl.

2 In another bowl, sift together the flours and cocoa powder. Using an electric whisk, whisk the sifted mixture into the chocolate mixture until smooth. Beat in the eggs and vanilla essence. Pour into the tin and bake in the preheated oven for 1¼ hours or until firm. Leave for at least 5 minutes before turning out onto a wire rack to cool.

3 Meanwhile, mix together 200 g/7 oz of the melted dark chocolate with the butter and icing sugar and beat until smooth. Leave to cool, then beat again. Reserve 4–5 tablespoons of the chocolate filling.

4 Cut the cooled cake in half to make 2 rectangles, then split each rectangle in 3 horizontally. Place 1 cake layer on a serving plate and spread thinly with the jam, then a thin layer of dark chocolate filling. Top with a second cake layer and sprinkle with a little liqueur, then spread thinly with filling. Repeat with the remaining cake layers, liqueur and filling.

5 Chill in the refrigerator for 2–3 hours or until firm. Cover the cake with the reserved chocolate filling and press the flaked almonds into the sides of the cake.

6 Place the remaining melted chocolate in a nonstick baking parchment piping bag. Snip a small hole in the tip and pipe thin lines 2 cm/¾ inch apart crossways over the cake. Drag a cocktail stick lengthways through the icing in alternating directions to create a feathered effect on the top. Serve.

INGREDIENTS
Cuts into 10–12 slices

175 g/6 oz butter
1 tbsp instant coffee granules
150 g/ 5 oz plain dark chocolate
350 g/12 oz caster sugar
150 g/5 oz self-raising flour
125 g/4 oz plain flour
2 tbsp cocoa powder
2 medium eggs
1 tsp vanilla essence
215 g/7½ oz plain dark
 chocolate, melted
125 g/4 oz butter, melted
40 g/1½ oz icing sugar, sifted
2 tsp raspberry jam
2½ tbsp chocolate liqueur
100 g/3½ oz toasted flaked
 almonds

Tasty Tip

Use dark chocolate which has 70 per cent cocoa solids in this cake for the best flavour.

Chocolate Mousse Sponge

1 Preheat the oven to 180°C/
350°F/Gas Mark 4, 10
minutes before baking. Lightly
oil and line a 23 cm/9 inch
round cake tin and lightly oil the
sides of a 23 cm/9 inch springform tin. Whisk the eggs, sugar
and vanilla essence until thick
and creamy. Fold in the flour,
ground almonds and dark
chocolate. Spoon the mixture
into the prepared round cake tin
and bake in the preheated oven
for 25 minutes or until firm. Turn
out onto a wire rack to cool.

2 For the mousse, soak the
gelatine in 50 ml/2 fl oz
of cold water for 5 minutes until
softened. Meanwhile, heat the
double cream in a small saucepan,
when almost boiling, remove
from the heat and stir in the
chocolate and vanilla essence. Stir
until the chocolate melts. Squeeze
the excess water out of the
gelatine and add to the chocolate
mixture. Stir until dissolved, then
pour into a large bowl.

3 Whisk the egg whites until
stiff, then gradually add
the caster sugar, whisking well
between each addition. Fold
the egg white mixture into the
chocolate mixture in 2 batches.

4 Split the cake into 2 layers.
Place 1 layer in the bottom
of the springform tin. Pour in
the chocolate mousse mixture,
then top with the second layer
of cake. Chill in the refrigerator
for 4 hours or until the mousse
has set. Loosen the sides and
remove the cake from the tin.
Dust with icing sugar and
decorate the top with a few
freshly sliced strawberries.
Serve cut into slices.

INGREDIENTS
Cuts into 8–10 slices

3 medium eggs
75 g/3 oz caster sugar
1 tsp vanilla essence
50 g/2 oz self-raising flour, sifted
25 g/1 oz ground almonds
*50 g/2 oz plain dark chocolate,
grated*
icing sugar, for dusting
*freshly sliced strawberries,
to decorate*

FOR THE MOUSSE:
2 sheets gelatine
50 ml/2 fl oz double cream
*100 g/3½ oz plain dark
chocolate, chopped*
1 tsp vanilla essence
4 medium egg whites
125 g/4 oz caster sugar

Tasty Tip
Sheet gelatine is very easy to use. Soak the gelatine as
described in step 2, then squeeze out the excess liquid. It must
be added to hot liquid, where it will melt on contact.

Chocolate Chiffon Cake

1 Preheat the oven to 170°C/ 325°F/Gas Mark 3, 10 minutes before serving. Lightly oil and line a 23 cm/9 inch round cake tin. Lightly oil a baking sheet. Blend the cocoa powder with 175 ml/6 fl oz boiling water and leave to cool. Place the flour and 350 g/12 oz of the caster sugar in a large bowl, and add the cocoa mixture, egg yolks, oil and vanilla essence. Whisk until smooth and lighter in colour.

2 Whisk the egg whites in a clean, grease-free bowl until soft peaks form, then fold into the cocoa mixture.

3 Pour into the prepared tin and bake in the preheated oven for 1 hour or until firm. Leave for 5 minutes before turning out onto a wire rack to cool.

4 To make the icing, cream together 125 g/4 oz of the butter with the icing sugar, cocoa powder and brandy until

smooth, then reserve. Melt the remaining butter and blend with 150 g/5 oz of the melted dark chocolate. Stir until smooth and then leave until thickened.

5 Place the remaining caster sugar into a heavy-based saucepan over a low heat and heat until the sugar has melted and is a deep golden brown.

6 Add the walnuts and the remaining melted chocolate to the melted sugar and pour onto the prepared baking sheet. Leave until cold and brittle, then chop finely. Reserve.

7 Split the cake into 3 layers, place 1 layer onto a serving plate and spread with half of the brandy butter icing. Top with a second cake layer and spread with the remaining brandy butter icing, arrange the third cake layer on top. Cover the cake with the thickened chocolate glaze. Sprinkle with the walnut praline and serve.

INGREDIENTS
Cuts into 10–12 slices

50 g/2 oz cocoa powder
300 g/11 oz self-raising flour
550 g/1¼ lb caster sugar
7 medium eggs, separated
125 ml/4 fl oz vegetable oil
1 tsp vanilla essence
75 g/3 oz walnuts
50 g/2 oz plain dark chocolate
200 g/7 oz plain dark chocolate,
  melted

FOR THE ICING:
175 g/6 oz butter
275 g/10 oz icing sugar, sifted
2 tbsp cocoa powder, sifted
2 tbsp brandy

Helpful Hint

Do not overmix the mixture in step 2 or the cake will be heavy instead of very light and spongy.

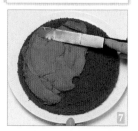

White Chocolate & Passion Fruit Cake

1 Preheat the oven to 180°C/ 350°F/Gas Mark 4 10 minutes before baking. Lightly oil and line 2 x 20.5 cm/8 inch cake tins.

2 Melt the white chocolate in a heatproof bowl set over a saucepan of simmering water. Stir in 125 ml/4 fl oz warm water and stir, then leave to cool.

3 Whisk the butter and sugar together until light and fluffy, add the eggs, one at a time, beating well after each addition. Beat in the chocolate mixture, soured cream and sifted flours. Divide the mixture into 8 portions. Spread 1 portion into each of the tins. Bake in the preheated oven for 10 minutes, or until firm, then turn out onto wire racks. Repeat with the remaining mixture to make 8 cake layers.

4 To make the icing, place 125 ml/4 fl oz of water

with 50 g/2 oz of the sugar in a saucepan. Heat gently, stirring, until the sugar has dissolved. Bring to the boil, simmer for 2 minutes. Remove from the heat and cool, then add 2 tablespoons of the passion fruit juice. Reserve.

5 Blend the remaining sugar with 50 ml/2 fl oz of water in a small saucepan and stir constantly over a low heat, without boiling, until the sugar has dissolved. Remove from the heat and cool. Stir in the remaining passion fruit juice and the seeds. Cool, then strain. Using an electric whisk, beat the butter in a bowl until very pale. Gradually beat in the syrup.

6 Place 1 layer of cake on a serving plate. Brush with the syrup and spread with a thin layer of icing. Repeat with the remaining cake, syrup and icing. Cover the cake with the remaining icing. Press the chocolate curls into the top and sides to decorate.

INGREDIENTS
Cuts into 8–10 slices

125 g/4 oz white chocolate
125 g/4 oz butter
225 g/8 oz caster sugar
2 medium eggs
125 ml/4 fl oz soured cream
200 g/7 oz plain flour, sifted
75 g/3 oz self-raising flour, sifted
125 g/4 oz white chocolate,
  coarsely grated, to decorate

FOR THE ICING:

200 g/7 oz caster sugar
4 tbsp passion fruit juice (about
  8–10 passion fruit, sieved)
1½ tbsp passion fruit seeds
250 g/9 oz unsalted butter

Food Fact

Passion fruit is available from large supermarkets. It adds a sweet/sour flavour that goes particularly well with white chocolate.

Sachertorte

1 Preheat the oven to 180°C/ 350°F/Gas Mark 4, 10 minutes before baking. Lightly oil and line a deep 23 cm/9 inch cake tin.

2 Melt the 150 g/5 oz of chocolate in a heatproof bowl set over a saucepan of simmering water. Stir in 1 tablespoon of water and leave to cool.

3 Beat the butter and 125 g/ 4 oz of the sugar together until light and fluffy. Beat in the egg yolks, one at a time, beating well between each addition. Stir in the melted chocolate, then the flour.

4 In a clean grease-free bowl, whisk the egg whites until stiff peaks form, then whisk in the remaining sugar. Fold into the chocolate mixture and spoon into the prepared tin. Bake in the pre-heated oven for 30 minutes until firm. Leave for 5 minutes, then turn out onto a wire rack to cool. Leave the cake upside down.

5 To decorate the cake, split the cold cake in 2 and place one half on a serving plate. Heat the jam and rub through a fine sieve.

6 Brush half the jam onto the first cake half, then cover with the remaining cake layer and brush with the remaining jam. Leave at room temperature for 1 hour or until the jam has set.

7 Place the plain dark chocolate with the butter into a heatproof bowl set over a saucepan of simmering water and heat until the chocolate melted. Stir occasionally until smooth, then leave until thickened. Use to cover the cake.

8 Melt the milk chocolate in a heatproof bowl set over a saucepan of simmering water. Place in a small greaseproof piping bag and snip a small hole at the tip. Pipe Sacher with a large 'S' on the top. Leave to set at room temperature.

INGREDIENTS
Cuts into 10–12 slices

150 g/5 oz plain dark chocolate
150 g/5 oz unsalted butter, softened
125 g/4 oz caster sugar, plus 2 tbsp
3 medium eggs, separated
150 g/5 oz plain flour, sifted

TO DECORATE:

225 g/8 oz apricot jam
125 g/4 oz plain dark chocolate, chopped
125 g/4 oz unsalted butter
25 g/1 oz milk chocolate

Food Fact

In 1832, the Viennese foreign minister asked a Vienna hotel to prepare an especially tempting cake. The head pastry chef was ill and so the task fell to second year apprentice, Franz Sacher, who presented this delightful cake.

Chocolate Roulade

1 Preheat the oven to 180°C/ 350°F/Gas Mark 4, 10 minutes before baking. Lightly oil and line a 33 cm x 23 cm/ 13 inch x 9 inch Swiss roll tin with nonstick baking parchment.

2 Break the chocolate into small pieces into a heatproof bowl set over a saucepan of simmering water. Leave until almost melted, stirring occasionally. Remove from the heat and leave to stand for 5 minutes.

3 Whisk the egg yolks with the sugar until pale and creamy and the whisk leaves a trail in the mixture when lifted, then carefully fold in the melted chocolate.

4 In a clean grease-free bowl, whisk the egg whites until stiff, then fold 1 large spoonful into the chocolate mixture.

5 Mix lightly, then gently fold in the remaining egg whites. Pour the mixture into the prepared tin and level the

surface. Bake in the preheated oven for 20–25 minutes or until firm.

6 Remove the cake from the oven, leave in the tin and cover with a wire rack and a damp tea towel. Leave for 8 hours or preferably overnight.

7 Dust a large sheet of nonstick baking parchment generously with 2 tablespoons of the icing sugar. Unwrap the cake and turn out onto the greaseproof paper. Remove the baking parchment.

8 Whip the cream with the liqueur until soft peaks form. Spread over the cake, leaving a 2.5 cm/1 inch border all round.

9 Using the paper to help, roll the cake up from a short end. Transfer to a serving plate, seam-side down, and dust with the remaining icing sugar. Decorate with fresh raspberries and mint. Serve.

INGREDIENTS
Cuts into 8 slices

200 g/7 oz plain dark chocolate
200 g/7 oz caster sugar
7 medium eggs, separated
300 ml/½ pint double cream
3 tbsp Cointreau or Grand Marnier
4 tbsp icing sugar for dusting

TO DECORATE:
fresh raspberries
sprigs of fresh mint

Tasty Tip

Leaving the cake in the tin overnight gives it a fudgy texture and also means that the cake is less likely to break when it is rolled up.

Supreme Chocolate Gateau

1 Preheat the oven to 180°C/350°F/Gas Mark 4, 10 minutes before baking. Lightly oil and line 3 x 20.5 cm/8 inch round cake tins. Place all the cake ingredients into a bowl and whisk together until thick, add a little warm water if very thick. Divide the mixture evenly between the prepared tins. Bake in the preheated oven for 35–40 minutes until a skewer inserted in the centre comes out clean. Cool on wire racks.

2 Very gently heat 2 table-spoons of hot water with 50 g/2 oz of chocolate and stir until combined. Remove from the heat and leave for 5 minutes. Place the gelatine into a shallow dish and add 2 tablespoons of cold water. Leave for 5 minutes then squeeze out any excess water and add to the chocolate and water mixture. Stir until dissolved. Whip the double cream until just thickened. Add the chocolate mixture and continue whisking until soft peaks form. Leave until starting to set.

3 Place 1 of the cakes onto a serving plate and spread with half the cream mixture. Top with a second cake and the remaining cream, cover with the third cake and chill in the refrigerator until the cream has set.

4 Melt 175 g/6 oz of the chocolate with the butter and stir until smooth, leave until thickened. Melt the remaining chocolate. Cut 12 x 10 cm/4 inch squares of tinfoil. Spread the chocolate evenly over the squares to within 2.5 cm/1 inch of the edges. Refrigerate for 3–4 minutes until just set but not brittle. Gather up the corners and crimp together. Return to the refrigerator until firm.

5 Spread the chocolate and butter mixture over the top and sides of the cake. Remove the foil from the giant curls and use to decorate the top of the cake. Dust with cocoa powder and serve cut into wedges.

INGREDIENTS
Cuts into 10–12 slices

FOR THE CAKE:
175 g/6 oz self-raising flour, sifted
1½ tsp baking powder, sifted
3 tbsp cocoa powder, sifted
175 g/6 oz margarine or butter, softened
175 g/6 oz caster sugar
3 large eggs

TO DECORATE:
350 g/12 oz plain dark chocolate
1 gelatine leaf
200 ml/7 fl oz double cream
75 g/3 oz butter
cocoa powder for dusting

Helpful Hint

If you prefer, make ordinary chocolate curls to decorate this cake.

Chocolate Hazelnut Meringue Gateau

1 Preheat the oven to 150°C/ 300°F/Gas Mark 2, 5 minutes before baking. Cut 3 pieces of nonstick baking parchment into 30.5 cm x 12.5 cm/12 inch x 5 inch rectangles and then place onto 2 or 3 baking sheets.

2 Whisk the egg whites until stiff, add half the sugar and whisk until the mixture is stiff, smooth and glossy. Whisk in the remaining sugar, 1 tablespoon at a time, beating well between each addition. When all the sugar has been added whisk for 1 minute. Stir in the hazelnuts.

3 Spoon the meringue inside the marked rectangles spreading in a continuous backwards and forwards movement. Bake in the preheated oven for 1¼ hours, remove and leave until cold. Trim the meringues until they measure 25.5 cm x 10 cm/10 inch x 4 inch. Reserve all the trimmings.

4 Melt the chocolate and the butter in a heatproof bowl set over a saucepan of gently simmering water and stir until smooth. Remove from the heat and beat in the egg yolks. Whisk the egg whites until stiff, then whisk in the icing sugar a little at a time. Fold the egg whites into the chocolate mixture and chill in the refrigerator for 20–30 minutes, until thick enough to spread. Whip the double cream until soft peaks form. Reserve.

5 Place 1 of the meringue layers onto a serving plate. Spread with about half of the mousse mixture, then top with a second meringue layer. Spread the remaining mouse mixture over the top with the third meringue. Spread the cream over the top and sprinkle with the chopped hazelnuts. Chill in the refrigerator for at least 4 hours and up to 24 hours. Serve cut into slices.

INGREDIENTS
Cuts into 8–10 slices

5 medium egg whites
275 g/10 oz caster sugar
125 g/4 oz hazelnuts, toasted and finely chopped
175 g/6 oz plain dark chocolate
100 g/3½ oz butter
3 medium eggs, separated plus 1 medium egg white
25 g/1 oz icing sugar
125 ml/4 fl oz double cream
hazelnuts, toasted and chopped, to decorate

Tasty Tip

This cake can be round. Make the meringues into circles measuring 20.5 cm/8 inches. Trim to 18 cm/7 inches before assembling.

Black Forest Gateau

1 Preheat the oven to 150°C/300°F/Gas Mark 2, 5 minutes before serving. Lightly oil and line a deep 23 cm/9 inch cake tin.

2 Melt the butter in a large saucepan. Blend the coffee with the hot water, add to the butter with the chocolate and sugar and heat gently, stirring until smooth. Pour into a large bowl and leave until just warm.

3 Sift together the flours and cocoa powder. Using an electric mixer, whisk the warm chocolate mixture on a low speed, then gradually whisk in the dry ingredients. Whisk in the eggs 1 at a time, then the vanilla essence.

4 Pour the mixture into the prepared tin and bake in the preheated oven for 1 hour 45 minutes or until firm and a skewer inserted into the centre comes out clean. Leave in the tin for 5 minutes to cool slightly before turning out onto a wire rack.

5 Place the cherries and their juice in a small saucepan and heat gently.

6 Blend the arrowroot with 2 teaspoons of water until smooth, then stir into the cherries. Cook, stirring, until the liquid thickens. Simmer very gently for 2 minutes, then leave until cold.

7 Whisk the double cream until thick. Trim the top of the cake if necessary, then split the cake into 3 layers.

8 Brush the base of the cake with half the kirsch. Top with a layer of cream and one-third of the cherries. Repeat the layering, then place the third layer on top.

9 Reserve a little cream for decorating and use the remainder to cover the top and sides of the cake. Pipe a decorative edge around the cake, then arrange the remaining cherries in the centre and serve.

INGREDIENTS
Cuts 10–12 slices

250 g/9 oz butter
1 tbsp instant coffee granules
350 ml/12 fl oz hot water
200 g/7 oz plain dark chocolate, chopped or broken
400 g/14 oz caster sugar
225 g/8 oz self-raising flour
150 g/5 oz plain flour
50 g/2 oz cocoa powder
2 medium eggs
2 tsp vanilla essence
2 x 400 g cans stoned cherries in juice
2 tsp arrowroot
600 ml/1 pint double cream
50 ml/2 fl oz kirsch

Helpful Hint

The cake can be assembled and served straightaway but will benefit from being refrigerated for 1–2 hours so that the cream sets slightly. This will make slicing easier.

Whole Orange & Chocolate Cake With Marmalade Cream

1 Preheat the oven to 180°C/ 350°F/Gas Mark 4, 10 minutes before baking. Lightly oil and line the base of a 900 g/ 2 lb loaf tin. Place the orange in a small saucepan, cover with cold water and bring to the boil. Simmer for 1 hour until completely soft. Drain and leave to cool.

2 Place 2 egg yolks, 1 whole egg and the sugar in a heatproof bowl set over a saucepan of simmering water and whisk until doubled in bulk. Remove from the heat and continue to whisk for 5 minutes until cooled.

3 Cut the whole orange in half and discard the seeds, then place into a food processor or blender and blend to a purée.

4 Carefully fold the purée into the egg yolk mixture with the ground almonds and melted chocolate.

5 Whisk the egg whites until stiff peaks form. Fold a large spoonful of the egg whites into the chocolate mixture, then gently fold the remaining egg whites into the mixture.

6 Pour into the prepared tin and bake in the preheated oven for 50 minutes, or until firm and a skewer inserted into the centre comes out clean. Cool in the tin before turning out of the tin and carefully discarding the lining paper.

7 Meanwhile, whip the double cream until just thickened. In another bowl, blend the soft cheese with the icing sugar and marmalade until smooth, then fold in the double cream.

8 Chill the marmalade cream in the refrigerator until required. Decorate with orange zest and serve the cake cut in slices with the marmalade cream.

INGREDIENTS
Cuts 6–8 slices

1 small orange, scrubbed
2 medium eggs, separated, plus
 1 whole egg
150 g/5 oz caster sugar
125 g/4 oz ground almonds
75 g/3 oz plain dark chocolate,
 melted
100 ml/3½ fl oz double cream
200 g/7 oz full fat soft cheese
25 g/1 oz icing sugar
2 tbsp orange marmalade
orange zest, to decorate

Tasty Tip

This cake contains no flour and is therefore likely to sink in the centre on cooling. This is normal and does not mean that the cake is not cooked.

Grated Chocolate Roulade

1 Preheat the oven to 180°C/350°F/Gas Mark 4, 10 minutes before serving. Lightly oil and line a 20.5 cm x 30.5 cm/8 inch x 12 inch Swiss roll tin. Beat the egg yolks and sugar with an electric mixer for 5 minutes or until thick, then stir in 2 tablespoons of hot water and the grated chocolate. Finally fold in the sifted flour.

2 Whisk the egg whites until stiff, then fold 1–2 tablespoons of egg white into the chocolate mixture. Mix lightly, then gently fold in the remaining egg white. Pour into the prepared tin and bake in the preheated oven for about 12 minutes or until firm.

3 Place a large sheet of non-stick baking parchment onto a work surface and sprinkle liberally with caster sugar. Turn the cake onto the baking parchment, discard the lining paper and trim away the crisp edges. Roll up as for a Swiss roll cake, leave for 2 minutes, then unroll and leave to cool.

4 Beat the double cream with the icing sugar and vanilla essence until thick. Reserve a little for decoration, then spread the remaining cream over the cake, leaving a 2.5 cm/1 inch border all round. Using the greaseproof paper, roll up from a short end.

5 Carefully transfer the roulade to a large serving plate and use the reserved cream to decorate the top. Add the chocolate curls just before serving, then cut into slices and serve. Store in the refrigerator

INGREDIENTS
Cuts 8 slices

4 medium eggs, separated

125 g/4 oz caster sugar

60 g/2½ oz plain dark chocolate, grated

75 g/3 oz self-raising flour, sifted

2 tbsp caster sugar, plus extra for sprinkling

150 ml/¼ pint double cream

2 tsp icing sugar

1 tsp vanilla essence

chocolate curls, to decorate

Helpful Hint

Make sure to leave a border around the cream before rolling up the roulade or all the cream will squeeze out of the ends.

White Chocolate & Raspberry Mousse Gateau

1 Preheat the oven to 190°C/ 375°F/Gas Mark 5, 10 minutes before baking. Oil and line 2 x 23 cm/9 inch cake tins. Whisk the eggs and sugar until thick and creamy and the whisk leaves a trail in the mixture. Fold in the flour and cornflour, then divide between the tins. Bake in the preheated oven for 12–15 minutes or until risen and firm. Cool in the tins, then turn out onto wire racks.

2 Place the gelatine with 4 tablespoons of cold water in a dish and leave to soften for 5 minutes. Purée half the raspberries, press through a sieve, then heat until nearly boiling. Squeeze out excess water from the gelatine, add to the purée and stir until dissolved. Reserve.

3 Melt 175 g/6 oz of the chocolate in a bowl set over a saucepan of simmering water. Leave to cool, then stir in the fromage frais and purée.

Whisk the egg whites until stiff and whisk in the sugar. Fold into the raspberry mixture with the rest of the raspberries.

4 Line the sides of a 23 cm/9 inch springform tin with nonstick baking parchment. Place 1 layer of sponge in the base and sprinkle with half the liqueur. Pour in the raspberry mixture and top with the second sponge. Brush with the remaining liqueur. Press down and chill in the refrigerator for 4 hours. Unmould onto a plate.

5 Cut a strip of double thickness nonstick baking parchment to fit around the cake and stand 1 cm/½ inch higher. Melt the remaining white chocolate and spread thickly onto the parchment. Leave until just setting. Wrap around the cake and freeze for 15 minutes. Peel away the parchment. Whip the cream until thick and spread over the top. Decorate with raspberries.

INGREDIENTS
Cuts 8 slices

4 medium eggs
125 g/4 oz caster sugar
75 g/3 oz plain flour, sifted
25 g/1 oz cornflour, sifted
3 gelatine leaves
450 g/1 lb raspberries, thawed if frozen
400 g/14 oz white chocolate
200 g/7 oz plain fromage frais
2 medium egg whites
25 g/1 oz caster sugar
4 tbsp raspberry or orange liqueur
200 ml/7 fl oz double cream
fresh raspberries, halved, to decorate

Helpful Hint

Do not try to wrap the chocolate-covered parchment around the cake before it is nearly set or it will run down and be uneven.

Chocolate Orange Fudge Cake

1 Preheat the oven to 180°C/ 350°F/Gas Mark 4, 10 minutes before baking. Lightly oil and line 2 x 23 cm/9 inch round cake tins with nonstick baking parchment. Blend the cocoa powder and 50 ml/2 fl oz of boiling water until smooth. Stir in the orange zest and reserve. Sift together the flour, baking powder, bicarbonate of soda and salt, then reserve. Cream together the sugar and softened butter and beat in the eggs, 1 at a time, then the cocoa powder and vanilla essence. Finally, stir in the flour mixture and the soured cream in alternate spoonfuls.

2 Divide the mixture between the prepared tins and bake in the preheated oven for 35 minutes, or until the edges of the cake pull away from the tin and

the tops spring back when lightly pressed. Cool in the tins for 10 minutes, then turn out onto wire racks until cold.

3 Gently heat together the butter and milk with the pared orange rind. Simmer for 10 minutes, stirring occasionally. Remove from the heat and discard the orange rind.

4 Pour the warm orange and milk mixture into a large bowl and stir in the cocoa powder. Gradually beat in the sifted icing sugar and beat until the icing is smooth and spreadable. Place 1 cake onto a large serving plate. Top with about one-quarter of the icing, place the second cake on top, then cover the cake completely with the remaining icing. Serve.

Cuts into 8–10 slices

60 g/2½ oz cocoa powder
grated zest of 1 orange
350 g/12 oz self-raising flour
2 tsp baking powder
1 tsp bicarbonate of soda
½ tsp salt
225 g/8 oz light soft brown sugar
175 g/6 oz butter, softened
3 medium eggs
1 tsp vanilla essence
250 ml/9 fl oz soured cream
6 tbsp butter
6 tbsp milk
thinly pared rind of 1 orange
6 tbsp cocoa powder
250 g/9 oz icing sugar, sifted

Helpful Hint

This cake keeps exceptionally well in an airtight container for up to 5 days.

Cranberry & White Chocolate Cake

1 Preheat the oven to 180°C/ 350°F/Gas Mark 4, 10 minutes before baking. Lightly oil and flour a 23 cm/9 inch kugelhopf tin or ring tin. Using an electric mixer, cream the butter and cheese with the sugars until light and fluffy. Add the grated orange zest and vanilla essence and beat until smooth, then beat in the eggs, 1 at a time.

2 Sift the flour and baking powder together and stir into the creamed mixture, beating well after each addition. Fold in

the cranberries and 175 g/6 oz of the white chocolate. Spoon into the prepared tin and bake in the preheated oven for 1 hour, or until firm and a skewer inserted into the centre comes out clean. Cool in the tin before turning out onto a wire rack.

3 Melt the remaining white chocolate, stir until smooth, then stir in the orange juice and leave to cool until thickened. Transfer the cake to a serving plate and spoon over the white chocolate and orange glaze. Leave to set.

INGREDIENTS
Serves 4

225 g/8 oz butter, softened
250 g/9 oz full fat soft cheese
150 g/5 oz light soft brown sugar
200 g/7 oz caster sugar
grated zest of ½ orange
1 tsp vanilla essence
4 medium eggs
375 g/13 oz plain flour
2 tsp baking powder
200 g/7 oz cranberries, thawed
  if frozen
225 g/8 oz white chocolate,
  coarsely chopped
2 tbsp orange juice

Tasty Tip

If fresh or frozen cranberries are not available substitute with either peeled and diced Bramley cooking apple, raisins, dried cranberries or ready-to-eat chopped dried apricots.

Helpful Hint

A kugelhopf tin is a ring tin with fluted sides that makes a decoratively shaped cake. A kugelhopf is a yeasted German cake, similar to a panettone.

Fresh Strawberry Sponge Cake

1 Preheat the oven to 190°C/ 375°F/Gas Mark 5 10 minutes before baking. Lightly oil and line the bases of 2 x 20.5 cm/8 inch round cake tins with greaseproof or baking paper.

2 Using an electric whisk, beat the butter, sugar and vanilla essence until pale and fluffy. Gradually beat in the eggs a little at a time, beating well between each addition.

3 Sift half the flour over the mixture and using a metal spoon or rubber spatula gently fold into the mixture. Sift over the remaining flour and fold in until just blended.

4 Divide the mixture between the tins, spreading evenly.

Gently smooth the surfaces with the back of a spoon. Bake in the centre of the preheated oven for 20–25 minutes, or until well risen and golden.

5 Remove and leave to cool before turning out on to a wire rack. Whip the cream with 1 tablespoon of the icing sugar until it forms soft peaks. Fold in the chopped strawberries.

6 Spread 1 cake layer evenly with the mixture and top with the second cake layer, rounded side up.

7 Thickly dust the cake with icing sugar and decorate with the reserved strawberries. Carefully slide on to a serving plate and serve.

INGREDIENTS
8–10 servings

175 g/6 oz unsalted
  butter, softened
175 g/6 oz caster sugar
1 tsp vanilla essence
3 large eggs, beaten
175 g/6 oz self-raising flour
150 ml/¼ pint double cream
2 tbsp icing sugar, sifted
225 g/8 oz fresh strawberries,
  hulled and chopped
few extra strawberries, to decorate

Helpful Hint

For sponge cakes, it is important to achieve the correct consistency of the uncooked mixture. Check it after folding in the flour by tapping a spoonful of the mixture on the side of the bowl. If it drops easily, 'dropping' consistency has been reached. If it is too stiff, fold in a tablespoon of cooled boiled water.

Almond Angel Cake with Amaretto Cream

1 Preheat the oven to 180°C/ 350°F/Gas Mark 4 10 minutes before baking. Sift together the 175 g/6 oz icing sugar and flour. Stir to blend, then sift again and reserve.

2 Using an electric whisk, beat the egg whites, cream of tartar, vanilla essence, ½ teaspoon of almond essence and salt on medium speed until soft peaks form. Gradually add the caster sugar, 2 tablespoons at a time, beating well after each addition, until stiff peaks form.

3 Sift about one-third of the flour mixture over the egg white mixture and using a metal spoon or rubber spatula, gently fold into the egg white mixture.

4 Repeat, folding the flour mixture into the egg white mixture in 2 more batches. Spoon gently into an ungreased angel food cake tin or 25.5 cm/ 10 inch tube tin.

5 Bake in the preheated oven until risen and golden on top and the surface springs back quickly when gently pressed with a clean finger. Immediately invert the cake tin and cool completely in the tin.

6 When cool, carefully run a sharp knife around the edge of the tin and the centre ring to loosen the cake from the edge. Using the fingertips, ease the cake from the tin and invert on to a cake plate. Thickly dust the cake with the extra icing sugar.

7 Whip the cream with the remaining almond essence, Amaretto liqueur and a little more icing sugar, until soft peaks form.

8 Fill a piping bag fitted with a star nozzle with half the cream and pipe around the bottom edge of the cake. Decorate the edge with the fresh raspberries and serve the remaining cream separately.

INGREDIENTS
Cuts into 10–12 slices

175 g/6 oz icing sugar, plus
 2–3 tbsp
150 g/5 oz plain flour
350 ml/12 fl oz egg whites
 (about 10 large egg whites)
1½ tsp cream of tartar
½ tsp vanilla essence
1 tsp almond essence
¼ tsp salt
200 g/7 oz caster sugar
175 ml/6 fl oz double cream
2 tablespoons Amaretto liqueur
fresh raspberries, to decorate

Food Fact

Angel cake has a very light and delicate texture, and can be difficult to slice. For best results, use 2 forks to gently separate a portion of the cake.

Luxury Carrot Cake

1 Preheat the oven to 180°C/ 350°F/Gas Mark 4 10 minutes before baking. Lightly oil a 33 x 23 cm/13 x 9 inch baking tin. Line the base with non-stick baking paper, oil and dust with flour.

2 Sift the first 6 ingredients into a large bowl and stir in the sugars to blend. Make a well in the centre.

3 Beat the eggs, oil and vanilla essence together and pour into the well. Using an electric whisk, gradually beat drawing in the flour mixture from the side until a smooth batter forms. Stir in the carrots, crushed pineapple and chopped nuts until blended.

4 Pour into the prepared tin and smooth the surface evenly. Bake in the preheated oven for 50 minutes, or until firm and a skewer inserted into the centre comes out clean. Remove from the oven and leave to cool before removing from the tin and discarding the lining paper.

5 For the frosting, beat the cream cheese, butter and vanilla essence together until smooth, then gradually beat in the icing sugar until the frosting is smooth. Add a little milk, if necessary. Spread the frosting over the top. Refrigerate for about 1 hour to set the frosting, then cut into squares and serve.

Food Fact

Carrots contain beta carotene, which on cooking converts in the body to Vitamin A. They are antioxidants, which help in the fight against heart disease and cancer. When buying carrots, choose bright coloured, firm, well-shaped specimens and where possible, avoid peeling as the vitamin content is located immediately under the skin.

INGREDIENTS
Cuts into 12 slices

275 g/10 oz plain flour
2 tsp baking powder
1 tsp bicarbonate of soda
1 tsp salt
2 tsp ground cinnamon
1 tsp ground ginger
200 g/7 oz dark soft brown sugar
100 g/3½ oz caster sugar
4 large eggs, beaten
250 ml/9 fl oz sunflower oil
1 tbsp vanilla essence
4 carrots, peeled and shredded
  (about 450 g/1 lb)
380 g/14 oz can crushed
  pineapple, well drained
125 g/4 oz pecans or walnuts,
  toasted and chopped

FOR THE FROSTING:

175 g/6 oz cream cheese, softened
50 g/2 oz butter, softened
1 tsp vanilla essence
225 g/8 oz icing sugar, sifted
1–2 tbsp milk

White Chocolate Cheesecake

1 Preheat the oven to 180°C/ 350°F/Gas Mark 4 10 minutes before baking. Lightly oil a 23 x 7.5 cm /9 x 3 inch springform tin. Crush the biscuits and almonds in a food processor to form fine crumbs.

2 Pour in the butter and almond essence and blend. Pour the crumbs into the tin and using the back of a spoon, press on to the bottom and up the sides to within 1 cm/½ inch of the top of the tin edge.

3 Bake in the preheated oven for 5 minutes to set. Remove and transfer to a wire rack. Reduce the oven temperature to 150°C/ 300°F/Gas Mark 2.

4 Heat the white chocolate and cream in a saucepan over a low heat, stirring constantly until melted. Remove and cool.

5 Beat the cream cheese and sugar until smooth. Add the eggs, one at a time, beating well after each addition. Slowly beat

in the cooled white chocolate cream and the Amaretto and pour into the baked crust. Place on a baking tray and bake for 45–55 minutes, until the edge of the cake is firm, but the centre is slightly soft. Reduce the oven temperature if the top begins to brown. Remove to a wire rack and increase the temperature to 200°C/400°F/Gas Mark 6.

6 To make the topping, beat the soured cream, sugar and almond or vanilla essence until smooth and gently pour over the cheesecake, tilting the pan to distribute the topping evenly. Alternatively spread with a metal palette knife.

7 Bake for another 5 minutes to set. Turn off the oven and leave the door halfway open for about 1 hour. Transfer to a wire rack and run a sharp knife around the edge of the crust to separate from the tin. Cool and refrigerate until chilled. Remove from the tin, decorate with white chocolate curls and serve.

INGREDIENTS
Cuts into 16 slices

FOR THE BASE:
150 g/5 oz digestive biscuits
50 g/2 oz whole almonds,
  lightly toasted
50 g/2 oz butter, melted
½ tsp almond essence

FOR THE FILLING:
350 g/12 oz good-quality white
  chocolate, chopped
125 ml /4 fl oz double cream
700 g/1½ lb cream
  cheese, softened
50 g/2 oz caster sugar
4 large eggs
2 tbsp Amaretto or
  almond-flavour liqueur

FOR THE TOPPING:
450 ml /¾ pint soured cream
50 g/2 oz caster sugar
½ tsp almond or vanilla essence
white chocolate curls,
  to decorate

Rich Devil's Food Cake

1 Preheat the oven to 180°C/ 350°F/Gas Mark 4 10 minutes before baking. Lightly oil and line the bases of 3 x 23 cm/9 inch cake tins with greaseproof or baking paper. Sift the flour, bicarbonate of soda and salt into a bowl.

2 Sift the cocoa powder into another bowl and gradually whisk in a little of the milk to form a paste. Continue whisking in the milk until a smooth mixture results.

3 Beat the butter, sugar and vanilla essence until light and fluffy then gradually beat in the eggs, beating well after each addition. Stir in the flour and cocoa mixtures alternately in 3 or 4 batches.

4 Divide the mixture evenly among the 3 tins, smoothing the surfaces evenly. Bake in the preheated oven for 25-35 minutes, until cooked and firm to the touch. Remove, cool and turn

out on to a wire rack. Discard the lining paper.

5 To make the frosting, put the sugar, salt and chocolate into a heavy-based saucepan and stir in the milk until blended. Add the golden syrup and butter. Bring the mixture to the boil over a medium-high heat, stirring to help dissolve the sugar.

6 Boil for 1 minute, stirring constantly. Remove from the heat, stir in the vanilla essence and cool. When cool, whisk until thickened and slightly lightened in colour.

7 Sandwich the 3 cake layers together with about a third of the frosting, placing the third cake layer with the flat side up.

8 Transfer the cake to a serving plate and, using a metal palette knife, spread the remaining frosting over the top and sides. Swirl the top to create a decorative effect and serve.

INGREDIENTS
Cuts into 12–16 slices

450 g/1 lb plain flour
1 tbsp bicarbonate of soda
½ tsp salt
75 g/3 oz cocoa powder
300 ml/½ pint milk
150 g/5 oz butter, softened
400 g/14 oz soft dark brown sugar
2 tsp vanilla essence
4 large eggs

CHOCOLATE FUDGE FROSTING:
275 g/10 oz caster sugar
½ tsp salt
125 g/4 oz plain dark chocolate, chopped
225 ml/8 fl oz milk
2 tbsp golden syrup
125 g/4 oz butter, diced
2 tsp vanilla essence

Italian Polenta Cake with Mascarpone Cream

1 Preheat the oven to 190°C/ 375°F/Gas Mark 5 10 minutes before baking. Butter a 23 cm/9 inch springform tin. Dust lightly with flour.

2 Stir the flour, polenta or cornmeal, baking powder, salt and lemon zest together. Beat the eggs and half the sugar until light and fluffy. Slowly beat in the milk and almond essence.

3 Stir in the raisins or sultanas, then beat in the flour mixture and 50 g/2 oz of the butter.

4 Spoon into the tin and smooth the top evenly. Arrange the pear slices on top in overlapping concentric circles.

5 Melt the remaining butter and brush over the pear slices. Sprinkle with the rest of the sugar.

6 Bake in the preheated oven for about 40 minutes, until puffed and golden and the edges of the pears are lightly caramelised. Transfer to a wire rack. Reserve to cool in the tin for 15 minutes.

7 Remove the cake from the tin. Heat the apricot jam with 1 tablespoon of water and brush over the top of the cake to glaze.

8 Beat the mascarpone cheese with the sugar to taste, the cream and Amaretto or rum until smooth and forming a soft dropping consistency. Serve with the polenta cake.

9 When cool, sprinkle the almonds over the polenta cake and dust generously with icing sugar. Serve the cake with the liqueur-flavoured mascarpone cream on the side.

INGREDIENTS
Cuts into 6–8 slices

1 tsp butter and flour for the tin
100 g/3½ oz plain flour
40 g/1½ oz polenta or
    yellow cornmeal
1 tsp baking powder
¼ tsp salt
grated zest of 1 lemon
2 large eggs
150 g/5 oz caster sugar
5 tbsp milk
½ tsp almond essence
2 tbsp raisins or sultanas
75 g/3 oz unsalted
    butter, softened
2 medium dessert pears, peeled,
    cored and thinly sliced
2 tbsp apricot jam
175 g/6 oz mascarpone cheese
1–2 tsp sugar
50 ml/2 fl oz double cream
2 tbsp Amaretto liqueur or rum
2–3 tbsp toasted flaked almonds
icing sugar, to dust

Autumn Bramley Apple Cake

1 Preheat the oven to 170°C/ 325°F/Gas Mark 3 10 minutes before baking. Lightly oil and line the base of a 20.5 cm/8 inch deep cake tin with non-stick baking or greaseproof paper. Sift the flour and baking powder into a small bowl.

2 Beat the margarine, sugar and vanilla essence until light and fluffy. Gradually beat in the eggs a little at a time, beating well after each addition. Stir in the flour.

3 Spoon about one-third of the mixture into the tin, smoothing the surface. Toss the apple slices in the lemon juice and cinnamon and spoon over the cake mixture, making a thick even layer. Spread the remaining mixture over the apple layer to the edge of the tin, making sure the apples are covered. Smooth the top with the back of a wet spoon and sprinkle generously with sugar.

4 Bake in the preheated oven for 1½ hours, or until well risen and golden, the apples are tender and the centre of the cake springs back when pressed lightly. (Reduce the oven temperature slightly and cover the cake loosely with tinfoil if the top browns too quickly.)

5 Transfer to a wire rack and cool for about 20 minutes in the tin. Run a thin knife blade between the cake and the tin to loosen the cake and invert on to a paper-lined rack. Turn the cake the right way up and cool. Serve with the custard sauce or cream.

INGREDIENTS
Cuts into 8–10 slices

225 g/8 oz self-raising flour
1½ tsp baking powder
150 g/5 oz margarine, softened
150 g/5 oz caster sugar, plus extra for sprinkling
1 tsp vanilla essence
2 large eggs, beaten
1.1 kg/2½ lbs Bramley cooking apples, peeled, cored and sliced
1 tbsp lemon juice
½ tsp ground cinnamon
fresh custard sauce or cream, to serve

Food Fact

Cooking apples are extremely versatile, as they can be baked, puréed, poached and used in cakes and pies as well as savoury foods. Apples have a good soluble fibre content and are an important aid for slimmers as they keep hunger pangs at bay.

Christmas Cranberry Chocolate Roulade

1 Preheat the oven to 200°C / 400°F/Gas Mark 6. Bring the cream to the boil over a medium heat. Remove from the heat and add all of the chocolate, stirring until melted. Stir in the brandy, if using, and strain into a medium bowl. Cool, then refrigerate for 6–8 hours.

2 Lightly oil and line a 39 x 26 cm/15 ½ x 10½ inch Swiss roll tin with non-stick baking paper. Using an electric whisk, beat the egg yolks until thick and creamy. Slowly beat in the cocoa powder and half the icing sugar and reserve. Whisk the egg whites and cream of tartar into soft peaks. Gradually whisk in the remaining sugar until the mixture is stiff and glossy. Gently fold the yolk mixture into the egg whites with a metal spoon or rubber spatula. Spread evenly into the tin.

3 Bake in the preheated oven for 15 minutes. Remove and invert on to a large sheet of greaseproof paper, dusted with cocoa powder. Cut off the crisp edges of the cake then roll up. Leave on a wire rack until cold.

4 For the filling, heat the cranberry sauce with the brandy, if using, until warm and spreadable. Unroll the cooled cake and spread with the cranberry sauce. Allow to cool and set. Carefully spoon the whipped cream over the surface and spread to within 2.5 cm/1 inch of the edges. Re-roll the cake. Transfer to a cake plate or tray.

5 Allow the chocolate ganache to soften at room temperature, then beat until soft and of a spreadable consistency. Spread over the roulade and, using a fork, mark the roulade with ridges to resemble tree bark. Dust with icing sugar. Decorate with the caramelised orange strips and dried cranberries and serve.

INGREDIENTS
Cuts into 12–14 slices

CHOCOLATE GANACHE FROSTING:
300 ml/½ pint double cream
350 g/12 oz plain dark chocolate, chopped
2 tbsp brandy (optional)

FOR THE ROULADE:
5 large eggs, separated
3 tbsp cocoa powder, sifted, plus extra for dusting
125 g/4 oz icing sugar, sifted, plus extra for dusting
¼ tsp cream of tartar

FOR THE FILLING:
175 g/6 oz cranberry sauce
1–2 tbsp brandy (optional)
450 ml/¾ pint double cream, whipped to soft peaks

TO DECORATE:
caramelised orange strips
dried cranberries

Buttery Passion Fruit Madeira Cake

1 Preheat the oven to 180°C/ 350°F/Gas Mark 4 10 minutes before baking. Lightly oil and line the base of a 23 x 12.5 cm/9 x 5 inch loaf tin with greaseproof paper. Sift the flour and baking powder into a bowl and reserve.

2 Beat the butter, sugar, orange zest and vanilla essence until light and fluffy, then gradually beat in the eggs, 1 tablespoon at a time, beating well after each addition. If the mixture appears to curdle or separate, beat in a little of the flour mixture.

3 Fold in the flour mixture with the milk until just blended. Do not over mix. Spoon lightly into the prepared tin and smooth the top evenly. Sprinkle lightly with the tea-spoon of caster sugar.

4 Bake in the preheated oven for 55 minutes, or until well risen and golden brown. Remove from the oven and leave to cool for 15–20 minutes. Turn the cake out of the tin and discard the lining paper.

5 Cut the passion fruits in half and scoop out the pulp into a sieve set over a bowl. Press the juice through using a rubber spatula or wooden spoon. Stir in the icing sugar and stir to dissolve, adding a little extra sugar if necessary.

6 Using a skewer, pierce holes all over the cake. Slowly spoon the passion fruit glaze over the cake and allow to seep in. Gently invert the cake on to a wire rack, then turn it back the right way up. Dust with icing sugar and cool completely. Serve the Madeira cake cold.

INGREDIENTS
Cuts into 8–10 slices

210 g/7½ oz plain flour
1 tsp baking powder
175 g/6 oz unsalted butter, softened
250 g/9 oz caster sugar, plus 1 tsp
grated zest of 1 orange
1 tsp vanilla essence
3 medium eggs, beaten
2 tbsp milk
6 ripe passion fruits
50 g/2 oz icing sugar
icing sugar, to dust

Food Fact

Regardless of its name, Madeira cake does not actually originate from the Portuguese-owned island of Madeira. It is, in fact, a traditional English favourite which acquired its name because the cake was often served with the fortified wine, Madeira.

French Chocolate Pecan Torte

1 Preheat the oven to 180°C/ 350°F/Gas Mark 4 10 minutes before baking. Lightly butter and line a 20.5 x 5 cm/8 x 2 inch springform tin with non-stick baking paper. Wrap the tin in a large sheet of tinfoil to prevent water seeping in.

2 Melt the chocolate and butter in a saucepan over a low heat and stir until smooth. Remove from the heat and cool.

3 Using an electric whisk, beat the eggs, sugar and vanilla essence until light and foamy. Gradually beat in the melted chocolate, ground nuts and cinnamon, then pour into the prepared tin.

4 Set the foil-wrapped tin in a large roasting tin and pour in enough boiling water to come

2 cm/¾ inches up the sides of the tin. Bake in the preheated oven until the edge is set, but the centre is still soft when the tin is gently shaken. Remove from the oven and place on a wire rack to cool.

5 For the glaze, melt all the ingredients over a low heat until melted and smooth, then remove from the heat. Dip each pecan halfway into the glaze and set on a sheet of non-stick baking paper until set. Allow the remaining glaze to thicken slightly.

6 Remove the cake from the tin and invert. Pour the glaze over the cake smoothing the top and spreading the glaze around the sides. Arrange the glazed pecans around the edge of the torte. Allow to set and serve.

INGREDIENTS
Cuts into 16 slices

200 g/7 oz plain dark
  chocolate, chopped
150 g/5 oz butter, diced
4 large eggs
100 g/3½ oz caster sugar
2 tsp vanilla essence
125 g/4 oz pecans, finely ground
2 tsp ground cinnamon
24 pecan halves, lightly toasted,
  to decorate

CHOCOLATE GLAZE:
125 g/4 oz plain dark
  chocolate, chopped
60 g/2½ oz butter, diced
2 tbsp clear honey
¼ tsp ground cinnamon

Food Fact

Although this recipe is French, the torte actually originates from Germany, and tends to be a very rich cake-like dessert. It is delicious served with a fruity mixed berry compote.

Lemony Coconut Cake

1 Preheat the oven to 180°C/350°F/Gas Mark 4 10 minutes before baking. Lightly oil and flour 2 x 20.5 cm/8 inch non-stick cake tins.

2 Sift the flour, cornflour, baking powder and salt into a large bowl and add the white vegetable fat or margarine, sugar, lemon zest, vanilla essence, eggs and milk.

3 With an electric whisk on a low speed, beat until blended, adding a little extra milk if the mixture is very stiff. Increase the speed to medium and beat for about 2 minutes.

4 Divide the mixture between the tins and smooth the tops evenly. Bake in the preheated oven for 20–25 minutes, or until the cakes feel firm and are cooked. Remove from the oven and cool before removing from the tins.

5 Put all the ingredients for the frosting, except the

coconut, into a heatproof bowl placed over a saucepan of simmering water. (Do not allow the base of the bowl to touch the water.)

6 Using an electric whisk, blend the frosting ingredients on a low speed. Increase the speed to high and beat for 7 minutes, until the whites are stiff and glossy. Remove the bowl from the heat and continue beating until cool. Cover with clingfilm.

7 Using a serrated knife, split the cake layers horizontally in half and sprinkle each cut surface with the Malibu or rum. Sandwich the cakes together with the lemon curd and press lightly.

8 Spread the top and sides generously with the frosting, swirling and peaking the top. Sprinkle the coconut over the top of the cake and gently press on to the sides to cover. Decorate the coconut cake with the lime zest and serve.

INGREDIENTS
Cuts into 10–12 slices

275 g/10 oz plain flour
2 tbsp cornflour
1 tbsp baking powder
1 tsp salt
150 g/5 oz white vegetable fat or soft margarine
275 g/10 oz caster sugar
grated zest of 2 lemons
1 tsp vanilla essence
3 large eggs
150 ml/¼ pint milk
4 tbsp Malibu or rum
450 g/1 lb jar lemon curd
lime zest, to decorate

FOR THE FROSTING:
275 g/10 oz caster sugar
125 ml/4 fl oz water
1 tbsp glucose
¼ tsp salt
1 tsp vanilla essence
3 large egg whites
75 g/3 oz shredded coconut

Coffee & Walnut Gateau
with Brandied Prunes

1 Preheat the oven to 180°C/ 350°F/Gas Mark 4 10 minutes before baking. Put the prunes in a small bowl with the tea and brandy and allow to stand for 3–4 hours or overnight. Oil and line the bases of 2 x 23 cm/ 9 inch cake tins. Chop the walnut pieces in a food processor. Reserve a quarter of the nuts. Add the flour, baking powder and coffee and blend until finely ground.

2 Whisk the egg whites with the cream of tartar until soft peaks form. Sprinkle in one-third of the sugar, 2 tablespoons at a time, until stiff peaks form. In another bowl, beat the egg yolks, oil and the remaining sugar, until thick. Using a metal spoon or rubber spatula, alternately fold in the nut mixture and egg whites until just blended.

3 Divide the mixture evenly between the tins, smoothing the tops. Bake in the preheated oven for 30–35 minutes, or

until the top of the cakes spring back when lightly pressed with a clean finger. Remove from the oven and cool. Remove from the tins and discard the lining paper.

4 Drain the prunes, reserving the soaking liquid. Dry on kitchen paper, then chop and reserve. Whisk the cream with the icing sugar and liqueur until soft peaks form. Spoon one-eighth of the cream into a pastry bag fitted with a star nozzle.

5 Cut the cake layers in half horizontally. Sprinkle each cut side with 1 tablespoon of the reserved prune-soaking liquid. Sandwich the cakes together with half of the cream and all of the chopped prunes.

6 Spread the remaining cream around the sides of the cake and press in the reserved chopped walnuts. Pipe rosettes around the edge of the cake. Decorate with walnut halves and serve.

INGREDIENTS
Cuts into 10–12 slices

FOR THE PRUNES:
225 g/8 oz ready-to-eat pitted dried prunes
150 ml/¼ pint cold tea
3 tbsp brandy

FOR THE CAKE:
450 g/1 lb walnut pieces
50 g/2 oz self-raising flour
½ tsp baking powder
1 tsp instant coffee powder (not granules)
5 large eggs, separated
¼ tsp cream of tartar
150 g/5 oz caster sugar
2 tbsp sunflower oil
8 walnut halves, to decorate

FOR THE FILLING:
600 ml/1 pint double cream
4 tbsp icing sugar, sifted
2 tbsp coffee-flavoured liqueur

Wild Strawberry & Rose Petal Jam Cake

1 Preheat the oven to 180°C/350°F/Gas Mark 4 10 minutes before baking. Lightly oil and flour a 20.5 cm/8 inch non-stick cake tin. Sift the flour, baking powder and salt into a bowl and reserve.

2 Beat the butter and sugar until light and fluffy. Beat in the eggs, a little at a time, then stir in the rosewater. Gently fold in the flour mixture and milk with a metal spoon or rubber spatula and mix lightly together.

3 Spoon the cake mixture into the tin, spreading evenly and smoothing the top.

4 Bake in the preheated oven for 25–30 minutes, or until well risen and golden and the

centre springs back when pressed with a clean finger. Remove and cool, then remove from the tin.

5 For the filling, whisk the cream, yogurt, 1 tablespoon of rosewater and 1 tablespoon of icing sugar until soft peaks form. Split the cake horizontally in half and sprinkle with the remaining rosewater.

6 Spread the warmed jam on the base of the cake. Top with half the whipped cream mixture, then sprinkle with half the strawberries. Place the remaining cake half on top. Spread with the remaining cream and swirl, if desired. Decorate with the rose petals. Dust the cake lightly with a little icing sugar and serve.

INGREDIENTS
Cuts into 8 servings

275 g/10 oz plain flour
1 tsp baking powder
¼ tsp salt
150 g/5 oz unsalted
  butter, softened
200 g/7 oz caster sugar
2 large eggs, beaten
2 tbsp rosewater
125 ml/4 fl oz milk
125 g/4 oz rose petal or
  strawberry jam, slightly warmed
125 g/4 oz wild strawberries,
  hulled, or baby strawberries,
  chopped
frosted rose petals, to decorate

ROSE CREAM FILLING:
200 ml/7 fl oz double cream
25 ml/1 fl oz natural
  Greek yogurt
2 tbsp rosewater
1–2 tbsp icing sugar

Food Fact

Rosewater is distilled from rose petals and has an intensely perfumed flavour. It has been popular in the cuisines of the Middle East, China and India for centuries.

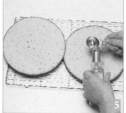

Celebration Fruit Cake

1 Preheat the oven to 170°C/ 325°F/Gas Mark 3 10 minutes before baking. Heat the butter and sugar in a saucepan until the sugar has dissolved, stirring frequently.

2 Add the pineapple and juice, dried fruits and peel. Bring to the boil, simmer 3 minutes, stirring occasionally, the remove from the heat to cool completely.

3 Lightly oil and line the base of a 20.5 x 7.5 cm/8 x 3 inch loose-bottomed cake tin with non-stick baking paper. Sift the flour, bicarbonate of soda, spices and salt into a bowl.

4 Add the boiled fruit mixture to the flour with the eggs and mix. Spoon into the tin and smooth the top. Bake in the

preheated oven for 1¼ hours, or until a skewer inserted into the centre comes out clean. (If the cake is browning too quickly, cover loosely with tinfoil and reduce the oven temperature.)

5 Remove and cool completely before removing from the tin and discarding the lining paper.

6 Arrange the nuts, cherries and prunes or dates in an attractive pattern on top of the cake. Heat the honey and brush over the topping to glaze.

7 Alternatively, toss the nuts and fruits in the warm honey and spread evenly over the top of the cake. Cool completely and store in a cake tin for a day or two before serving to allow the flavours to develop.

INGREDIENTS
Cuts into 16 slices

125 g/4 oz butter or margarine
125 g/4 oz soft dark brown sugar
380 g can
    crushed pineapple
150 g/5 oz raisins
150 g/5 oz sultanas
125 g/4 oz crystallised ginger,
    finely chopped
125 g/4 oz glacé cherries,
    coarsely chopped
125 g/4 oz mixed cut peel
225 g/8 oz self-raising flour
1 tsp bicarbonate of soda
2 tsp mixed spice
1 tsp ground cinnamon
½ tsp salt
2 large eggs, beaten

FOR THE TOPPING:

100 g/3½ oz pecan or walnut
    halves, lightly toasted
125 g/4 oz red, green and yellow
    glacé cherries
100 g/3½ oz small pitted prunes
    or dates
2 tbsp clear honey

Tasty Tip

The fruit used in this cake will make all the difference in flavour – try to use natural glacé cherries, which tend to have a fruitier taste. California prunes, raisins and sultanas are usually more flavoursome.

Toffee Walnut Swiss Roll

1 Preheat the oven to 190°C/ 375°F/Gas Mark 5 10 minutes before baking. Lightly oil and line a Swiss roll tin with non-stick baking paper. Beat the egg whites and cream of tartar until softly peaking. Gradually beat in 50 g/2 oz of the icing sugar until stiff peaks form.

2 In another bowl, beat the egg yolks with the remaining icing sugar until thick. Beat in the vanilla essence. Gently fold in the flour and egg whites alternately using a metal spoon or rubber spatula. Do not over mix.

3 Spoon the batter into the tin and spread evenly. Bake in the preheated oven for 12 minutes, or until well risen and golden and the cake springs back when pressed with a clean finger.

4 Lay a clean tea towel on a work surface and lay a piece of baking paper about 33 cm/ 13 inches long on the towel and dust with icing sugar. As soon as the cake is cooked turn out on

to the paper. Peel off the lining paper and cut off the crisp edges of the cake. Starting at one narrow end, roll the cake with the paper and towel. Transfer to a wire rack and cool completely.

5 For the filling, put the flour, milk and syrup into a small saucepan and place over a gentle heat. Bring to the boil, whisking until thick and smooth. Remove from the heat and slowly beat into the beaten egg yolks.

6 Pour the mixture back into the saucepan and cook over a low heat until it thickens and coats the back of a spoon.

7 Strain the mixture into a bowl and stir in the chopped walnuts or pecans. Cool, stirring occasionally, then fold in about half of the whipped cream.

8 Unroll the cooled cake and spread the filling over the cake. Re-roll and decorate with the remaining cream. Sprinkle with the icing sugar and serve.

INGREDIENTS
Cuts into 10–12 slices

4 large eggs, separated
½ tsp cream of tartar
125 g/4 oz icing sugar, plus extra to dust
½ tsp vanilla essence
125 g/4 oz self-raising flour

TOFFEE WALNUT FILLING:

2 tbsp plain flour
150 ml/¼ pint milk
5 tbsp golden syrup or maple syrup
2 large egg yolks, beaten
100 g/3½ oz walnuts or pecans, toasted and chopped
300 ml/½ pint double cream, whipped

Food Fact

Using a clean tea towel to roll up the sponge in this recipe, turns the steam into condensation which helps to keep the cake fairly flexible and therefore prevents it from cracking.

Raspberry & Hazelnut Meringue Cake

1 Preheat the oven to 140°C/ 275°F/Gas Mark 1. Line 2 baking sheets with non-stick baking paper and draw a 20.5 cm/8 inch circle on each. Whisk the egg whites and cream of tartar until soft peaks form then gradually beat in the sugar, 2 tablespoons at a time.

2 Beat well after each addition until the whites are stiff and glossy. Using a metal spoon or rubber spatula, gently fold in the ground hazelnuts.

3 Divide the mixture evenly between the 2 circles and spread neatly. Swirl 1 of the circles to make a decorative top layer. Bake in the preheated oven for about 1½ hours, until crisp

and dry. Turn off the oven and allow the meringues to cool for 1 hour. Transfer to a wire rack to cool completely. Carefully peel off the papers.

4 For the filling, whip the cream, icing sugar and liqueur, if using, together until soft peaks form. Place the flat round on a serving plate. Spread over most of the cream, reserving some for decorating and arrange the raspberries in concentric circles over the cream.

5 Place the swirly meringue on top of the cream and raspberries, pressing down gently. Pipe the remaining cream on to the meringue and decorate with a few raspberries and serve.

INGREDIENTS

Cuts into 8 slices

FOR THE MERINGUE:

4 large egg whites
¼ tsp cream of tartar
225 g/8 oz caster sugar
75 g/3 oz hazelnuts, skinned,
  toasted and finely ground

FOR THE FILLING:

300 ml/½ pint double cream
1 tbsp icing sugar
1–2 tbsp raspberry-flavoured
  liqueur (optional)
350 g/12 oz fresh raspberries

Helpful Hint

It is essential when whisking egg whites that the bowl being used is completely clean and dry, as any grease or oil will prevent the egg whites from gaining the volume needed.

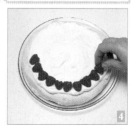

Chocolate & Almond Daquoise with Summer Berries

1 Preheat the oven to 140°C/ 275°F/Gas Mark 1 10 minutes before baking. Line 3 baking sheets with non-stick baking paper and draw a 20.5 cm/8 inch round on each one.

2 Whisk the egg whites and cream of tartar until soft peaks form.

3 Gradually beat in the sugar, 2 tablespoons at a time, beating well after each addition, until the whites are stiff and glossy.

4 Beat in the almond essence, then using a metal spoon or rubber spatula gently fold in the ground almonds.

5 Divide the mixture evenly between the 3 circles of baking paper, spreading neatly into the rounds and smoothing the tops evenly.

6 Bake in the preheated oven for about 1¼ hours or until crisp, rotating the baking sheets halfway through cooking. Turn off the oven, allow to cool for about 1 hour, then remove and cool completely before discarding the lining paper

7 Beat the butter, icing sugar and cocoa powder until smooth and creamy, adding the milk or cream to form a soft consistency.

8 Reserve about a quarter of the berries to decorate. Spread 1 meringue with a third of the buttercream and top with a third of the remaining berries. Repeat with the other meringue rounds, buttercream and berries.

9 Scatter with the toasted flaked almonds, the reserved berries and sprinkle with icing sugar and serve.

INGREDIENTS

Cuts into 8 servings

ALMOND MERINGUES:

6 large egg whites
¼ tsp cream of tartar
275 g/10 oz caster sugar
½ tsp almond essence
50 g/2 oz blanched or flaked almonds, lightly toasted and finely ground

CHOCOLATE BUTTERCREAM:

75 g/3 oz butter, softened
450 g/1 lb icing sugar, sifted
50 g/2 oz cocoa powder, sifted
3–4 tbsp milk or single cream
550 g/1¼ lb mixed summer berries such as raspberries, strawberries and blackberries

TO DECORATE:

toasted flaked almonds
icing sugar

Orange Fruit Cake

1 Preheat the oven to 180°C/ 350°F/Gas Mark 4 10 minutes before baking. Lightly oil and line the base of a 25.5 cm/10 inch ring mould tin or deep springform tin with non-stick baking paper.

2 Sift the flour and baking powder into a large bowl and stir in the sugar.

3 Make a well in the centre and add the butter, eggs, grated zest and orange juice. Beat until blended and a smooth batter is formed. Turn into the tin and smooth the top.

4 Bake in the preheated oven for 35–45 minutes, or until golden and the sides begin to shrink from the edge of the tin. Remove, cool before removing from the tin and discard the lining paper.

5 Using a serrated knife, cut the cake horizontally about one-third from the top and remove the top layer of the cake.

If not using a ring mould tin, scoop out a centre ring of sponge from the top third and the bottom two-thirds of the layer, making a hollow tunnel. Reserve for a trifle or other dessert. Sprinkle the cut sides with the Cointreau.

6 For the filling, whip the cream and yogurt with the vanilla essence, Cointreau and icing sugar until soft peaks form.

7 Chop the orange fruit and fold into the cream. Spoon some of this mixture on to the bottom cake layer, mounding it slightly. Transfer to a serving plate.

8 Cover with the top layer of sponge and spread the remaining cream mixture over the top and sides.

9 Press the chopped nuts into the sides of the cake and decorate the top with the Cape gooseberries, blueberries and raspberries. If liked, dust the top with icing sugar and serve.

INGREDIENTS
Cuts into 10–12 slices

ORANGE CAKE:
225 g/8 oz self-raising flour
2 tsp baking powder
225 g/8 oz caster sugar
225 g/8 oz butter, softened
4 large eggs
grated zest of 1 orange
2 tbsp orange juice
2–3 tbsp Cointreau
125 g/4 oz chopped nuts
Cape gooseberries, blueberries,
 raspberries and mint sprigs
 to decorate
icing sugar, to dust (optional)

FOR THE FILLING:
450 ml/¾ pint double cream
50 ml/2 fl oz Greek yogurt
½ tsp vanilla essence
2–3 tbsp Cointreau
1 tbsp icing sugar
450 g/1 lb orange fruits, such as
 mango, peach, nectarine, papaya
 and yellow plums

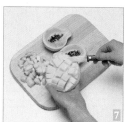

Chocolate Mousse Cake

1 Preheat the oven to 180°C/ 350°F/Gas Mark 4 10 minutes before baking. Lightly oil and line the bases of 2 x 20.5 cm/8 inch springform tins with baking paper. Melt the chocolate and butter in a bowl set over a saucepan of simmering water. Stir until smooth. Remove from the heat and stir in the brandy.

2 Whisk the egg yolks and the sugar, reserving 2 table-spoons of the sugar, until thick and creamy. Slowly beat in the chocolate mixture until smooth and well blended. Whisk the egg whites until soft peaks form, then sprinkle over the remaining sugar and continue whisking until stiff but not dry.

3 Fold a large spoonful of the egg whites into the choco-late mixture. Gently fold in the remaining egg whites. Divide about two-thirds of the mixture evenly between the tins, tapping to distribute the mixture evenly. Reserve the remaining one-third of the chocolate mousse mixture

for the filling. Bake in the preheated oven for about 20 minutes, or until the cakes are well risen and set. Remove and cool for at least 1 hour.

4 Loosen the edges of the cake layers with a knife. Using the fingertips, lightly press the crusty edges down. Pour the rest of the mousse over one layer, spreading until even. Carefully unclip the side, remove the other cake from the tin and gently invert on to the mousse, bottom side up to make a flat top layer. Discard lining paper and chill for 4–6 hours, or until set.

5 To make the glaze, melt the cream and chocolate with the brandy in a heavy-based saucepan and stir until smooth. Cool until thickened. Unclip the side of the mousse cake and place on a wire rack. Pour over half the glaze and spread to cover. Allow to set, then decorate with chocolate curls. To serve, heat the remaining glaze and pour round each slice, and dot with cream.

INGREDIENTS
Cuts into 8–10 servings

FOR THE CAKE:
450 g / 1 lb plain dark chocolate, chopped
125 g / 4 oz butter, softened
3 tbsp brandy
9 large eggs, separated
150 g / 5 oz caster sugar

CHOCOLATE GLAZE:
225 ml / 8 fl oz double cream
225 g / 8 oz plain dark chocolate, chopped
2 tbsp brandy
1 tbsp single cream and white chocolate curls, to decorate

Food Fact

Wonderfully rich and delicious served with a fruity compote – why not try making cherry compote using either fresh, if in season or otherwise tinned in fruit juice. Stone the cherries, or drain and then simmer on a low heat with a little apple juice until reduced.

Chocolate Box Cake

1 Preheat the oven to 180°C/ 350°F/Gas Mark 4 10 minutes before baking. Lightly oil and flour a 20.5 cm/8 inch square cake tin. Sift the flour and baking powder into a large bowl and stir in the sugar.

2 Using an electric whisk, beat in the butter and eggs. Blend the cocoa powder with 1 tablespoon of water, then beat into the creamed mixture.

3 Turn into the tin and bake in the preheated oven for about 25 minutes, or until well risen and cooked. Remove and cool before removing the cake from the tin.

4 To make the chocolate box, break the chocolate into small pieces, place in a heatproof bowl over a saucepan of gently simmering water and leave until soft. Stir it occasionally until melted and smooth. Line a Swiss roll tin with non-stick baking paper then pour in the melted

chocolate, tilting the tin to level. Leave until set.

5 Once the chocolate is set, turn out on to a chopping board and carefully strip off the paper. Cut into 4 strips, the same length as the cooked sponge, using a large sharp knife that has been dipped into hot water.

6 Gently heat the apricot preserve and sieve to remove lumps. Brush over the top and sides of the cake. Carefully place the chocolate strips around the cake sides and press lightly. Leave to set for at least 10 minutes.

7 For the topping, whisk the cream to soft peaks and quickly fold into the melted chocolate with the brandy.

8 Spoon the chocolate whipped cream into a pastry bag fitted with a star nozzle and pipe a decorative design of rosettes or shells over the surface. Dust with cocoa power and serve.

INGREDIENTS
Cuts into 16 slices

CHOCOLATE SPONGE:
175 g/6 oz self-raising flour
1 tsp baking powder
175 g/6 oz caster sugar
175 g/6 oz butter, softened
3 large eggs
25 g/1 oz cocoa powder
150 g/5 oz apricot preserve
cocoa powder, to dust

CHOCOLATE BOX:
275 g/10 oz plain dark chocolate

CHOCOLATE WHIPPED CREAM TOPPING:
450 ml/¾ pint double cream
275 g/10 oz plain dark chocolate, melted
2 tbsp brandy
1 tsp cocoa powder to decorate

Index